PUBLICATIONS OF THE
SCOTTISH COUNCIL FOR RESEARCH
IN EDUCATION

61

A HISTORY OF THE TRAINING OF TEACHERS
IN SCOTLAND

A HISTORY
OF THE TRAINING OF
TEACHERS IN SCOTLAND

MARJORIE CRUICKSHANK

UNIVERSITY OF LONDON PRESS LTD

LB
1725
D6
C7

ISBN 0 340 11752 4

Copyright © 1970 The Scottish Council for Research in Education,
46 Moray Place, Edinburgh

University of London Press Ltd
St Paul's House, Warwick Lane, London EC4

Printed and bound in Great Britain by
T and A Constable Ltd, Edinburgh

CONTENTS

		PAGE
ACKNOWLEDGMENTS		7
INTRODUCTION		9

CHAPTER

1	The Scottish Tradition of Education	13
2	The Pioneers of Teacher Training	26
3	State Control, 1841-1872	51
4	Response to Challenge, 1872-1900	85
5	The New Pattern of Teacher Training, 1900-1921	126
6	The Inter-War Period	160
7	Expansion and Reorganisation since 1945	186
8	Conclusion	214

APPENDICES

A	Education legislation, etc	218
B	Heads of institutions and leading officials connected with teacher training, 1835 to the present day	221
C	Short biographies: George Combe and John Kerr	229
D	Salaries of Scottish school teachers, statistics for schools, teachers and teachers in training	234
E	Early examples of timetables, duties, etc	238
F	Examples of early university courses in education	246
G	Examples of inter-war courses and of common examination papers	251
	SELECTED BIBLIOGRAPHY	258
	INDEX	267

ACKNOWLEDGMENTS

This study was written at the invitation of the Scottish Council for Research in Education. I wish to thank the Director and his staff for their help and advice. I am appreciative of the assistance of the Secretary, Miss J M Gray, particularly during the final stages of preparation. I have been greatly aided by the bibliographical lists on the history of Scottish education prepared by Dr James Craigie, Vice-President of the Council.

I am grateful to the Principal of Jordanhill College of Education, Sir Henry Wood, who gave me facilities to undertake the work when I was a member of the college staff. I was fortunate in being able to consult him during my research and, later, in having his comments on my script.

I owe a great deal to Dr R R Rusk who wrote in 1928 the first history of the training of teachers in Scotland, and who has eased my path by his numerous kindnesses. At all stages, I have drawn deeply on his knowledge and profited from his wisdom.

My work has taken me to many libraries and brought me into contact with many people. I am grateful to those who have given me access to materials in their possession, and, in particular, to Mr G D Gray, Registrar of the General Teaching Council for Scotland, and to the Principals of the Colleges of Education. Among those whose advice I have sought I should like to thank particularly Dr W B Inglis, formerly Principal of Moray House, Miss E M Rennie, Principal of Craigie College, Dr Nan Shepherd, formerly on the staff of Aberdeen College, and Miss E G Malloch, Principal of Madeley College, near Crewe. Dr Inglis has placed me further in his debt by reading my script.

I am grateful to Professor A C F Beales, Editor of *The British Journal of Educational Studies*, for permission to reproduce part of my article, "David Stow, Scottish Pioneer of Teacher Training in Britain", vol XIV, no 2, May 1966.

My especial thanks are due to my husband, who has sustained me through all difficulties and has been my most cogent critic.

University of Keele
July 1969

7

INTRODUCTION

"Every reform in education centres round the teachers and
every advance depends almost solely upon their intelligence,
character and skill."

Alexander Morgan [1]

Ideally, teachers should be like poets and painters, born not
made. The natural production rate, however, does not permit
their supply to be left to chance. Almost a century and a half
ago, one of the pioneers of Scottish teacher training, David
Stow, estimated that only one in fifty of his students had a
natural genius for teaching, but that at the end of a course of
training there were only five out of fifty who could not teach
efficiently.

It could be claimed that teacher education goes back to the
medieval universities, when the Master's degree was a certificate of admission to the guild of professional teachers. Indeed,
the arts degree in Scotland was long associated with teaching,
and the parish dominie was respected for his scholarship. Long
before the Reformation, education had been a means of escape
from the natural poverty of the land, and many Scotsmen were
to be found among the wandering scholars and teachers of
Europe. The Reformation gave a great stimulus to learning.
For centuries, education drew strength from a strong religious
tradition and from a keen popular interest in the nation's
schools. In a stable rural society the schoolmaster ranked next
to the minister, and parents and dominie alike took great pride
in the "lad o' pairts".

Teacher training in Scotland came as a by-product of the
factory age. The needs of the spawning child-population of
the streets roused a spirit of missionary zeal. Pioneer Sunday
schools in the slums of Edinburgh and Glasgow gave rise to
day schools, each geared to a distinctive method of teaching.
Day schools in turn expanded into "model" schools for student
observers and subsequently into full-scale training seminaries.

---

[1] *Rise and Progress of Scottish Education.* Oliver and Boyd, 1927, p 212.

9

Even in its infancy the Scottish movement derived strength from the study of Continental practice and, during the latter years of the nineteenth century it was, in its quest for a science of education, drawn more towards the European than the English pattern.

Today the two systems of teacher training in Britain remain distinct. In both England and Scotland, teacher training is part of a national system of education. The transient visitor to Scotland has to be reminded that, with a school population of almost a million, the northern kingdom forms an administrative unit comparable in size with one of the Scandinavian countries. He may nevertheless regard with whimsical interest divergencies which impede the two-way traffic of students and teachers between north and south Britain.[1] The native-born Englishman or Scot who domiciles himself over the border, however, is soon conscious of the deeper differences revealed in organisation, atmosphere and personal relationships. Today both systems face many similar challenges, yet each has its own particular problems. Even amid the surge of mass communications and the trend towards uniformity, current practice in the two countries reflects the vitality of different culture patterns.

Salient features of the Scottish system can only be appreciated against the canvas of the past. Firstly, the secular control of the colleges (apart from the two smaller Roman Catholic colleges) corresponds to the simplicity of the "Scottish solution" to the problem of denominational schools. Secondly, the emphasis on intellectual standards and universal qualification stems, on the one hand, from the traditional respect for learning and, on the other, from the native belief in the professional, the trained expert. Thirdly, the pre-eminence of the comprehensive, co-educational day college, is a consequence of the need of early industrial society to mass-produce teachers as cheaply as possible.

In the past, Scottish education was held in high regard for its

[1] Fewer than 1% of home students in colleges of education in Scotland came (in 1962-3) from England and Wales and fewer than 1% of home students in colleges in England and Wales came from Scotland. (The Robbins Report, Appendix 2 (B), Cmnd 2154 II-I, 69.) There is some movement of teachers, though the migration of English teachers is discouraged by the fact that certain English qualifications are not recognised by the Scottish authorities. Each country has its own salary scales.

achievements of widespread literacy and academic learning. Among emigrants, Scottish trained teachers were much sought after and, as headmasters, administrators and inspectors, they helped to mould education overseas. Today these associations are proudly recalled in the older countries of the Commonwealth which still claim affinity with the traditional ideals of Scottish education.

It was particularly experience in rural schools which served the emigrants well. Training authorities were always conscious of the need to provide suitable preparation for the rural teacher. Today preparation is made realistic by special courses of rural studies and by periods of teaching practice in remoter areas. Probably no country of similar size presents such diversity of school conditions for which teachers must be prepared. With half the total area designated "mainly heath and moorland" and the greater part of the remaining area "mainly rural", over 40 per cent of the schools have fewer than 100 children (about 17 per cent have fewer than 25 children). At the other extreme, among the highly concentrated population in the central belt – Edinburgh and Glasgow alone account for almost a third of the entire population – schools are large, and even primary schools may cater for upwards of a thousand children.[1]

The scale and complexity of the task of colleges of education today is without parallel. In the 1870s, as training colleges, they adapted themselves to cater for the rapidly expanding school system which demanded order, organisation and unity of method; in the early 1900s, they were remodelled to produce a hierarchy of teachers corresponding to a stratified school system. The demands of the past were limited in the earlier years to the achievements of universal literacy and subsequently to the provision also of academic secondary education. Today, when education has become part of the social programme as well as a necessity of economic survival, teachers of quality are required in ever-increasing numbers for a widening arena of education.

Never has teacher training been subject to so many outside pressures as at the present time. Never has it been under such compulsion to re-interpret educational content and to provide

[1] *Scottish Educational Statistics*, 1968, table 5.

courses which will challenge students by their rigour and their contemporary relevance. If teachers are to prepare the young for the varied demands of technological society they must themselves be open to change. Their education therefore must be humanistic as well as technical, for essentially the quality of their teaching will depend, as David Stow, the early pioneer of training, insisted, on a liberal education, on liveliness of mind and on personal relationships.

Chapter 1
THE SCOTTISH TRADITION OF EDUCATION

THE BACKGROUND

The Scot, unlike the Englishman, is not a man of compromise. His genius lies in rationality. He looks to first principles rather than to precedent. He is logical rather than flexible. Historically his links are with the Continent, and in his philosophical thinking and in his attitudes he belongs to the European rather than to the insular tradition.

Scotland was never conquered by the English. Following the Union of the Crowns in the seventeenth century, the two countries formed a single political and economic structure in 1707. In religion, law and education, however, the native usages were retained. Thus in Scotland the tradition of centuries of independence was proudly preserved and national exclusiveness was perpetuated by the moral and intellectual discipline associated with Church and school.

There was a symbolic difference in the Reformation settlements adopted north and south of the border. The English erected in the Church of England a middle-way establishment, which owed much of its breadth and comprehensiveness to the mixture of old and new. The Scots, on the contrary, broke completely with the past and in doctrine embraced the logical system of Calvin. While the English Church, identified with the Crown and with the nobility, enjoyed a secure dignity, the Scottish Kirk, poverty-stricken and beset by political adversaries, had to assert and maintain itself independently of the State. In the early years, its very existence depended on popular allegiance, on the devotion of believing congregations. By instruction of the intellect and by discipline of the will therefore the Kirk sought to train "a priesthood of all believers", a people who could endure, even exult in, the tensions of private judgment and who could strive with unrelaxed aspiration for the

13

greater glory of God. Patriotism was associated with the Presbyterian creed. Perhaps nowhere did Calvinism take root in such
congenial soil as in Scotland. What Burckhardt called "the
certainty of unique chosenness" gave militancy to the faith and
inspired successive generations of Covenanters to defy their
foes.

By elevating the importance of the ordinary man, the Kirk
did much to mould national character, to kindle a desire for
knowledge and to inculcate a sense of purpose and a stern
morality. The Scots became a people of the Book. Natural
austerity was confirmed by the discipline of the Church and
qualities of self-denial, industry and perseverance were branded
in by emphasis on Law, Duty and Restraint. Religion was the
central fibre of life in a people essentially "Hebraic" in their
outlook, in their disdain for pleasure and in their moral
endeavour.

The requirements of the ministry and the need of an instructed laity demanded organisation of education on a national
level. All, irrespective of sex or degree, must be able to read the
word of God. All must be equipped for the duties incumbent on
laymen in the new ecclesiastical system. Education, long associated with the Church, was therefore systematically planned
so that family training should be buttressed by the teaching of
the school, by ministerial catechising and by Sabbath exercises.
Already, in 1560, John Knox in his *Book of Discipline* had outlined a plan for "the vertue and godlie upbringing of the youth
of this Realm". Rights of parents were to be circumscribed, no
father might "use his children at his own fantasie". The pattern
of education for rich and poor alike was to consist of parish and
burgh schools, and gifted boys were to proceed to university
"so that the commonwealth may have some comfort by
them".

Economic difficulties and political upheavals impeded the
execution of the plan. In the burghs, town councils assumed
responsibility for the grammar schools, many of which were of
old foundation, but in the parishes the provision varied. Sometimes the minister acted as schoolmaster, sometimes schools,
which had struggled into existence, foundered amid the violence
and tumult of the times. Yet during the years of conflict with

Episcopacy, the ideal of the parish school was never lost sight of, and when, at the end of the seventeenth century, Presbyterianism was finally restored, the Kirk assumed as part of ecclesiastical organisation the supervision of schools, including the trial of faith and qualifications of the schoolmaster. Church and State were as one. By legislation of 1696[1] therefore the heritors of every parish were required to maintain a schoolhouse and to provide for a schoolmaster a salary fixed at 100 merks minimum and 200 merks maximum, in sterling £5.11.1½ and £11.2.3, a sum which, together with school fees, was estimated to give the same standard of living as a farmer. The State system of schools and the public office of schoolmaster in Scotland thus date from the seventeenth century. By the closing years of the eighteenth century few parishes in the Lowlands were without a school.

Though not compulsory, education was looked upon as a necessity of life and in some areas "a man would be looked upon as a monster who could keep his child from means of instruction within his reach."[2] The school was an integral part of the community, and newcomers quickly fell into the accepted custom of sending their children. As Dr Thomas Chalmers later remarked, "There is more than may appear at first sight, in the very circumstance of a marked and separate edifice standing visibly out to the eye of the people, with its familiar and often repeated designation. There is also much in the constant residence of the teacher of recognised office and distinction."[3]

In a country where many communities were physically isolated and where there were no great differences of wealth to separate rich and poor, the common school was a practical arrangement. In a very real sense the parish school was a *Volkschule*, in which the son of the minister or the laird might share the same bench as the bare-legged boy of the ploughman or shepherd. Over a wide area there was a great respect for learning and family pride in the son who aspired to the pulpit.

Scotland was a poor country. Many travellers were moved to comment on the inhospitable conditions, the rigorous climate

[1] *Act for Settling of Schools*, William III, cap 26.
[2] *Report of Select Committee on the State of Education*, 1834, p 37. (Evidence of Professor Pillans.)
[3] *Edinburgh Review*, June 1827, vol xci, p 108.

and infertile land. Emerson, for example, remarked on the contrasts between England and Scotland. He noticed as he travelled north the poverty and coarseness of the Scots, "the rapid loss of grandeur of mien and manner", but he was also struck by the shrewdness of the people and their "provincial eagerness and acuteness".[1] Reared to the necessity of struggle and fortified by a sense of divine mission, many Scots owed their advancement in life to their education and to their spirit of self-help. Some of them got on and got out, and there was a good deal of truth in Dr Johnson's saying that the noblest prospect which a Scotchman ever saw was the high road that led him to England.

The growth in prosperity of the country in the eighteenth century was in part attributed to the school system. In particular the parish schools were credited with the high standard of morality, the sobriety and industry of peasant families who "considered it worse than death to come on the parish roll".[2] Energies, which elsewhere had been spent in rebellion and dis- affection, in Scotland had been directed to self-help and enlightenment, so that, in the words of Macaulay, "wherever the Scotchman went he carried his superiority with him . . . in America, in India, in trade and in war, the advantage he derived from his early training raised him above his competitors. . . . Mixed with Englishmen or mixed with Irishmen, he rose to the top as surely as oil rises to the top of water."[3]

THE DOMINIE

What sort of man was the parochial schoolmaster? Much of course depended on the traditions and prosperity of the area. The scholarship of many a schoolmaster made him a figure of distinction. The heritors at his appointment – a comparative trial if there was more than one candidate – might ask him to explain one of the Odes of Horace "grammaticallie, logicallie and rhetoricallie". At his best he was a university man, who had attended for one or two sessions even if he had not grad-

---

[1] R W Emerson, *English Traits*. Boston: Phillips, 1857, p 59.
[2] Alex Christison, *The General Diffusion of Knowledge, one great cause of prosperity of North Britain*, P Hill, 1802, p 20.
[3] *Lord Macaulay's Speeches*, Longmans, 1886, p 230.

uated. He had to subscribe the Confession of Faith,[1] and he was licensed by the Presbytery, which approved his appointment on grounds of faith and which examined his teaching by annual visitation. His tenure was for life, *ad vitam aut culpam*, and, though he was the social inferior of the minister, his scholarly attainments and recognised office frequently gave him a position of dignity. The poorer parishes could not attract scholarly candidates. Sometimes there was a boy in charge of the school or a man who had little pretension to learning, but who had once served as a private tutor. Even decayed tradesman were employed in some of the outlying regions.

The emoluments of the schoolmaster varied from place to place. Salaries were usually paid at the minimum rate and in many parishes children's fees, 1s 6d to 2s a quarter for reading, with an additional 6d each for writing and arithmetic, and as much as 3s for Latin, formed the largest item of remuneration. Sometimes, too, the master could make a little profit from boarding in his house pupils who came from a distance. He felt the pinch, of course, when children were kept away from school for a variety of seasonal work, such as herding the cattle, lifting the "neeps", cutting and drying the peat. Indeed in some areas children came to school only for the winter "spate" from November until spring. Though cases of poverty could be referred to the Kirk Session, parents, restrained by a sense of pride, often preferred to send two children on alternate days for the single fee, or perhaps they despatched only one of a numerous brood and expected him to teach the rest at home.

At New Year and Candlemas the traditional children's "offerings" brought in a little extra income and, if he was fortunate, the dominie might expect an occasional present of books, a snuff-box or even a suit of clothing from a grateful parent. Customarily he supplemented his income by acting as clerk and precentor. Sometimes with his skills in calculating and book-keeping he was called upon to serve as land-surveyor, auctioneer or even as temporary factor, but very often he took on the menial work of beadle, acting as bell-ringer, grave-digger, keeper of the mort cloth and custodian of the public clock.

[1] A document of 40 pages of print.

B

There were schoolmasters who were shopkeepers, cattle dealers, publicans and even smugglers.[1] At the best, the schoolmaster's extra-mural activities kept him in touch with the outside world, at the worst, they degraded him and brought his office into disrepute.

The physical conditions in which the parish schoolmaster worked were often deplorable. In some localities a church steeple, a family vault, a granary, a byre or stable served as a school. Even when a building was specially erected, it was a low one-room structure. The furniture usually consisted of rough wooden benches and a single writing desk. Probably the description of an Aberdeenshire school, written in the early nineteenth century by a former pupil, was fairly typical: "A part of the schoolroom was taken up with a pile of peats. This store was kept up by each scholar bringing a peat every morning under his arm. . . . The floor was of earth and usually well worn into holes. The duty of removing the ashes, kindling the fire and sweeping the floor devolved on a censor appointed weekly. The sweeping was mostly confined to the middle space of the floor; the dust under the desks was rarely disturbed and generally lay about an inch deep."[2] It was little wonder that visitors to schools referred to the offensive smell, a consequence of the dirt and lack of ventilation.

To ambitious young men, teaching was a stepping-stone to the Church. The vocational urge, the scholarly aspirations associated with the pulpit and the attraction of the minister's status and salary, often three or four times that of the school-master, all spurred him to further study. The common practice was to combine teaching duties with theological reading and, during the single session of attendance required at Divinity Hall, to employ a substitute in the school. There were many complaints about masters who "could not see the school for the steeple" and who found the office of schoolmaster merely a

[1] *Select Committee on the State of Education*, 1838. The investigation extracted from all the Presbytery books the charges brought against parish schoolmasters from the beginning of the century. Some of their illicit activities are described in "The Parish Schoolmaster in the Bad Old Days", Marjorie Cruickshank, *Times Educational Supplement (Scotland)*, 31 December 1965.
[2] Description of the 1820s, quoted in S S Laurie, *Report to the Trustees of the Dick Bequest*, Constable, 1890, pp 58-9.

convenient means of support, while talents, thoughts and energies were absorbed elsewhere. Indeed some advertisements stated that "applicants must not have the kirk in view". Yet the schools often benefited from the services of aspirants to the ministry. "If", as one defender expressed it, "we have a succession of young men, each devoting 8 to 10 years of the flower of their lives to their laborious office, are we not better with a series of minds of such strength and culture than we should be with a whole life destitute, in present occupation or future occupation, of any antidote to the narrowing influence of a limited path of duty incessantly trodden?"[1] In the absence of a system of promotion within the teaching profession itself, the Church served the interests of education by attracting able young men into the schools.

Among the parish schoolmasters there were always a number who had failed to obtain their qualifications in divinity and who remained in the schools as "stickit ministers". Perhaps they bore their disappointment as best they could, or they became embittered even to the extent of losing their usefulness. Indeed the isolation of their surroundings often bore heavily on many and the lack of congenial company and of access to books had a dispiriting effect on their work. Because he was appointed *ad vitam aut culpam*, the parochial schoolmaster was practically irremovable. The security of his tenure was one of the prized privileges of office which made him master in his own domain, able to express himself in his work, but there was little safeguard against inefficiency. In the absence of any provision for old age it was customary for the schoolmaster to cling to office until death despite illhealth or even senility, and it was not uncommon to find men in their 70s still teaching without assistance. Possibly the record for service was held by a schoolmaster in Inverness-shire who, when he died at the age of 89, had been teaching for 70 years.[2] It was true that schools were subject to annual visitation by the Presbyteries which, in turn, reported to the General Assembly of the Church. In fact, what usually happened was that the members of the Presbytery

[1] G Allan Menzies, *Report to the Trustees of the Dick Bequest*, Constable, 1854, p 104.
[2] James Barron, *The Northern Highlands in the Nineteenth Century*, printed in Inverness, 1907, vol II, p xxxv.

witnessed a well-rehearsed show on which they reported in perfunctory terms to higher authority.

The Highlands and Islands were a region distinct from the Lowlands. It was true that in the north-eastern counties there was a great respect for learning and a steady stream of scholars proceeded to the university, but even here, where the school-master received his salary in kind, it was not unknown in years of frosted corn for the tenants to dispose of some of their bad meal to him.[1] The parish school system was at its weakest in the West Highlands and in the Islands. Many of the parishes, larger even than whole counties of the Lowlands, were so vast and so intersected by mountain and loch that parish schools could cater for only a small proportion of the children. Yet even in the desolate areas there were among the farmers, inn-keepers and shepherds many who appreciated the benefits of education and encouraged their children to acquire the means of self-advancement. Thus on encountering among the islanders of Coll a tenant whose son made his way each year to Aberdeen University, Dr Johnson had been moved to exclaim – "There is something noble in a young man's walking two hundred miles and back again every year for the sake of learning."[2]

The Highlanders, however, were a race apart. The disciplines of learning and religion had done little to curb their natural turbulence or to combat their carefree fecklessness, and they remained content to live at subsistence level. Lowlanders had long regarded the Highlands and Western Isles as the home mission field, a sphere for philanthropic and evangelical endeavour. From the early years of the eighteenth century they established through the Society in Scotland for Propagating Christian Knowledge a system of charity schools in an endea-vour to extirpate Popish heresy and to inculcate a sense of moral discipline and urge for self-help.

The masters of the schools were poorly paid, often receiving only £3 a year together with a house, ground for a kailyard and grass for a cow. Like the parish schoolmasters, they devised their own methods of teaching. However, since it was difficult

----

[1] William Barclay, *The Schools and Schoolmasters of Banffshire*, printed in Banff, 1925, p ix.
[2] James Boswell, *Journal of a Tour to the Hebrides*, (first published 1785), Dent, 1906, vol II, p 69.

to recruit enough Gaelic-speaking teachers who were "Men of Piety, Loyalty, Prudence, Gravity, Competent Knowledge and Literature", the Society decided on a form of apprenticeship. Promising poor scholars were encouraged to stay on at school and equip themselves for the office of schoolmaster. Maintenance allowances of "twelve pennies Scots everyday including Lord's days" were to be paid to youths of 12 to 14 during the first two years of preparation, at the end of which they were to be given a suit of clothes and a pair of shoes. If they stayed on for a further year, they would receive "eighteen pennies Scots" each day together with another suit of clothes and a pair of shoes.[1] Some of the boys were maintained briefly while they observed the teaching in Raining's School, Inverness, which had been specially endowed and was in some respects the model school of the society. The system was a precursor in miniature of the nineteenth century pupil-teacher system, and, like the later State scheme, it produced teachers of very limited attainments. Nevertheless, however rudimentary, it is significant as the first recorded attempt at teacher training in Scotland.

Visitors to parish and burgh schools were often impressed by the Scotsman's natural flair for teaching, which they attributed to national temperament and to intellectual training. The very fact that the dominie had fought his way to university, often as a boy of 14 to 15, and once there had endured conditions of physical discomfort and loneliness gave him moral stamina and dignity of character.[2] He had worked in an atmosphere of competition, had "scorned delights and lived laborious days". At his best, he was an energetic devoted teacher, stimulating his pupils to intensity of effort. His background of struggle, however, often made him an austere figure, more likely to command the awe and respect of his pupils than their friendship and affection.

In the smaller towns, the burgh school was often indistinguishable from the parish school. It took girls as well as boys for the elementary subjects, though by custom it was only boys

---

[1] *The State of the Society in Scotland for Propagating Christian Knowledge,* 1729, p 17 *et seq.*
[2] Bursaries were particularly numerous at Aberdeen and St Andrews but the scholar usually took many of his provisions from home. There are details of a student's life at St Andrews 1819-26 in Duncan Dewar, *A Student of St Andrews 100 years ago. His Accounts,* Jackson, 1926.

who were instructed in the "higher branches", the classics and mathematics. In the larger towns, the burgh schools and later the private subscription schools, the "academies", were exclusively secondary schools. Indeed Edinburgh had its own "English" schools, feeders to the High School. The position of Rector of the Edinburgh High School was one of esteem, but in many burgh schools there was no one with the post or even the title of Rector. Each individual master was a law unto himself, to whom the parents paid fees directly. Since the salaries, paid out of the "common good" by the town councils, were very small, dependence on fees put the teachers on their mettle, but it also led to great rivalry and popularity-hunting as well as large classes. Nevertheless, the burgh schoolmaster, even the assistant or "doctor", was usually a man of learning and repute who would have resented a position of subordination within the school. "Place-taking" made the classroom the scene of great activity, with pupils competing for places by order of merit and especially for the most coveted position of dux.

Unlike many burgh schoolmasters, who taught pupils of similar age, the village dominie was teaching perhaps 30 or more children of all ages. Most children entered school at the age of 6 or 7. They began with the alphabet, learnt from the cover page of the Shorter Catechism, specially published under the title of "The A B C and Shorter Catechism for catechising such as are of weaker capacity". Thereafter they progressed to the Proverbs of Solomon,[1] and then to the Bible itself. A sprinkling of the older pupils might be learning Latin and mathematics, sometimes even navigation, book-keeping or surveying. Only a few children learned writing and arithmetic, and they were joined by "grown up lads", farm labourers often, who returned to school in the slack season. Many pupils never progressed beyond reading the Catechism or the Proverbs. "Frequently reading was miserably bad. . . . The scholar stumbling through the verse as best he could and when he came to a word he could call nothing, he was whipped."[2] Religion was thus learned at the cost of bitter tears, and Saturdays, which were specially

---

[1] The *Proverbs* were printed separately and used as a schoolbook for at least two centuries.

[2] G Allan Menzies, *Report to the Trustees of the Dick Bequest*, p 30.

devoted to the repetition of the Psalms, the Paraphrases and the Shorter Catechism, were designated "punishment days". Of course, many a child never grasped the meaning of the words he memorised. For the repetition exercise he would be given the first word. Then in the words of a critic, "he will move on rapidly like a machine that has been wound up, and, like it, perhaps continue to move till he regularly runs out. But in some instances before running out, the automaton may unfortunately become entangled with answers to a very different question...."[1]

Calvinism had always taken a severe view of human frailty and in his "godly upbringing" of the young, the schoolmaster was unsparing in his use of the tawse. Indeed the traditional asperity of school life was reflected in the expression, "Fa fuppit the laddie?", meaning "Who whipped the boy?", that is, "Who was the boy's teacher?" With children working at different stages, the parish schoolroom was often noisy and in disorder. Finally, when the master could stand it no longer, he lashed the worst of the offenders. Frequently he had little patience with the youngest children and after the briefest instruction left them to get on in terror of the tawse. For many pupils the harshness of school life clouded their childhood. It was the same in the burgh schools, where in later years many who had risen to fame remembered with revulsion their schooldays. Lord Cockburn, the famous judge, recalling his youth at Edinburgh High School at the end of the eighteenth century, spoke of being stupefied by the daily beatings he received.[2] Horace Mann, who wrote admiringly of the Scottish teacher's vigour and drive, nevertheless commented on the awesome discipline. He said, "the general character of the nation was distinctly visible in the schools. Could the Scottish teacher add something more of gentleness to his prodigious energy and vivacity, and were the general influences which he imparts to his pupils modified in one or two particulars, he would become a model teacher for the world."[3]

---

[1] John Wood, *Account of the Edinburgh Sessional School*, Oliver and Boyd, 5th edition, 1840, p 61.
[2] Henry Cockburn, *Memorials of His Time*, Grant, 1872, pp 3-4.
[3] Horace Mann, *Report of an Educational Tour of Germany, France, Holland, and of Great Britain and Ireland* (ed W B Hodgson), Simpkin, 4th edition, 1857, pp 161-2.

In the higher departments of the large burgh schools it was customary for the masters to keep the same pupils year after year. Promotion to the next class was a matter of routine and not of merit. Teaching was by the time-honoured method of place-taking. There was little variety in the course of study and, despite the introduction of new subjects in the academies, the classics still carried greatest weight and formed the staple fare of the majority of schoolboys. Many of them must have felt like James Nasmyth, the engineer, a pupil at Edinburgh High School some years after Cockburn. He recalled the large classes of 200 and said, "It was a mere matter of rote and cram. I learnt by heart a number of Latin rules and phrases, but what I learnt soon slipped from my memory. My young mind was tormented by the tasks set before me." Despite the unhappiness of his schooldays, however, he considered he had learnt much from the necessity of carrying out disagreeable tasks. He wrote, "This is an exercise in early life that is very useful in later years".[1]

In the parish school the dominie worked in isolation, devising his own methods, guided only by experience and corrected by failure. Sometimes he taught those of his pupils who had reached the "higher branches" before the rest of the school assembled, or after school in the evening. During the day the "Latin boys" had to work on their own; the less able became listless and lost heart, the others won through by sheer perseverance. School life was thus a preparation for the rigours and austerities of university, where survival in the large junior classes demanded qualities of persistence and toughness. Knowledge was not acquired with leisure and ease. It was burnt in by the red hot iron of necessity. Under the hard husk of Calvinism, the Scottish scholar often developed acute suppleness and excelled in analysis, but he lacked *la grande culture* and the power of being dissatisfied with his own possessions.

There were many university students, however, who got no more than, in modern terminology, a secondary education. As "soft milky boys" of 14 or 15 or as "unkempt lumbering clowns" straight from the fields they went ill-prepared for the highest

[1] James Nasmyth, *An Autobiography* (ed S Smiles), Murray, 1885, p 81.

study.[1] Many stayed for only one or two sessions, but some had graduated by the age of 18. John Stuart Blackie, who attended university in Aberdeen in the 1820s, wrote after further study at Göttingen, "The scales fell from my eyes. I perceived that at Marischal College they had degraded the university pretty much into a school; that they drilled boys when they might have been stimulating young men; that our academical system was prominently puerile and our standards of attainment lamentably low."[2] Blackie was to become a university reformer. Indeed, much of the impulse for educational reform in Scotland was to come from men sufficiently detached and independent to look critically at existing practice.

Education in Scotland in the pre-industrial age was widely diffused. Indeed, in the Lowlands, there was almost universal literacy. However, the peculiar mixed character of Scottish education and the lack of gradation of schools tended to keep standards low. It is easy to see the faults of the time-honoured system, the shoddy buildings, the lack of equipment and the limited curriculum. Many children must have felt the bodily and mental weariness of sitting long hours, staring often with little comprehension at the same page. The academic tradition was self-perpetuating, since schools were in charge of men who had themselves been reared to the university and who were often engaged in further study. Visitors criticised the veneration for the classics, and commented on the need for a more realistic curriculum, designed to improve the rural economy. Nevertheless, they acknowledged the popular character of education, seen in the sacrifice of parents and the perseverance of children, who struggled to school through flood and fell. By hard work and competition, by patience and self-discipline, youth learned to shun the pleasures of life. The ethos of the nation was reflected in its schools.

[1] J S Blackie, Professor of Greek, Edinburgh University, Letter to the Rt Hon the Lord Provost and Town Council of Edinburgh, *On the Advancement of Learning in Scotland*, 1855.
[2] Anna M Stoddard, *John Stuart Blackie*, Blackwood, 1896, p 41.

Chapter 2

THE PIONEERS OF TEACHER TRAINING

The parish system of schools had been geared to a stable rural society. By the early years of the nineteenth century, economic and social change was transforming conditions of life. Already in the previous century, commercial growth had brought new wealth to Scotland. Glasgow in particular had become a centre of trade with America and the West Indies. Its tobacco and sugar "barons" had been among the richest merchants in Britain, and its growing wealth had been reflected in the cultural and intellectual life of the city. Yet the population of Glasgow had increased at a leisurely rate and, even at the beginning of the century, had reached only 84,000.

Already, however, new industries in the Forth-Clyde valley were attracting an immigrant population. The Carron Iron-works in Stirlingshire dated from 1759; the collieries, foundries and factories of Lanarkshire and Renfrewshire were all attracting labour, while the construction of roads and canals brought in temporary unskilled workers. The widescale introduction of steam power coinciding with the Napoleonic war stimulated the growth of manufacturing and the process of urbanisation. From where did the great mass of people come? The depression of cottage industries brought many from neighbouring areas, others came from further afield: Highlanders evicted from the glens to make room for sheep, Irish peasants driven by semi-starvation to seek a passage to the nearest mainland port. Some became skilled workers, highly paid artisans, and by the principle of self-help improved themselves, but many sank in the alien, harsh environment and sought solace for their misery and degradation in the dram shops and gambling dens. Theirs was a savage brutalised existence and their young children, adrift in the wynds and vennels, were the flotsam and

26

jetsam of the urban underworld. In the past, the ignorance of
the Highlanders had roused compassion; now the educational
destitution of many townsfolk was no less compelling.

Meanwhile wartime inflation had struck the parish schoolmasters. With salaries unchanged for over a century, their
earnings had sunk to those of agricultural labourers whose
families existed on oatmeal and milk; in trade, even journeymen
were better off. In the words of the *Statistical Account* (1799),
the schoolmaster's "cultivated mind, improved sensibility . . .
(his) acquaintance with the comforts of life and previous hopes
of attaining these comforts, all conspired to deepen the gloom of
present poverty".[1] By Act of Parliament in 1803, salaries were
raised to £16.13.4 minimum, £22.4.5 maximum, equivalent
to 1½ or 2 chalders of oatmeal.[2] Provision was also made for the
regular review of salaries every quarter of a century so that
adjustments could be made depending on the price of oatmeal.
The schoolmaster, moreover, was to be provided with a house,
a "but an' ben" (room and kitchen), and he was also to have a
garden of one-fourth of a Scots acre so that he could keep a cow
and grow grain and potatoes for his own use. In order to extend
education in large parishes, heritors were permitted to raise an
additional £10 a year for the salary of a teacher of a "side"
school.

The Act did nothing to relieve educational destitution in the
towns, and it was left to voluntary enterprise to cater for the
children of the labouring population. Already in the whole
country there were twice as many private schools as parish
schools with twice as many pupils taught in them.[3] But,
despite the variety of works' schools and adventure schools in
the towns, there were 50,000 children attending no school.
Many were employed in the bleach fields, dye-works, mines and
foundries, where from the age of 7 upwards they could earn
1s or 1s 6d a week, a valuable addition to the family income.
Others were simply wandering the streets, picking up what they
could by begging or running errands.

The problem of the "lapsed masses" assumed dramatic form

[1] J Sinclair, *First Statistical Account*, vol 21, Creech, 1799, p 506.
[2] 43rd *Geo III*, cap 54.
[3] Figures from *Parliamentary Digest*, 1811.

in Edinburgh at "Hogmanay" in 1811, when youths, known as
"keelies", rioted and stormed into a midnight gathering at the
Tron Church. The law took savage reprisals. Church folk,
however, were stirred by the event to subscribe towards Sunday
schools in every parish in the city. The schools, opened in
April 1812, had paid superintendents in charge to ensure
efficient scriptural teaching, but their work was severely handicapped because the children could not read. In order therefore
to give the Sunday schools a fair chance, the Kirk Sessions of
the city resolved to open a day school to teach reading.

Already a new method of teaching large numbers of children
was in vogue. In England, rival societies representing the
Established Church and the Nonconformist Churches had
launched the monitorial system. Two men, Dr Andrew Bell,
a clergyman of the Church of England (and a native of St
Andrews, where he had also graduated), and Joseph Lancaster,
a Quaker, claimed the distinction of discovering that children
could teach one another. Their organisation differed in detail –
Lancaster's monitors had charge of 10 children, Bell's of 30 –
but the new system effectively solved the problem of finding
teachers, and it was, of course, cheap. As Lancaster said, "By
this system . . . above 1,000 children may be taught and governed
by one master only."

Even before Lancaster's visit to Edinburgh in 1812, the
monitorial system had been introduced in the Edinburgh High
School by the Rector, James Pillans.[1] Appointed in 1810,
Pillans had no previous experience of teaching large classes and,
when he took over, the school was in a state of disorder. He
divided his own class, consisting of boys of varying ability, into
groups of 10, each with a monitor in charge. From time to
time the monitors changed their groups so that individuals
could have experience of different instructors. By a combination
of class and group teaching he proved that the monitorial
principle, interpreted with skill and discrimination, could be as
successfully applied to the teaching of the classics as to the
elementary subjects. Indeed, so popular was his method that
the numbers in his class rose to 250.

[1] "Rationale of Discipline", in *Contributions to the Cause of Education*,
Longman, 1856, p 317 *et seq.*

He claimed that the monitorial system infused fresh life and spirit into the school, but he emphasised that the method could not be combined with brute force. "There must be a feeling of kindliness and confidence between master and scholar. . . . He must treat his monitors as gentlemen, and they will speedily become so." Even as Professor of Humanity at the University, he applied the same methods to his large junior classes, though he dignified the monitors with the name of "inspectors". His own practical experience, and his extensive knowledge of schools in his own country and abroad, made Pillans one of the powerful advocates of educational reform.

The monitorial system was the basis of organisation of the new day school, opened in Leith Wynd in April 1813. It was maintained by the Kirk Sessions of the various parishes, each of which was allowed to send 5 scholars free of charge and 10 others on payment of 6d a month. The master had a salary of £15 a year, payable half-yearly. First conducted on the Lancasterian model, it was later found more practicable with the increase of numbers to adopt the larger monitorial groups of Bell's system. Desks were placed round the walls of the schoolroom and the rest of the floor was left empty save for the master's desk. "One half of the scholars always sit at the desks with their faces to the wall, employed in learning to write or cipher, while the other half stand on the floor, either reading or practising the rules of arithmetic. . . ." The classes on the floor were arranged in segments facing the master and in front of each group stood the monitor and his assistant whose duty it was to keep order. At the end of one hour the divisions changed over, and those who had been sitting at desks exchanged places with those who had stood to read and to spell.[1]

In 1819, John Wood, an advocate and Sheriff of Peebles, began visiting the school to look after some unemployed apprentices who had been put under his care. His visits became so frequent that he was soon coming daily to the school, examining the progress of the children and taking classes himself. He was troubled by the emphasis on rote learning, and doubted whether the children "had been made such masters of their own language as in future life to give them any pleasure in reading or enable

[1] John Wood, *Account of the Edinburgh Sessional School*, p 84.

them to derive much profit by it". His criticism of the mechanical routine of instruction led him to evolve his own "explanatory" method, with emphasis on understanding the meaning of words. The pupil had to be constantly on the alert, ready to answer the stream of questions which tested his comprehension of a word or passage and required his re-expression. He was spurred to distinguish himself by the spirit of competition fostered by rewards. Wood prepared new textbooks to suit his methods. After the initial stages, there were "no more tables of unconnected words, nor even any more detached sentences". Instead, the pupil went straight on to read "interesting and instructive passages" of biblical and natural history.

Wood became effective head of the Sessional School, which in 1824 moved to new premises, a single schoolroom 83 ft by 35 ft, in Market Street. By coincidence there survives a description of the environs of the school written by an English medical student, James Kay, who was later to make his mark in education. In 1825, his work as dispensary assistant took him to the nearby wynds and closes. He has described his visits to the lofty houses, once the pride of the Old Town, but "now almost universally converted into barracks, in the separate rooms of which lodged the poorest and most suffering portion of the Scotch and Irish poor".[1] Living in conditions of filth and squalor the slum dwellers were an easy prey to the periodic outbreaks of fever and cholera.

The children were drawn from among the poorest families. Wood himself described the daily routine. School hours were short, from 10 am until noon and from 1 pm to 3 pm, with a morning session on Saturday. Monitors were required to attend earlier to prepare the books, slates and pencils and to receive instruction. There was in fact a hierarchy of monitors: a head monitor who was paid 1s a week, monitors who were paid 6d and assistant monitors, who kept order while the monitors taught and who were paid 4d.[2]

Wood infused a new spirit into the monitorial system. For him the man was more important than the mechanism. In

[1] B C Bloomfield (ed), *The Autobiography of Sir James Kay-Shuttleworth*, Education Libraries Bulletin, supplement seven, University of London Institute of Education, 1964, p 3.
[2] John Wood, *Account of the Edinburgh Sessional School*, p 116.

Lancasterian schools, the master was "a silent bystander and inspector", and in National schools he was forbidden to depart from the "beautiful and efficient simplicity" of the system. Wood, however, insisted that the master must be the very life and soul of the school, that he "ought seldom or never to be found in his desk, but always on the floor among his pupils, and almost always in the act of teaching".[1] He was to visit each class and, in particular, was to examine the lowest class before it could pass on to a new lesson. No system, he said, could supersede "the necessity of diligence or zeal, of earnestness and kindliness of manner on the part of the instructor". His "enlivening spirit" must be communicated to the monitors who were themselves to be capable of correcting their pupils' answers and of adapting their illustrations to the "capacities and inclinations" of the pupils.

In addition to reading, writing and arithmetic, grammar was taught by the method of analysis and geography with the aid of maps. Despite the large numbers in the school (sometimes as many as 600 children aged between 4 and 14) and the military precision of the movements following such commands as "recover slates", "give pencils", there were endearing touches of informality. For example, children who had finished their allotted tasks were encouraged to consult the classroom library. Wood wrote, "Times without number when examined by strangers on matters, which, we were aware, had not fallen under their instruction in school, have we heard them return answers which surprised us, and on enquiry we found that their information had been derived from their library". Wood also expressed "secret delight" when a child who had completed his arithmetic, left his place in order to examine an atlas. Indeed he advocated, to use a contemporary expression, "setting", and referred by example to a boy who was in the highest class for reading but in a lower class for arithmetic.[2]

Save for the external framework, the "Explanatory" or "Intellectual System" owed nothing to the original monitorial method. Its emphasis was on the personal qualities of the master and his understanding of the children. According to Wood it

[1] *ibid*, p 192.
[2] *ibid*, p 122.

was "natural teaching", an extension simply of the instruction given at the mother's knee. The approach was enlightened and sensitive. Yet, though a lively and vivacious master could inspire and direct his monitors, could encourage flexibility of approach and aptness of illustration, he could not endow them with the sense of judgment and discrimination which experience and maturity alone could foster. The weakness was inherent in the monitorial organisation.

DAVID STOW AND THE GLASGOW INFANT SCHOOL SOCIETY

The novel methods employed in the Edinburgh Sessional School had their parallel in Glasgow, in an infant school opened by David Stow. Like Wood, Stow was stirred to help the unfortunate children of the city streets. The son of a Paisley merchant, born in 1793, he was sent to Glasgow as a young man to train in one of the leading textile firms. His daily route took him through the city streets, where he was appalled by the squalor and wretchedness which he saw. Urban barbarism, which was everywhere associated with the factory age, was at its worst in Glasgow. Already the extremes of poverty and wealth were plainly visible: in the east, the congestion of closes and wynds, in the west the Georgian mansions and terraces. The distinction was between "the respectable" and the rest; "on the one side, an ordered living, comfort and decorum, a church connexion and a hope for the next generation; on the other, spiritual indifference, waste and want".[1] In the years after 1815, the "economic rhythm" brought recurring crises of depression and unemployment, while periodic scourges of fever and cholera took a deadly toll of the overcrowded, under-nourished population. It was an age of turbulence and violence reaching a climax in the "Radical rising" of 1819.

Stow was one of a number of young men attracted to missionary and social work by Thomas Chalmers, minister of the Tron Church, Glasgow. He soon realised, however, that charity was a mere expedient, which could touch only the surface of the problem, and that the real hope lay in training the young to resist the viciousness of their surroundings. Accordingly, in

[1] L J Saunders, *Scottish Democracy 1815-40*, Oliver and Boyd, 1950, p 111.

1816, he collected about 30 children into a Sabbath school, where over a period of years he evolved methods which he was later to apply in day school. To children arranged in parallel forms, an anticipation of his later gallery structure, he interpreted the Scriptures and made them relevant to everyday life.[1] He soon realised, however, that Sunday schools could make little impression on children exposed to corruption for the rest of the week, and his thoughts turned to day schools. With the help of like-minded citizens, he succeeded in 1826 in founding an Infant School Society, which two years later opened a school in Drygate, on a site near the Cathedral. Stow was not the first to establish an infant school in Scotland. Already in 1816, in connexion with his factory at New Lanark, Robert Owen had organised an infant or nursery school on enlightened lines, but his had been an isolated experiment, wholly secular in its inspiration.

For many of his ideas on infant education, Stow drew on the experience of others.[2] He had visited schools, and he had studied the children's literature of the period. Much of his organisation was modelled on Wilderspin's school in Spitalfields, London, and it was Wilderspin's help and advice he sought in the initial stages of the Drygate school. Wilderspin himself had applied to mass education many of the ideas of Pestalozzi, including the emphasis on objects and prints, which, by exercising the eye, were intended to direct the thoughts and develop the understanding. While Pestalozzi, in a homely rural setting, had preserved the family atmosphere of his school, Wilderspin, in a very different environment, had contrived devices for classroom and playground.

Stow followed Wilderspin in his emphasis on the development of the senses by the use of pictures and shapes, in his stress on emotional and physical development by music and movement, and in his insistence on the employment of a female assistant. But his fundamental aim was much more explicitly moral and religious than that of Wilderspin. Whereas the latter had confined his Bible teaching to a few precepts illustrated by pictures of miracles, Stow sought to mould character by

[1] David Stow, *The Training System*, Blackie, 1845 edition, pp 2-5.
[2] David Stow, *National Education*, Hatchard, 1847, p 26 *et seq*.

C

moral training based on the Scriptures, to cultivate habits of mind and conduct.[1] For in the same way as the young plant was nurtured, pruned and watered, so must the child be encouraged, curbed and directed.

The Drygate School, which admitted children between 2 and 6, became the model for other infant schools in neighbouring towns and cities. A master – David Caughie—and his wife were put in charge. The school itself, a transformed cottage, had a main room specially fitted with a gallery of tiered seats so that a hundred children could see the master and the illustrations he used.[2] There was also a small room for the children's coats, and outside the school there was a large gravel playground. In fact Stow was really breaking new ground, for infant education was contrary to accepted custom in Scotland. The physical hardships of weather and terrain and the frugality of parents, who sought maximum value for the fees they paid, had usually combined to postpone the beginning of schooling to the age of 7.

In his *Moral Training* published in 1834, a work which went to many editions under the later title *The Training System*, Stow described his "simultaneous" method of teaching a hundred children at once. Books were excluded. Instead the emphasis was on descriptive narrative, on "picturing out" in suitable simple and graphic language, and on questioning in order to ensure that children understood and remembered what had been taught. A favourite form of question was the ellipsis, the omission of a vital word or phrase to be filled in by the children. In fact, pupils were never told anything "which by analysis, comparison or illustration they can be made to find out for themselves".[3]

Scripture was an essential part of the daily instruction, but the children were not given the Shorter Catechism to learn. Stow's methods were more time-consuming than the old-fashioned memory work, and, in his popular dialogue *Granny and Leezy*, Granny expresses the impatience of his critics when she says: "Ye may keep the weans till they are auld men and

[1] David Stow, *The Training System*, pp 14-16.
[2] Stow claimed this was the first gallery. *Granny and Leezy*, Longman, 1860 edition, p 65.
[3] *2nd Report of the Glasgow Educational Society's Normal Seminary*, 1836, p 11.

women, afore they get through the mother's carritches, let
alone thinking to get through the Shorter Catechism".[1]

A great variety of secular subjects were taught with the aid of
objects, prints, flora or fauna. Counting was taught by means of
frames of coloured beads, the science of everyday things by
reference to food and articles of furniture, and natural history
with the aid of pictures and specimens. Children were encouraged to tend the plants and flowers bordering the playground, and Stow even advocated school museums and expedi-
tions to collect specimens. Sometimes the children were
divided into groups of 5 or 6 under the superintendence of
monitors, so that they could move round and examine pictures
mounted on lesson boards, returning to the gallery at the end of
the lesson for class questions. Rhymes set to well-known tunes
were designed to make learning pleasurable. There was the
multiplication table which began:

> "Two times one are two good boys
> Who came in time to school;
> Two times two are four large swans
> Now swimming in yon pool.
>
> Two times three are six strong ropes
> On which we children swing;
> Two times four are eight church bells
> How merrily they ring."

A less happy example, perhaps, was the song set to the tune of
"Scots wha hae" which explained orthography, geometry,
chronology, and so on, the vital word coinciding with the final
beat of each verse.[2]

Schoolroom routine included marching and singing, clapping
hands and exercises, all designed to enable the children to "let
off steam" and make them more attentive, orderly and obedient.
Indeed, they were rarely in their seats for more than fifteen
minutes at a time without some form of exercise. Physical
exercise, however, was much more than an outlet for super-
fluous energy. It was an essential part of character training for,

[1] David Stow, *Granny and Leezy*, p 24.
[2] *The Infant School Magazine*, 2nd edition, 1834, pp 160-1 and p 76.

according to Stow, it was no more possible to develop good habits in children within the restraint of the classroom than it was "to train a bird to fly in a cage, or a race-horse to run in a stable".[1] The playground was the "uncovered school", the "child's little world", where unselfconsciously he revealed himself. Playground equipment included circular swings, tall gymnastic poles with six ropes attached. While children whirled themselves round, others counted aloud to forty, and then claimed their turn. Contemporary prints show the delights of the "uncovered school" with the children engaged in a variety of play: swinging, building with bricks, skipping, gardening, or even having a tug-of-war with the master who, in his supervision of the children, often joined in their games.

Observation of children out-of-doors gave him an insight into character, for he could pick out the solitary children, the natural leaders and the docile followers. It was an essential part of his supervision in the playground to note acts of generosity or kindness, aggressiveness or brutality, so that later in the classroom he could, without mentioning the child by name, comment on some act of unselfishness or misdemeanour. Then he would appeal to the assembled gallery, to the "sympathy of numbers", to arouse appropriate feelings of joy or shame in the individual concerned. As the master David Caughie himself expressed it, the children were the jury, the master the judge.[2] Great stress was put on the "sympathy of numbers" which in early life could be powerfully directed at applying moral principles and fostering habits of cleanliness and neatness.[3] Public opinion was thus substituted for the traditional tawse.

Stow's school with its emphasis on varied curriculum, skilful organisation and sympathetic contact was thus very different from the unmethodical, authoritarian school regime of the past. It was very much in contrast, also, to the stark regimentation of the new monitorial system with its reliance on child instructors. Essentially, Stow held that teacher and class formed a unity and

[1] David Stow, *National Education*, p 6.
[2] The principle of the jury and the judge was made by David Caughie. *Address on the presentation to him on the occasion of his Jubilee as a teacher*, 6 January 1868. Transcribed from MS by R R Rusk.
[3] He referred to the honesty of the children who left the strawberry plants and blackberry bushes to ripen untouched. David Stow, *The Training System*, p 50.

that as companion and leader the teacher was to inspire confidence in children and to supervise them carefully and constantly. By tact and understanding he was to encourage each child to control his emotions and to develop his capacity for hard work. Visitors to the school commented on the devoted "maternal care" of the schoolmaster's wife, on the healthy, happy appearance of the young children, and on their obvious pleasure in attending school.[1] Indeed many of the children preferred to come to school even at holiday time for, they said, "We get better fun at school than we do in the street; we get swinging, and balls and tops and all we want".

Wood and Stow had much in common. Both were men of substance with a family background very different from that of so many dominies who had obtained their university class tickets only by vigorous self-discipline and self-denial. They were inspired not by classical scholarship but by love of humanity. Both were in sympathy with child nature and were able to appeal directly to the understanding of the child. They were alike in requiring of the teacher more than technical skill: liveliness of mind, flexibility and, above all, humanity. But Wood's emphasis on rivalry, on rewards based on individual testing, was much more in keeping with the fiercely competitive tradition of Scottish education. Nor did he eschew corporal punishment, though he used it sparingly and had no truck with Lancaster's elaborate devices of logs and shackles and badges of disgrace. Stow was much more revolutionary. He excluded prizes and place-taking which he considered fostered jealousy and ill-will, and he condemned corporal punishment which would destroy the desired relationship between teacher and pupil. Indeed, his practice was very different from that of Wilderspin, who confessed that he had found it necessary to whip even an infant of 15 months.[2]

On principle, as well as from necessity, both pioneers charged small school fees, for they felt that parents would value education all the more if they paid for it. Fees they found were no barrier, for children flocked to their schools. Indeed it was the

---

[1] *Committee Book*, 1829-31. Entries in manuscript.
[2] *Report of the Select Committee appointed to inquire into the Present State of Education of the People in England and Wales*, 1835, p 17.

necessity to cater for large numbers which gave an unfortunate rigidity to some of their methods. Though Wood described the monitorial system as the "shell" and the spirit of his teaching as the "kernel", his child instructors were hardly fitted for the delicacy of their task. By careful selection and training he claimed they were able to "explain . . . exemplify . . . illustrate, in a manner which has frequently excited the astonishment of strangers." Some "apparently slow, idle and heedless" boys were transformed by the responsibility of their office.[1] Yet it is clear that what they most excelled in was "drilling" and "riveting attention". While Wood, with a wide age-range of children, classified them, and gave them to immature instructors, Stow had infants of disparate ages and abilities taught together in the belief that the younger pupils learnt from the answers of their elders. Both methods had their drawbacks. With six or seven classes going on at the same time, the general noise of the Edinburgh Sessional School was described by a visitor as "deafening and intolerable".[2] On the other hand, with the large classes conducted on the "simultaneous" method, few teachers were able to achieve the family relationships which Stow desired, and instead of stimulating the "sympathy of numbers" they tended to impose their own ideas with formalism and rigidity.

Principally the two men differed in their aims. Wood, with his interest in intellectual training, preferred to take children over 6 years of age. Stow, concerned with character formation, wanted to influence children in their tenderest years. In our own terminology, his was a nursery school which children attended as soon as they could walk. When he later extended his operations to other age-groups, he was keen that teachers in training should start with infants. "If the student succeeds . . . with young children," he said, "he never fails in training the older ones in any branch, mentally or morally." He saw that, to avoid the depravity of urban life, children must go early to school. Prevention was better than cure. The "training system" was a necessary part of the "moral economy" of society,

[1] John Wood, *Account of the Edinburgh Sessional School*, p 102.
[2] "Hartvig Nissen's Impressions of the Scottish Educational System in the Mid-Nineteenth Century", Lawrence Stenhouse, *British Journal of Educational Studies*, vol IX, no 2, May 1961, p 146.

for it would "enable the close confined labourer or artisan in
a crowded city to bring up his child as free from evil example as
his forefathers did, or as his brother, the farmer, perhaps now
does in the scene of country life".[1]

Stow was convinced that no master should be without a
female helper who, with the gentleness of her sex, would readily
give the care and comfort required by young children. "Without a female hand," he said, "no infant school can be perfect."
Infant schools were to be models of family training and therefore there was need of both master and mistress to represent
father and mother.[2] Cleanliness and tidiness were insisted upon;
on arrival each morning, children were inspected while they
sang and mimed, "This is the way we wash our hands. . . . This
is the way we comb our hair. . . ." The classroom was kept
well ventilated and was regularly scrubbed.

As far as possible Stow tried to reproduce conditions of real
life so that children could be trained to apply moral standards in
their everyday conduct and intercourse with others. The equipment of the playground and the fruit trees in the garden were
therefore means of teaching children lessons of mutual forbear-
ance, of self-denial and honesty. Thus "sympathy of numbers"
and careful superintendence in a selected environment sup-
planted the immoral training of the city streets. Essentially,
Stow was concerned with the development of the whole child,
physically, intellectually and emotionally. Joyous activity was
therefore an important part of school life both in the classroom
and in the playground, a defiance of the tradition that "a school
canna be the richt sort when they hae sae muckle fun".

THE EVOLUTION OF THE EDINBURGH NORMAL SCHOOL

The pioneer schools made a great appeal. Wood very soon
had to restrict visitors to two days a week. From the Drygate
School, groups of infants were taken to neighbouring towns to
demonstrate Stow's system, and sets of apparatus, pictures and
woodcuts, similar to those used in the school, were sold to

---

[1] David Stow, *Infant Training*, Collins, 1833, p 16.
[2] *2nd Report of the Glasgow Educational Society's Normal Seminary*, 1836,
p 24 note.

admirers. Indeed, following a lecture tour by Wilderspin, public interest was such that schools were founded in Edinburgh, Dundee, Kinghorn, Dunfermline, Inverness and Dingwall, and the Glasgow Society launched an Infant School Magazine to illustrate and explain the training system. Both Wood and Stow attracted observers, often practising teachers, who came at their own expense.

The Edinburgh Sessional School became a "model" school as early as 1826 when teachers, intended for remote districts of the Highlands, were sent there by the General Assembly of the Church of Scotland. Already in 1824 the Church had launched an appeal for "Assembly" schools in the Highlands and Islands to supplement the system of parish schools established by law. Within a year £5,500 had been raised to provide teachers' salaries, and an Education Committee had been appointed to superintend the establishment of schools. Gaelic-speaking teachers were recruited, since it was recognised that children should first be taught in their home language before they progressed to English. Arithmetic and sometimes navigation and book-keeping were also taught. Many of the teachers, however, were of low attainment and before appointment to their stations were required to spend a brief period of observation in the Sessional School.[1] Others from their localities attended during the school vacation. By 1835, 50 teachers in assembly schools, nearly half the entire number, had attended the Sessional School.

Already, the Committee of the General Assembly had extended operations to include the establishment of schools in destitute areas in the towns, and applications for schools were flooding in. Members were now convinced that the mere planting of schools was not enough, that it must be accompanied by the systematic training of teachers both "to a knowledge of the branches usually taught and to the actual business of teaching". Originally selected Highland students had come as spectators to the Sessional School. Now it was arranged that all appointed to assembly schools should receive instruction in

---

[1] Report of the Committee of the General Assembly of the Church of Scotland for increasing the means of Education in Scotland particularly in the Highlands and Islands, 1835, p 9. Retrospective account.

elementary subjects and, by serving as monitors, should practise
the most approved method of teaching.[1] The period of attendance varied, but it was rarely over six months and diplomas were
awarded to students who were considered proficient. In return
for a pledge to remain in the service of the Assembly for at least
two years, students were given a maintenance allowance of 10s
a week (or 3s a week if they were already receiving a salary).

The scheme was considered highly successful. Indeed, so
enthusiastic were the authorities that they looked forward to
the establishment of "model seminaries" in Glasgow, Perth,
Aberdeen, and in Shetland, where the heritors of Lerwick had
already voted £500 for the purpose. In 1837, the Sessional
School was transferred to the Committee of the General
Assembly under the title of the Normal and Sessional School.
It now therefore combined a school and a teacher-training
centre. In its original character as a school, it had some 300
pupils; as a training institution it had over 100 students passing
through in the course of a year, including an increasing proportion of private students who paid a guinea entrance fee, but
who rarely stayed long enough to gain the diploma. On the
assumption that the course could be covered in three months
the students spent three hours a day on elementary subjects
and devoted the rest of their time to professional training.

The "Intellectual System" was very popular. The Gaelic-
speaking teachers, trained by Wood, became models for their
areas, and monitorial methods were also adopted by the new
assembly and sessional schools in the towns. Some of the
teachers disseminated Wood's ideas more widely. For example,
Horne, who had served in the Sessional School, became an
outstanding success as organising master in English workhouse
schools. His energy and technical skill were irresistible. "Everything was transformed where he appeared. When he left one
workhouse to proceed to another school he left behind him
deep traces of his influence. The master and the scholars alike
had been awakened from a torpor into which they could not at
once sink back."[2]

[1] *ibid*, p 12.
[2] B C Bloomfield (ed), *The Autobiography of Sir James Kay-Shuttleworth*,
p 3.

Meanwhile an Infant School Society had been founded in Edinburgh in 1829 and was attracting wide support. Indeed, in 1835, Wilderspin said that in the whole of Britain Scotland led in founding infant schools, and he had especial praise for the Edinburgh infant school which numbered Pillans among its directors.[1] The success of each system, however, depended on the particular training as well as on the personality of the teacher.

THE FOUNDATION OF THE GLASGOW NORMAL SCHOOL

The Edinburgh Sessional School had evolved into a training centre because of the requirements of the Gaelic-speaking students appointed to assembly schools. In Glasgow, Stow's infant school had from its early days attracted student observers. Indeed, there is evidence that Stow gradually began to give systematic instruction in the principles of his system, and that by 1832 he was awarding certificates to successful practitioners.[2] In its early days, however, the attendance of students was incidental to the main purpose of the school. Its later transformation into a normal school, specially designed for professional training, was the result of deliberate planning influenced by Continental practice.

The impulse for reorganisation came from a voluntary body, the Glasgow Educational Society, founded in 1834. Headed by a local MP, the Society, which drew on the support of a large number of professional and business men, reflected the reforming mood of the 'thirties. In the Scottish cities, and in Glasgow in particular, the agitation for parliamentary reform had roused great enthusiasm and the impetus given by the Reform Act of 1832 to all questions affecting popular interest had brought education to the fore. Local working men's organisations now aimed at social reform, and many of their most responsible members, skilled and reliable craftsmen and artisans, who had raised themselves by their own industry and endeavour, looked

[1] *Report of the Select Committee appointed to inquire into the Present State of Education of the People in England and Wales*, 1835, 16.
[2] William Fraser, *State of our Educational Enterprises*, Blackie, 1858, p 98. Fraser wrote, "I have before me a certificate headed 'Normal Seminary for Glasgow and the West of Scotland' signed D Stow, date 1832-3".

to education to advance their cause. Even at the national level, Parliament had, in 1833, made its first timorous gesture of support.

The defined aims of the Glasgow Educational Society were to awaken public interest, to inform public opinion of the educational needs of the country and to secure parliamentary investigation and support. The secretary and chief propagandist of the Society was George Lewis, editor of the *Scottish Guardian*. In his tract, *Scotland a Half Educated Nation*, published in 1834, he made a stirring appeal for relief of educational destitution in industrial areas where, he said, "ignorance and profligacy have now their strongholds". In the past, parish schools had imbued the rural population with the spirit of moral enterprise and self-reliance. Now there was need of a network of urban schools which would cater as effectively for the new proletariat. He referred to the impressive achievements of Prussia where the State had organised a comprehensive system of schools, staffed by trained teachers.[1]

Prussian education was the subject of the inaugural lecture of the Society, given at the first of a series of winter soirées by Dr Welsh, Professor of Church History at Edinburgh University, and formerly Minister of St David's Church, Glasgow. Welsh had visited Prussia in the summer of 1834, and he described the professional training of Prussian teachers and the respect in which they were held in their communities. There were, he said, over 30 training institutions in Prussia which gave a two- or a three-year course based on philosophy and which inspired teachers with a professional zeal. He urged his fellow countrymen to recognise education as "a science separate and distinct from all others", and to set up similar training centres.[2]

The Continental pattern of teacher training had also attracted Welsh's colleague in Edinburgh, Professor Pillans. Writing in *The Edinburgh Review* in 1834, he commented on the recent report by the famous French philosopher, Victor Cousin,[3] on

---

[1] Published Glasgow, p 44.
[2] Extracts of Welsh's address in R R Rusk, *The Training of Teachers in Scotland*, Educational Institute of Scotland, 1928, pp 65-68, and in *Edinburgh Review*, vol lix, p 490.
[3] Victor Cousin was a member of the Council of Public Instruction in France. In 1840 he became minister of public instruction under Thiers.

the "State of Education in Prussia". He then went on to extol the merits of the French residential normal training schools. These gave a three-year course of theoretical and practical work, at the successful conclusion of which the student received the much valued *brevet de capacité*. He referred particularly to the inclusion within the course of agricultural work, which gave students insight into the best methods of farming, an asset for the future country schoolmaster. He wrote – "skilful and effectual teaching will never be the ordinary, far less the uniform practice of schools, till all public teachers be required, previously to their appointment, to go through a regular course of professional discipline, and obtain upon examination, a certificate of qualification".[1] The brief courses sponsored by the two English organisations, the National Society and the British and Foreign School Society (formerly the Royal Lancasterian Institution) were "superficial and perfunctory", confined to initiation into "a set of mechanical evolutions, with the precision and promptitude of military drilling", and not to be compared with the didactic systems of Prussia and France.

Pillans himself had lectured on the art of teaching and, in particular, during one Christmas vacation, had given a course of lectures to schoolmasters. He urged that "superior attainments" were not enough in the schoolmaster. He should be able "to conceive even the embarrassments that entangle the beginner; to become identified with the feelings and faculties of children; . . . to lead, by short and easy steps, through a path that to them is a rugged one, leading them, as it were, in arms over the worst of the road, and strewing it with flowers instead of planting it with thorns". He proposed the endowment of "Lectureships on Didactics" in all the Scottish Universities. Besides their term-time duties the lecturers should, during their vacations, regularly inspect schools and diffuse the best methods of teaching.[2]

By its soirées and publications the Glasgow Society attracted

[1] "Seminaries for Teachers", James Pillans, *Edinburgh Review*, July 1834, vol 59.
[2] *ibid*, pp 501-2. James Simpson, advocate, and friend of George Combe, (see Appendix C, I) also proposed university chairs of education. *The Necessity of Popular Education as a National Object*. Black, 1834, p 227.

wide interest and support. Within months of its foundation, it resolved to sponsor teacher training based on a systematic study of principles as well as on practical experience. Initially, it proceeded on the advice of Cousin. "Choose the best conducted primary school . . . that which is in the hands of the master of greatest ability, and trustworthiness; annex to this school a class called Normal, in which the same master shall teach his art to a certain number of young men. . . ." After investigation, it selected as model schools the infant school associated with Stow and, for older children, St John's Parochial School, Annfield. The masters of the two schools were to be responsible for students in training.

In fact Stow's "simultaneous" system was enthusiastically adopted. Stow himself became energetic joint-secretary with Lewis and, from 1835, the informative reports of the Society are unmistakably from his hand. He had already adapted his system to children between the ages of 6 and 10, and he expressed his belief in "its perfect applicability to our ordinary parochial and private schools".[1] Indeed, many of the city parishes had already taken over the system and were defraying school expenses from fees and Church contributions. The Glasgow Educational Society was not connected directly with the Kirk. Members were to be "attached to the principles of a National Religious Establishment", however, and every student in training had to produce a certificate of moral character signed by a minister or clergyman. As was the custom for private as well as public institutions, it was to open its training centre to inspection by the local presbytery.

In 1835, students were admitted to the two model schools. They were required to have a background of elementary education and had to promise to stay at least three months. Some were said to have studied at the University. Professional training was by observation of model lessons and by criticism lessons, where students taught before their fellows. Instruction was also given in grammar and the roots of words, in scripture, geography and history.[2]

---

[1] *2nd Report of the Glasgow Educational Society's Normal Seminary*, 1836, p 12.
[2] *ibid*, pp 14-17.

The use of existing schools was a temporary measure. Already the Society was planning to build a combined normal and model school which would take 100 students and 1,000 children. In November 1836, at a civic ceremony representative of all aspects of public life, the foundation stone was laid of the first normal school in Britain. (The term "normal" was adopted from France, and referred to the norm or pattern of teaching.) The building itself was truly ambitious; the site alone, one acre in Dundas Vale, cost over £2,500 and when all was completed the total bill was well over £17,000.[1] It was designed for a normal department and for three model schools – an infant school, a juvenile school and a female school of industry, where, in addition to the elementary subjects, children should be taught sewing, darning, patching and knitting. There were in all 16 classrooms, a students' hall and 5 playgrounds.[2] A Rector was engaged at a generous salary of £300 and, according to the terms of his appointment, he visited educational institutions in Germany and France.

His death within a few months of his return was an unexpected setback. Stow himself temporarily filled the gap until a new Rector could be appointed, and even afterwards he continued to play an active part in the life and organisation of the college. He insisted that the student should start his training – now a six-month course – in the infant department and then, after experience in other departments, should return there "to receive his highest polish". Stow was convinced that only the most accomplished and cultivated teachers had the degree of tact and delicacy required for infants. It was not, as was commonly thought, a job for any sort of person, for young children resembled "exotic rather than forest trees, tender rather than hardy plants" in their need of the most devoted care.[3] The weekly criticism lesson was the core of the professional training. "Novel and trying as it is," wrote Stow, "the student could never otherwise acquire the system in a limited

[1] J Kay-Shuttleworth, *Public Education as affected by the Minutes of the Committee of Privy Council from 1846 to 1852*, Longman, 1853, p 66.

[2] Combe, who had visited the institution, described the lay-out of the buildings, see Appendix C, I, pp 229-30. (Today, the former normal school is used by Glasgow education authority as a Teachers' Centre.)

[3] *5th Report of the Glasgow Educational Society's Normal Seminary*, 1839, p 26.

attendance of 6 or 8 months. This exercise rubs off many incrustations which, but for this, must have remained. . . ."[1]

Meanwhile the Society was struggling beneath a burden of debt. After the initial surge of enthusiasm, subscriptions declined, and appeals had to be made for government help to clear the debt. In 1839, a grant of £1,000 was made on condition that the Society agreed to government inspection. In 1840, a further £3,500 was given, partly in payment for the training of a large number of teachers for service in English Poor Law schools. It was perhaps in order to alleviate the financial position that in 1839 there was opened an additional school department charging high fees, a private seminary for the children of wealthier citizens, who were instructed in Latin as well as the elementary subjects. Normal school students paid an entrance fee of three guineas. They were required to find lodgings with respectable families in the neighbourhood and, of course, to pay for their own maintenance. In 1839, the Wesleyan Conference began to send students from England for training, allowing them maintenance grants of 12s a month. According to Stow "some spent more and many less".[2]

The trained teachers were greatly in demand. In Scotland they were appointed to the large sessional and subscription schools but, as Stow said, "the largest proportion of our best educated and most accomplished teachers have gone to England, where larger salaries have been offered". Many were appointed to Poor Law schools. Indeed, James Kay (later Kay-Shuttleworth), now one of the Poor Law Commissioners, was so impressed by his visit to the normal school in 1837, that he appointed five of its former students to his own school at Norwood.[3] Subsequently, he appointed another former student, McLeod, to be master of the model school and master of method at his own training institution in Battersea, the first teacher-training college in England. As Secretary of the new Committee of Council in charge of education, he invited Stow to become the

[1] *4th Report of the Glasgow Educational Society's Normal Seminary*, 1837, p 18.
[2] Letter to George Combe, 16 October 1847. National Library, MS 7288, f 53.
[3] *5th Report of the Glasgow Educational Society's Normal Seminary*, 1839, p 11.

first of Her Majesty's Inspectors of Schools in Scotland, a compliment which Stow, however, felt unable to accept.

THE APPEAL FOR STATE AID

It was to Kay's Department that the Glasgow Educational Society made a further appeal for funds in 1841. Before responding to the appeal, their lordships of the Privy Council directed one of the Scottish inspectors to report on the work of the normal school. He was specially instructed to investigate the nature and extent of the moral training of the students and to consider "what expedients are adopted to preserve them from the contaminating influence of a great city, to imbue them with a love of their art".[1] The injunction reflected Kay's own concern for student welfare as seen in his careful oversight of the residential institution at Battersea.

The inspector described in detail the organisation and work of the seminary.[2] It was, he reported, co-educational, though women numbered only 14 compared with 41 men. Students, however, were only permitted to live in recommended lodgings, so that "it is not probable that any cause of conduct unbecoming to their profession can escape detection". Of the male students, the majority had been teachers in small adventure schools and, for the rest, 1 had been a carpenter, 1 a teacher of dancing, 1 a portrait painter, 1 a baker, while 3 had been shopmen and 5 had been university students. Though there was an entrance examination, many had meagre attainments.

The students spent eight hours a day in the institution, about a third of the time being devoted to a varied, though somewhat elementary and unsystematic, course of study, and the rest to practical training. Distinctive features of the training were the model lessons given by the tutors, and the public criticism lessons where students taught before their fellows. Every week 4 students in succession gave brief gallery lessons of a quarter of an hour, each commencing with physical exercises and concluding with the reading of a verse of a psalm which the children sang. Then they and their fellow-students, who had been busy recording their criticisms, proceeded to the hall,

[1] *Minutes of Committee of Council*, 1841-2, p 6 *et seq.*
[2] *ibid*, 1840-1, p 412 *et seq.*

1 Drygate School

2 *Edinburgh Sessional School*

where "in the presence of the rector and secretary, and occasionally of the heads of the various departments of the school, they state their opinion of the manner in which the business of the gallery had been conducted. Mr Stow then delivers . . . his views; the masters of the Model schools give the results of their observations, and the whole is wound up by the remarks of the rector." So great were the terrors of the public criticism lesson that "the female students take no active share in this exercise; they sit attentive and interested auditors".

Their lordships decided to give assistance to the normal schools of both Glasgow and Edinburgh, but they insisted on conditions which would bring them into line with English institutions. In return for a capital sum of £5,000 and an annual grant of £500 towards maintenance, the Glasgow Normal Seminary was to be transferred free of debt to the General Assembly of the Church of Scotland.[1] A similar offer was made to the Church authorities in Edinburgh who had appealed for assistance for rebuilding their institution. The State had thus for the first time assumed a measure of financial responsibility for teacher training, but it had also imposed terms which would ensure efficient and uniform management and control. The finances of the Glasgow Educational Society had long been precarious, and the Government insisted on the Church connexion as a guarantee of survival. The Church of Scotland thus had new responsibilities thrust upon it. It was a situation never contemplated by Stow himself and, with the transfer, something of the spirit of catholicity disappeared. The religious strife of the future was to have its repercussions in the world of teacher training.

The year 1841 was the end of an era. Two Scottish training institutions were now recognised and assisted by the State. Both had germinated from missionary efforts, from Sabbath schools for the offspring of the godless proletariat. Both owed their initial success to inventive amateurs, men of intuitive understanding and imagination, who brought a new humanity into teaching. In the 'thirties, philanthropic and religious zeal had transformed the schools into training institutions, the first normal schools in Britain.

[1] *ibid*, 1841-2, pp 50-1.

D

While the Edinburgh institution grew up in response to immediate needs, the development of the Glasgow training centre reflected much more the native philosophic approach: the recognition of the need of a science of education, a study which should strengthen and illumine practice in the schools, and enhance the professional status of the teachers. By observation, by teaching small groups of children, and by "simultaneous" gallery lessons the student learnt mastery of the whole inductive process. In their quest for a theory of education and in the scale of their operations, the promoters of the Glasgow institution were far ahead of the times. Circumstances, however, had compelled them to appeal for government aid. As a result the State had extended its commitments to teacher training. In the future as it paid the piper, so increasingly it was to call the tune.

Chapter 3
STATE CONTROL, 1841-1872

The transition of the entire training system to ecclesiastical authority came at a time of growing conflict within the Church. A powerful section of evangelicals ("High Flyers") led by Thomas Chalmers, now Professor of Theology in Edinburgh, strenuously objected to the practice of lay patronage in the presentation of ministers. The whole intellectual and moral vigour of Scotland was thrown into the controversy, which was resolved in 1843 by the dramatic exodus of 470 ministers from the General Assembly of the Church of Scotland to found a new Free Church. In the gale of popular enthusiasm, they were joined by about a third of the laity, and many parish churches were bereft of congregations.

The Disruption split the nation. Ministers who left the Establishment gave up their homes and livelihood. Teachers took similar risks, for 360 of them "outed" including 80 parochial schoolmasters. Free churchmen responded nobly and on such a scale that building funds soon covered not only churches and manses but also schools and colleges. Within six years, a capital sum of over £40,000 was raised for education, sufficient to build 500 schools. A further £3,500 a year was contributed for teachers' salaries.[1] The same spirit of devotion which raised such large sums – collected often in coppers and shillings – also provided the Church with expert advice. In particular, John Gibson gave up his appointment as Her Majesty's Inspector of Schools belonging to the Established Church and became Superintendent of Free Church Schools.

At the apex of the "Education Scheme" were two new normal schools. In Edinburgh the Rector, successor to John Wood,

---

[1] *Report of the Proceedings of the General Assembly of the Free Church of Scotland*, 1845, p 235.

who had emigrated in 1840, the teachers and the great majority of students and children had "come out" of the Established Church College in 1843. In Glasgow, where there had been delay in transferring the new college free of debt to the Church of Scotland, Stow himself in May 1845 led a mass exodus from the institution which embodied so much of his life work. It was a dramatic occasion as the procession of staff, students and pupils, about 800 strong, moved solemnly from the grand building, with the janitor bringing up the rear after he had locked the doors for the last time.[1] For Stow, the Disruption was a poignant episode, but it proved to be the beginning of a new chapter with the harnessing of Free Church energies to new training institutions.

Within a few months of the Glasgow exodus, the whole body of staff, students and children, housed in the meantime in tents and wooden huts, assembled in imposing new premises, finished off with a clock tower.[2] In Edinburgh, there was some difficulty in acquiring a suitable site, but eventually Moray House in the Canongate, famous as the lodging of the Earl of Moray, was purchased, and new buildings, erected in the garden, were ready for the students in 1848.[3] By 1848, the Education Committee of the Free Church announced with pride that both institutions, built at a cost of £18,500, of which £6,000 had been contributed by the State, were free of debt.[4] In response to an appeal, donors also furnished books for the libraries and specimens for the museums, while a bursary fund yielded £250 a year.

In the meantime, the Established Church colleges had been hard hit by the secession. In Glasgow, the inherited building was on a magnificent scale, but no Rector was appointed for four years and visitors' references to the slovenliness of the students and to the shockingly dirty classrooms bear witness to the low morale of the institution.[5] In Edinburgh, where a

[1] W Fraser, *Memoir of the Life of David Stow*, Nisbet, 1868, pp 177-9.
[2] *Report of the Proceedings of the General Assembly of the Free Church of Scotland*, 1846, p 182.
[3] *Report of the Proceedings of the General Assembly of the Free Church of Scotland*, 1847, p 150.
[4] *Report of the Proceedings of the General Assembly of the Free Church of Scotland*, 1849, p 251.
[5] *Visitors' Book*, Glasgow Church of Scotland Normal Committee, comments in October-November 1849.

new structure was urgently required, the Church was compelled to make such modest provision that on a £ for £ basis it was able to claim only £4,000 of the promised government grant of £5,000.[1] This later proved a false economy, for the newly acquired premises in Johnston Terrace, on sloping ground near the castle, were both depressing and inconvenient and within ten years became quite inadequate for their purpose.

The effect of the Disruption had been to double the number of training institutions. Each institution was on a similar pattern, a normal school attached to a large model school with accommodation for up to 1,000 children. Since students stayed for varying lengths of time, their numbers fluctuated from month to month. Many of them were the nominees of clergymen who had prepared them for admission. All, of course, had to present a certificate from a minister of religion testifying to moral character. Almost half the students in the Glasgow Free Church College, as many as 60 or 70 a year, were sent by the Wesleyan Conference and there was a sudden drop in numbers when the Wesleyan College in London was opened in 1851.[2] Both Churches took in Gaelic-speaking students, but whereas the Free Church training colleges placed them in lodgings in the vicinity, the Church of Scotland Seminary in Edinburgh boarded them with other male students who paid 8s a week. Altogether about 25 Highlanders, aged between 19 and 30, were selected for residential training on the basis of an entrance examination. The committee made sure, however, that unsuccessful candidates were not thrown on their charity, for they stipulated that all candidates "must, previous to the examination, consign with the Secretary a sufficient sum of money to defray their travelling expenses back to their homes".[3]

The timetable of the boarding establishment shows the intensive programme of the student day beginning at 6 am and ending at 10.30 pm.[4] "Each hour in the day," wrote an in-

[1] *Report of the Committee of the General Assembly for increasing the means of Education in Scotland particularly in the Highlands and Islands*, 1844, Appendix, p 41.
[2] *Minutes of the Committee of the Glasgow Free Church Normal Seminary*, 3 November 1851.
[3] *Report of the Committee of the General Assembly for increasing the means of Education in Scotland particularly in the Highlands and Islands*, 1845, p 43.
[4] See Appendix E, p 238.

spector, "has its allotted occupation, fixed by rules which are unvarying and . . . invariably observed."[1] Since most of the students had poor background (some even found it difficult to follow instruction in English), they required to learn "not merely *how* to teach but *what* to teach" and, in order to make good the deficiencies of their previous education, their course included reading, writing, arithmetic, grammar, syntax, English composition, geography and religious knowledge.[2] Five hours a day were spent in professional training: two and a half hours in actual teaching and the rest of the time in observation and recording. There was also regular instruction in Latin, at a rudimentary level for beginners and at a more advanced stage for others, and a weekly lecture in pedagogy.

Both Churches were keen to preserve Latin in the curriculum so that some at least of the schoolmasters could carry on the intellectual tradition of the parish schools. Ideally they would have liked the normal schools to confine themselves to the art of instruction, and they were hopeful that in the future large numbers of university students would be attracted to a course of professional training. In the meantime, they compromised by including subject matter in the curriculum. Stow himself, however, was most reluctant to accept a combined course and expressed a preference for separate academies for the instruction of poorly-prepared trainees.[3]

Schools conducted by teachers from the Established Church and Free Church normal schools reflected the different methods of training. Under the one system, intellectual culture was the master's chief concern; under the other, moral training and discipline. As one of the inspectors wrote, "While the pupils of those schools conducted on the Intellectual System possess a large measure of information, and have their intellectual faculties more fully developed and strengthened, the pupils of schools conducted on the Training System greatly excel them in habits of cleanliness, of strict order, cheerful obedience, earnest attention and steady application".[4] The best teachers

---

[1] *Report of the Committee of Council on Education*, 1846, vol II, p 505.
[2] *Report of the Committee of the General Assembly for increasing the means of Education in Scotland particularly in the Highlands and Islands*, 1847, p 13.
[3] W Fraser, *Memoir of the Life of David Stow*, p 193.
[4] *Report of the Committee of Council on Education*, 1848-50, vol II, p 611.

were able to combine both methods, but the majority lacked both the experience and the capacity to examine them on their merits. Devotees of one particular system, they were either so fascinated by the interrogatory procedure, by the minute analysis of words and meaning, that they neglected everything else, or they were so absorbed by the external arrangements of the schoolroom that they allowed themselves to be deceived by the showiness of the simultaneous response.[1]

By the mid-'forties, the State had subsidised the establishment of 13 training institutions in Britain – 9 in England, and 4 in Scotland. There were wide diversities of standards and practice, and even in the Scottish seminaries there were contrasts and anomalies. Though all four seminaries were co-educational, women students were very much on the fringe and were ineligible for church bursaries. Only the Church of Scotland seminary in Edinburgh included a "domestic establishment" for some of the male students. The other institutions were non-residential on the pattern of the universities. There were no fixed criteria for entry, which depended more on personal recommendation and ability to pay than on formal qualification. Each institution awarded its own diploma, but placed no embargo on students coming and going when they pleased. The result was a heterogeneous assortment of students who got a smattering of elementary instruction and an initiation into a particular method of teaching.

THE MINUTES OF 1846

The Minutes of Council of 1846 inaugurated a new system of teacher training.[2] Within the schools, promising recruits were to be selected at the age of 13 for a five-year apprenticeship, serving as teachers by day and devoting themselves to further instruction and private study outside school hours. Tested by annual examinations conducted by Her Majesty's Inspectors, the most able of them at the conclusion of their apprenticeship were to be awarded Queen's Scholarships tenable at normal schools. The scheme was designed to achieve a dual purpose:

[1] *ibid*, p 612 *et seq.*
[2] *Minutes*, 25 August and 21 December 1846. Pupil teachers were not to exceed 1 for every 25 scholars.

to replace in the schools child monitors by teenage assistants and to provide normal schools with better-qualified candidates. At the conclusion of each year of the normal school course, which could extend up to three years, students were to take a common examination in general and professional subjects. Leaving Certificates, awarded on the results of the examinations, would carry with them augmentation of salary from state funds.

The new system was widely condemned as an English imposition, a measure of assimilation which had no relevance to Scotland. Though the actuality had often fallen short of the ideal, the country had always prided itself on having teachers of scholarship. The pupil-teacher system was identified with the English elementary school, a conception which was wholly alien, for it limited the range of education and created an unbridgeable gulf between the schools and the universities. Certainly in introducing the system, Kay-Shuttleworth had in mind English conditions and, in particular, the need to improve the standards and prospects of the elementary schoolmaster.[1] By early selection and training, he hoped to rear "a body of skilful and highly instructed masters". Stipends of £10 at the age of 13 rising by annual increments to £20 would cover living expenses of the pupil teacher, while competitive Queen's Scholarships at the conclusion of the apprenticeship would single out the élite for further training. Teachers' certificates, based on courses of uniform length and content, would improve standards of normal schools and would give incentive to ambitious recruits.

Despite the outcry in Scotland, the pupil-teacher system was an obvious improvement on the monitorial method of instruction, for it guaranteed a minimum knowledge as well as a degree of practical skill. It was therefore suited to the large urban schools, of which the Church of Scotland alone had between 200 and 300. As for the quality of normal school entrants, the Scottish ideal – the university student, was rare indeed. From the evidence of those best qualified to judge, the inspectors, it

---

[1] J Kay-Shuttleworth, *Public Education as affected by the Minutes of the Committee of Privy Council*, p 60. (Kay-Shuttleworth had imported the system from Holland.)

seems clear that the average entrant had limited attainments. "It does not include," John Gibson had written, "anything of which a boy of 13 or 14 years of age, in the highest class of a well taught primary school, should be ignorant."[1] As nominees of clergymen, students were apparently selected for their moral and religious qualities rather than for their intellectual calibre. Few had any knowledge of the "higher branches", and Stow himself had found it necessary to extend instruction to those elementary subjects which the students would have to teach. Even so, many left as they had entered "with very shallow attainments indeed", and the term, "normal teachers" was accompanied by the inevitable sneer.[2]

Free Churchmen responded quickly to the government injunctions. During the first flush of enthusiasm they had built schools and seminaries. Now the strain of supporting these institutions was such that they were eager to avail themselves of state aid. They therefore lost no time in adapting their normal seminaries to train large numbers of students, and they encouraged older teachers to study externally for the government certificate, which automatically brought state support to their schools.[3] Stow apparently was a lone dissentient to the generally accepted policy of combining general and professional education in normal school. Free Churchmen in general, though they considered university education the ideal, recognised that it was unattainable in the circumstances.[4] They therefore wholeheartedly welcomed the new state scheme, which in fact offered prospect of complete support for their seminaries and of free maintenance, by means of Queen's Scholarships, to numbers of their students. They lengthened the course of training to a year and appointed new members of staff to teach drawing, mathematics, classics and chemistry.[5]

---

[1] *Report of the Committee of Council on Education*, 1840-1, p 4.
[2] Retrospective account from *Report of the Committee of Council on Education*, 1870-1, p 411.
[3] *Report of the Proceedings of the General Assembly of the Free Church of Scotland*, 1846, p 182.
[4] *Report of the Proceedings of the General Assembly of the Free Church of Scotland*, 1847, p 130.
[5] Stow asked for the appointment of a sub-committee to investigate the effect of adding "direct teaching in Mathematics and Classics upon our students during their limited course of twelve months' training". 4 March 1850. *Minutes of the Committee of the Glasgow Free Church Normal Seminary.*

Members of the Established Church were much more critical of the new financial terms. Grants based on examination results seemed a precarious substitute for the £1,000 annual grant they had received under the previous arrangements. They objected to a fixed length of course which would prevent them from filling vacancies as they occurred in their schools. They also took strong exception to the pupil-teacher system, for, while they admitted that standards had fallen during the crisis years following the Disruption, they looked forward to fulfilling the high ideals associated with the past.[1]   Kay-Shuttleworth, however, reminded them of the grave defects of organisation, discipline and curriculum of their colleges, which indeed had lost them half their annual grant in recent years.[2]   Finally, by a compromise arrangement, the Privy Council agreed to pay half the original grant to the two seminaries on condition that the Church contributed a matching sum.[3]   In order to cover major expenses, the authorities were left with no alternative but to remodel the course of training and to appoint additional staff.

The Minutes of 1846 revolutionised teacher training. Students were now taught by special instructors instead of relying on the teachers of the model school. In response to the emphasis placed on subject matter in the certificate examinations, the whole pattern of training changed. The minimum course was fixed at one year, and of a working week of 30 to 40 hours only 5 or, at the most, 10 hours were now devoted to practical teaching. The Free Church authorities reaped the reward of their prompt reorganisation. By 1852, they were receiving an annual grant of £3,000, four times the sum earned by the colleges of the Established Church.[4] Very soon even the Church of Scotland admitted that its institutions were better off under the new regime and discouraged students from coming for brief periods.[5] Examiners noted how efficiently the Scottish

---

[1] *Report of the Committee of the General Assembly for increasing the means of Education in Scotland particularly in the Highlands and Islands*, 1848, p 24.

[2] *ibid*, p 88 *et seq.*

[3] *Report of the Committee of the General Assembly for increasing the means of Education in Scotland particularly in the Highlands and Islands*, 1855, p 14.

[4] *Report of the Committee of Council on Education*, 1852-3, p 1112.

[5] *Report of the Committee of the General Assembly for increasing the means of Education in Scotland particularly in the Highlands and Islands*, 1855, p 37.

candidates had been taught. Their parsing was particularly sound. In other respects, hower, the scripts were heavy-going. "The papers are often very good in point of knowledge, but dreadfully hard and dry," wrote Frederick Temple.[1]

At the school level, the new system brought incentives to both teachers and school managers. The teachers gained financially (they were paid £5 for one pupil teacher, £9 for two, £12 for three and £3 for every additional apprentice over three), and the managers gained by the fact that their schools could get teaching assistants free of charge. Though the standards demanded by the yearly examination of pupil teachers were much lower than the best schools might hope to achieve, they served as a stimulus to many other schools.[2] Moreover, in the long run, schools benefited from the requirement that only certificated teachers, or those whom HMIs judged competent to instruct apprentices, should participate in the scheme, and from the insistence on reasonable standards of furniture, apparatus and books.

Pupil teachers were in the words of Matthew Arnold the "drudges" of the profession. Occasionally in the parish schools they attended advanced classes in Latin or mathematics, but in general they were engaged in teaching the whole of the school day. The teachers in charge were required to give them one and a half hours of private instruction, but in fact the practice varied. Some teachers took great personal interest in the progress of their apprentices, others devoted much less than the required time to them, and even that within school hours. The *Scottish Educational Journal*, which was launched in the 1850s, made a special feature of catering for pupil teachers. Exercises were specially prescribed, and the best answers were selected for publication.

The annual examinations conducted by Her Majesty's

[1] Quoted from the Kay-Shuttleworth papers, Nancy Ball, *Her Majesty's Inspectorate 1839-1849*, Educational Monographs, University of Birmingham Institute of Education, 1963, p 181.

[2] Candidates at the age of 13 had to take an examination in elementary subjects, and to teach a class in front of an Inspector of Schools. At the end of the fifth year, pupil teachers were examined in syntax, etymology, prosody, composition and religious knowledge. Boys had also to show proficiency in the rudiments of algebra or the practice of surveying and in geography, girls in sewing, knitting and historical geography. All had to teach a gallery lesson in front of the inspector.

Inspectors were a spur to individual effort.[1] In general, pupil teachers in parish and burgh schools achieved the highest standards in the compulsory subjects and had, in addition, some knowledge of mathematics and classics. Those best trained in practical teaching came from the large urban schools, such as the sessional school in Dundee where, according to the inspector, "one master with the aid only of pupil teachers keeps 600 children above the average state of progress, and in better than average condition as to discipline".[2] Pupil teachers were selected on moral as well as intellectual grounds. Indeed only apprentices from respectable homes were engaged in the first place,[3] and illegitimate children were excluded from employment in their own parishes where all the circumstances of their birth were known. The indenture of apprenticeship laid great emphasis on moral qualities; the pupil teacher was required to "conduct himself with honesty, sobriety and temperance and not be guilty of any profane or lewd conversation or conduct, or of gambling or any other immorality". He was also required to attend church every Sunday.

Inspectors welcomed the improvement in organisation and industry of those schools which had pupil teachers. The greatest single revolution in the school, due directly to the employment of apprentices, was the disappearance over the years of the monster galleries which were replaced by classrooms.[4] The simultaneous method with ellipses and "picturing out" had often sacrificed thoroughness to display and had not catered for the wide diversity of age. Now, as girl apprentices were recruited into what had previously been regarded as a male profession, it was recognised that they had special aptitude with younger children. Indeed, because they were so good with infants, masters frequently neglected to give them a range of

[1] The HMIs were keen that pupil teachers should profit by their mistakes. One of them described how, when he visited the schools, he took the pupil teachers' written papers with him "marked in red ink where erroneous". He attributed their improvement to the personal contact. *Report of the Committee of Council on Education*, 1861-2, p 199.

[2] *Report of the Committee of Council on Education*, 1850-1, p 846.

[3] There was some question whether publicans' children could become pupil teachers. *Official Papers*, No 25, March 1857, Scotch Education Department.

[4] Even in the 1930s a HMI referred to "the obsolete galleries in Highland schools". *Education in Scotland*, 1933-4, p A97.

experience with other classes.[1] With their constant duties and regular examinations the apprentices had little opportunity of extending their horizons. They mastered the technicalities of teaching; they could purvey information and drill their classes by questioning, but they could not probe the child mind. To them a response was right or wrong.

At the age of 18, those pupil teachers who wished to remain in the profession competed for Queen's Scholarships which, valued at up to £25 a year (women's awards were only two-thirds the value of the men's), covered maintenance at college. The scholarships were restricted to 25 per cent of normal school entrants and went to those apprentices "who appeared most proficient in their studies and skilful in the art of teaching, and concerning whose character and zeal for the office of Teacher the Inspector is able to give the most favourable report". For the highest award, male candidates had to offer one of the advanced subjects: Euclid, algebra, mensuration or mechanics. Females, who were exempted from answering questions on vulgar fractions and decimals in the arithmetic paper, qualified for the maximum award by offering book-keeping or domestic economy.[2] Apart from Queen's Scholars, some of the men were assisted with Church bursaries, but many others were deterred by poverty from going to normal school. They either took other jobs or they remained in the schools as assistants (ex-pupil teachers) and tried to prepare themselves for the certificate examination.

It is significant that the new regulations gave recognition to women students.[3] They could compete for Queen's Scholarships, but the majority came as private students. Unlike the men, who were usually the sons of labourers and required either a scholarship or bursary, many of the women were the daughters of shopkeepers and clerks who could afford to maintain them during their course.[4] Indeed, the women students, who were very much in a minority at first, seem to have had altogether more poise and polish than the men. Hitherto, publicly

[1] *Report of the Committee of Council on Education*, 1861-2, p 226.
[2] *Pupil Teachers' Broadsheet*, issued under the *Minutes*, 1846-7.
[3] Relatively few women were employed in teaching in Scotland.
Report of the Committee of Council on Education, 1852-3, tables of statistics:
In inspected schools in Scotland   100 women and   531 men
In inspected schools in Britain   2,062 women and 3,879 men
[4] *Report of the Argyll Commissioners*, vol I, 1865, Appendix, p 126.

supported schools had been a male preserve, and women had been compelled to confine themselves to inferior dame schools. Now, teaching offered women altogether more attractive prospects, the opportunity of self-support in a respectable and rewarding occupation.

By liberal extension of grants in the 1850s, teacher-training institutions were able to attract a wider range of students and to establish a regular two-year course. More Queen's Scholarships, now no longer restricted to pupil teachers, became available and could be extended for a second year.[1] The four Presbyterian seminaries were flourishing.[2] By 1857, student numbers had risen to over 500, of whom one-third were women. By the end of the decade, the Glasgow Free Church College was recording annual surpluses of £400 to £500 and was renting additional accommodation.[3] In 1855, a small fifth college had been founded by the Episcopal Church in Minto House, Edinburgh, to cater for the needs of the Scottish Episcopal schools.[4] Exclusively male, the college was run on the English residential pattern, and was staffed by tutors from St Mark's College, Chelsea. Minto House, however, had great difficulty in filling its twenty-six places and had to draw on English students.

Already the Privy Council had taken measures to improve the standard and extend the range of work. From 1853, it paid £100 a year (over and above the £150 salary required of the authorities) to normal school lecturers who could pass an examination in one of several subjects: history, geography, physical science and applied mathematics.[5] Within two years, five of the Free Church lecturers had qualified for the new grant. Some members of the Free Church expressed apprehension lest the

[1] *Minutes*, July 1851 and August 1853. The value of the awards was increased to cover books and travel.

[2] The Church of Scotland in 1858 established special preparatory classes for the scholarship examination. *Report of the Committee of the General Assembly for increasing the means of Education in Scotland particularly in the Highlands and Islands*, 1858, p 12.

[3] *Minutes of the Committee of the Glasgow Free Church Normal Seminary*. March 1857.

[4] *Report of the Committee of Council on Education*, 1859-60, p 469. There were 95 Episcopal schools in Scotland under inspection.

[5] *Minutes*, 20 August 1853. *Report of the Committee of Council on Education* 1853-4, vol I, p 24.

term "lecturer" implied that the practical training of the student might be neglected. They were reassured by the Rector of the Edinburgh Normal School who wrote, "lecturers lecture and also show students how to impart knowledge . . . how to simplify what is difficult and to cast a charm round what seems repulsive".[1] (The Privy Council examination in fact tested not only knowledge of subject matter, but also "skill in adapting it to elementary instruction".) Including their augmentation, several of the lecturers were paid £300 a year, and the Rectors received princely salaries of £500.

New subjects such as music and drawing had already come into the curriculum. Drill was first introduced in the Glasgow Free Church College in 1858,[2] when the students were charged an extra 2s a year to cover the cost of hiring a visiting instructor. Geometry, mechanics, higher mathematics, physical science and classics were all studied by men. As an optional subject, Latin was none too popular with many of the lads who came up with little or no knowledge of the subject, and, in one seminary at least, numbers of students refused to take it seriously.[3]

The Free Church authorities were keen to encourage the teaching of science and in 1857 they appointed the Rev John Kerr to teach mathematics and natural science in their Glasgow college. Kerr was a former student of Professor W Thomson, later Lord Kelvin, who described him in 1892 as "one of the most distinguished scientific investigators in the whole world".[4] Indeed, he was a born research worker and, like his mentor, who had constructed his physical laboratory in the professorial wine cellar, he organised his own laboratory in the college cellar. Here, despite a heavy timetable, he pursued his researches throughout his forty years at the college.[5]

---

[1] *Report of the Proceedings of the General Assembly of the Free Church of Scotland,* 1857, p 258.

[2] A teacher of gymnastics and calisthenics was appointed 3 May 1858. *Minutes of the Committee of the Glasgow Free Church Normal Seminary.*

[3] *ibid,* 3 August 1857. The lecturer, who had apparently taught English efficiently, was reprimanded for the indiscipline of his Latin classes.

[4] *Scottish Universities Commission,* Minutes of Evidence, 1892 (published 1900), cd 276, p 307. (See Appendix C, II, pp 231-3, for Kerr's career.)

[5] His teaching was clearly enlightened. In arithmetic, for example, students were trained to "discard mere dogmatic rules, substituting in their stead those easy principles by which almost all questions in arithmetic may be solved". *Report of the Committee of Council on Education,* 1858-9, p 408.

Students attended normal school for 5½ days a week and were expected to study on their own in the evenings. The timetable varied slightly from college to college, but the array of subjects to be covered was formidable. The course of study for men students included: religious knowledge, church history, grammar, reading, penmanship, geography, history, music, logarithmic arithmetic, mathematics, arithmetic, algebra, science, English literature, Latin, Gaelic, school management and practical teaching. Dickens poked fun at the brimmingly confident "Mr M'Choakumchild", the prototype of the numerous Scottish teachers who came to teach in England. He wrote, "He and some one hundred and forty other schoolmasters, had been lately turned at the same time, in the same factory, on the same principles, like so many pianoforte legs. He had been put through an immense variety of paces, and had answered volumes of head-breaking questions. Orthography, etymology, syntax, and prosody, biography, astronomy, geography and general cosmography, the sciences of compound proportion, algebra, land surveying and levelling, vocal music, and drawing from models, were all at the ends of his ten chilled fingers. . . . He . . . had taken the bloom off the higher branches of mathematics and physical science, French, German, Latin and Greek. He knew all about all the histories of all the people, and all the names of all the rivers and mountains. . . . Ah, rather overdone, M'Choakumchild. If he had only learnt a little less, how infinitely better he might have taught much more!"[1]

COMMENTARIES ON THE NEW SYSTEM

There were many regrets that the new type of teachers lacked the depth of knowledge of their predecessors, but there was universal agreement that they could teach better. Certainly they were capable of organising the large numbers of children in the sessional and subscription schools to which they were usually appointed. Her Majesty's Inspectors were full of praise for the work of the normal schools. As one of them said, "They

---

[1] Charles Dickens, *Hard Times*, book I, chapter 2. In fact *Hard Times* was published in 1854, barely in time to have judged the effect of the new regulations.

3 *Dundas Vale Normal School*

4   *Sir John Adams*

(the students) are taught daily by the most skilful and experienced masters and lecturers. They see in them the best models for imitation . . . there are no teachers to be compared with those who have been at normal schools."[1] Probably the fairest assessment, however, came from the inspector who said, "The former (parish schoolmasters) knew much more and had more general culture, but could not teach so well, the latter (trained teachers) know much less but can teach better what they do know".[2] Already in the early 1850s there were those who looked forward to combining university study with the normal school training. Indeed the colleges themselves recorded the numbers of their students who had proceeded to university (no fewer than 30 from the Free Church institutions alone between 1854-8)[3] with the intention of entering the Church, or securing promotion to burgh schools or academies.

Could the numbers of teachers required at the time have been produced by any other means than normal school training? One of the most severe critics of the training system was Simon S Laurie, the newly appointed Secretary of the Church of Scotland Education Committee. It was probably Laurie, writing under the initials, "S S", in the *Scottish Educational Journal*, who suggested that would-be teachers should attend burgh schools rather than normal seminaries.[4] By mixing with children of the middle class they would "acquire the manners and habits of gentlemen. . .". "Why," he asked, "set down Normal schools in low localities and assemble together an innumerable (*sic*) number of ill-trained unmannerly children and educate our future teachers on the same forms with these children?" Teachers should have the best education the country could give, and in the best society possible, "for society educates the man as much, nay more, than systems of technology". Laurie was in fact suggesting a system of secondary education for intending teachers. However, secondary education as such was confined to the few larger centres; elsewhere, burgh schools combined elementary and secondary education. It was lack of a graded

---

[1] *Report of the Argyll Commission*, vol II, 1867, p cxlv.
[2] *Report of the Committee of Council on Education*, 1865-6, p 304.
[3] *Report of the Proceedings of the General Assembly of the Free Church of Scotland*, 1858, p 253.
[4] *Scottish Educational Journal*, April 1856, p 62 *et seq.*

E

system of schools which compelled the normal schools to instruct students as well as to train them for teaching.

In his official capacity, Laurie had recently become acquainted with the Established Church seminaries. His own experience of teaching, however, was confined to that of a private tutor, and he had the disdain of a young man of culture for the low aims and puritanical atmosphere of training institutions. Like his scholarly contemporary, Derwent Coleridge, Principal of St Mark's College, Chelsea, he was repelled by the "lurking meanness"[1] of the normal schools, by the notion that young men should be conditioned to working with the lowest of the low. Practising schools were certainly attended by some of the poorest children and there are references in time of hardship to bread being distributed to the pupils.[2] Many of the students, however, would find themselves teaching in similar circumstances and it was questionable whether, if they had been educated as gentlemen, they would have taken willingly to teaching barefooted urchins.

Later, Laurie expressed regret that preparation for teaching had been severed from the universities and confined, as he put it, to the "hot-house system" of normal seminaries. Such arrangements might be suited to England, where the universities were separated from the poorer classes of the population, but not to Scotland with its opportunities for university study where at small cost men "may enjoy the highest education which the country affords". Normal school training might be necessary for women, but men should be prepared in the universities by extension of university bursaries and by the endowment of Chairs of the Principles and Practice of Teaching.[3] As official visitor under the terms of the Dick Bequest,[4] Laurie was

[1] The phrase is from R W Rich, *Training of Teachers in England and Wales during the Nineteenth Century*, Cambridge University Press, p 88.
[2] *Minutes of the Committee of the Glasgow Free Church Normal Seminary*, 10 February 1853.
[3] *The Museum*, July 1862, p 199 *et seq.*
[4] Under the terms of the Dick Bequest (an early nineteenth century endowment) parish schoolmasters in Aberdeen, Moray and Banff were rewarded for high qualifications and for teaching Classics. "The Dick Bequest: The Effect of a Famous Nineteenth-century Endowment on the Parish Schools of North East Scotland", Marjorie Cruickshank, *History of Education Quarterly*, vol V, no 3, University of Pittsburg Press, September 1965.

familiar with the achievements of the parish schoolmasters of
the North-East. As university products, they had, he said, "a
superiority and dignity of character which belongs to men of
considerable cultivation". Their own exertions had given
them moral qualities which he felt to be lacking in youths,
who at the age of 13 had exercised premature authority, who
as protégés of the Government had had their training paid for,
and who only too often were confirmed in self-esteem by the
superficial studies of the normal school. Nevertheless, Laurie
commented on the wastefulness of effort of some of the North-
Eastern schoolmasters, and he encouraged them to spend short
periods of observation in the training institutions.[1]

LIFE IN THE NORMAL SCHOOLS

Normal students were given experience in the different
divisions of the practising school. By observation, by teaching
and by criticism lessons, they became familiar with the work of
each section. Instructing separate classes in a large model
school, however, was not the best preparation for those country
students who would be expected to organise small all-age
schools. The Free Church Training College in Glasgow
therefore experimented with a new model department, a "village
school", resembling as nearly as possible the small parish
unit.[2]

The Rectors themselves controlled and spent much of their
time in the practising schools. As masters of method, their
lectures on the principles of teaching, the art of school-keeping
as it was sometimes called, were directly related to the classroom.
While Principals of English training colleges were often distinguished clergymen, graduates of the ancient universities and
somewhat remote from the day-to-day work of the schools,
Scottish Rectors were able teachers, appointed direct from
schools or promoted within their own institutions. Some of
them were extremely youthful. Thomas Morrison, for example,

---

[1] *Report of the Colebrooke Commission* (on Endowed Schools and Hospitals),
vol II, 1874, p 217.
[2] *Report of the Committee of Council*, 1851-2, p 1073. (Similarly, students
from Kay-Shuttleworth's country residential training college found themselves unsuited to work in urban schools.)

was only 25 when he was appointed to the Glasgow Free Church
College in 1852, and Maurice Paterson only 28 when he was
appointed to Moray House in 1864. All were versatile teachers
and instructed students in a range of subjects. Many of them
wrote their own textbooks; there was, for example, Morrison's
Manual of School Management, Sime's *Manual of Religious
Knowledge* and Currie's *Principles and Practice of Early Infant
School Education*.

Members of the college committees maintained close oversight over their institutions. Often they judged candidates for
staff vacancies by trial lectures delivered in their presence to the
students. They made it their business to visit the various
college departments and listen to the tutors' classes. (Stow
himself, of course, attended the students' criticism lessons to
within a few years of his death.) In his early years as Secretary
of the Church of Scotland Education Committee, Laurie felt
his reforming zeal frustrated, and he confessed to a desire to be
rid of the "close ecclesiastical connexion" which he found so
stifling and restrictive.[1]

Ladies' committees, composed of wives or relatives of officials,
were charged with a special oversight of the boarding houses
which were established for women students. There was now
general consensus that the infant school was the province of the
mistress, and women were encouraged to train in increasing
numbers. Their course was less arduous than that of the men,
and instead of the various branches of higher mathematics and
physical science they were required to show proficiency in
domestic economy and industrial skill. They were taught
separately from the men students. In fact, in the Church of
Scotland colleges, the courses were so organised that there were
"two distinct institutions under one roof".[2] The Free Church
allowed joint classes in music, an arrangement which apparently
had an adverse effect on the results in that subject.[3]

Already in 1849 the Edinburgh Church of Scotland College
had established a boarding house for women students from the

---

[1] Letter to George Combe, 1 July 1858. National Library of Scotland
MS 7372, f 132.
[2] *Report of the Committee of the General Assembly for increasing the means
of Education in Scotland particularly in the Highlands and Islands*, 1857, p 11.
[3] *Report of the Committee of Council on Education*, 1860-1, p 405.

country. It was Laurie's idea that a larger "Industrial Boarding House" should be fitted up so that women students could qualify for the Privy Council examination in household economy and teach in the new industrial schools. There was a great demand that girls should be instructed at school in house-craft: sewing, knitting and domestic economy, a knowledge of which would enable them to make their homes pleasant and attractive and to keep their husbands away from "the wretched excitement of the village change-house".[1] Students (referred to in the Committee Reports as "inmates") in the Industrial Boarding House paid 8s a week for their board and lodging including a seat in church with the Matron. They were to be neat and modest in their dress since, in the words of the regula-tions, "all extravagance and finery are inconsistent with the objects of the Institution".[2] Their fare was plain and solid to sustain them for their hard physical work as well as their daily two-mile walk to and from the normal school and their six-hour day there. It was a rigorous life for young women, who rose at 6 am to begin their domestic drudgery of cleaning and washing. Even the inspector commented on the excessive length of their family worship. Under such a strict regime it was hardly surprising that, despite the superior accommodation of the boarding house, the students "seem to prefer lodgings where they have more liberty to go out as they please".[3]

Other seminaries established boarding houses for those women students who came from a distance. On principle, however, the Church authorities were opposed to male residence, to the provision of "collegiate halls" of the Battersea type. "We prefer," said the Free Church Committee, "the good old Scottish plan, which has nothing in it of the monastic, or hospital character, crowding the persons under discipline into one artifi-cial household, and subjecting them to one uniform martinet domiciliary routine."[4] Only the small Episcopal College was

---

[1] Report of the Committee of the General Assembly for increasing the means of Education in Scotland particularly in the Highlands and Islands, 1849, p 8.
[2] Report of the Committee of the General Assembly for increasing the means of Education in Scotland particularly in the Highlands and Islands, 1859, p 16.
[3] Report of the Committee of Council on Education, 1858, p 384. See Appendix E, II, p 240.
[4] Report of the Proceedings of the General Assembly of the Free Church of Scotland, 1849, p 259.

organised on a residential basis.[1] It was true that the Church of
Scotland had regarded the Gaelic-speaking students as a special
category and had provided them with bed and board in the
early days, but even this arrangement was dissolved in 1856. All
men students, who did not live at home or with relatives, chose
lodgings from an approved list and were carefully supervised
by the college staff. The students of Moray House, for example,
were "visited from time to time by the Rector, usually in the
evening, and unexpectedly, such visits being repeated probably
six or eight times in the session of six months". They were
expected to attend family worship in the homes and indeed to
conduct it frequently themselves. They served as missioners in
the destitute districts, where they went in organised groups of
two or three to visit the poor, distribute religious tracts and hold
prayer meetings.[2]

In order to qualify for the "parchment", the training college
student had to serve two probationary years in school after
passing the certificate examination. The precise grade of
certificate which was awarded depended on the examination
result and on the inspector's report on service in school.[3]
Thereafter, revision every five years depended on the inspector's
comments recorded annually on the certificate. The certificate
therefore represented much more than examination success.
It bore testimony to each year's exertions, to the diligence and
character of the teacher and to progress in different schools and
under different circumstances.

Practising teachers, including former pupil teachers who remained in the schools as assistants, could study independently
for the certificate examination. Candidates in the early years
included many who had left normal school after only a brief
course and were teaching in the church assembly or sessional
schools, or in the Free Church schools. Apparently, parish
schoolmasters were reluctant to submit themselves to examination. They disliked competing with younger candidates
who had been specially prepared, and they were apprehen-
sive lest failure to obtain the highest certificate would be lowering

[1] See Appendix E, III, p 241.
[2] *Report of the Committee of Council on Education*, 1851-2, p 128.
[3] There were 3 classes and 3 divisions in each class, in all 9 grades.

to their prestige.[1] Inspectors were instructed to show tact and discretion with such candidates, often their seniors in years.

THE EFFECT OF THE NEW SYSTEM

By 1860 there were over 1,200 certificated teachers in the inspected schools of Scotland. Already there was a hierarchy of teachers: certificated teachers, assistant teachers and pupil teachers. As a class, the certificated schoolmasters with salaries of over £90 a year were more prosperous than many of the parish schoolteachers. They were also much more mobile. The old dominie, if he had moved at all, had usually stayed within the same county. The new teachers with their widely recognised qualifications moved with ease. Some of them went to England or abroad, others changed to better posts within Scotland, to positions in burgh schools or academies. Indeed, there were complaints that as careerists they were worse than the old schoolmasters who could not see the school for the steeple. Many of the men teachers joined the Educational Institute of Scotland, the first professional union of teachers. Founded in 1847, chiefly by the efforts of the burgh and parochial schoolmasters, the Institute sought to restrict entry to the profession to those whose qualifications it had approved.[2] It was also active in campaigning for a national, as distinct from a denominational system, of education, which should be universal and compulsory.

It was in response to the widespread demand for the abolition of religious tests that in 1861 the parish schoolmaster was released from the obligation to sign the Confession of Faith.[3] Appointees now had to submit their secular qualifications to trial by university examiners rather than ecclesiastical authority. Salaries were increased to a minimum of £35. However, in the North-Eastern counties, the prized positions were worth as much as £135. Without exception, the Dick Bequest schools were in charge of university men, who, though untrained, had

[1] *Report of the Committee of Council on Education*, 1850-1, p 850.
[2] EIS Diploma could be gained by examination. A J Belford, *Centenary Handbook of the Educational Institute of Scotland*, EIS, 1946, p 72.
[3] The Parochial and Burgh Schoolmaster (Scotland) Act, 1861, opened the office of schoolmaster to any member of the Presbyterian Church.

been initiated in the techniques of teaching and of school-keeping. Elsewhere the incentive of government augmentation encouraged increasing numbers of parish schoolmasters to submit themselves to examination.[1]

As the teacher-training schemes gathered momentum, government expenditure rose rapidly. By the early 1860s, the annual grant to Scotland was over £100,000 of which normal schools alone absorbed £20,000. As holders of Queen's Scholarships, almost all the men students and half the women were receiving free training and maintenance. In the day institutions of Scotland, where there was no limitation on expansion such as was imposed by the residential requirements of English seminaries, numbers of students by 1863 had reached 765. The Minutes of the Privy Council had effected a great transformation. Schools built with government aid (available from the 1830s) had served as models for others, for the heritors had not infrequently been compelled, either by the contrast with neighbouring schools or by the necessity of qualifying for grant, to replace the low ill-ventilated and earthen-floored buildings. School furniture, books and maps had been provided. Above all, a new class of teachers had been trained. Though they could not compare with the parish schoolmaster at his best, they were far superior to the many others who had simply been picked up wherever they could be found. Whereas for the majority of the children of the past the school curriculum had been confined to religion and reading, now under the trained teachers from the normal schools, children were learning grammar, history, geography, drawing, sewing, as well as the "3 Rs".

THE REVISED CODE

The early 1860s brought drastic changes. Following the investigation of English elementary education by the Newcastle Commission, Robert Lowe's Revised Code imposed on English schools a system of payment by results based on the examination of all children in the "3 Rs". The education of the masses was

---

[1] *Report of the Argyll Commission, Report on the State of Education in the Country Districts of Scotland*, 1866, p 38. By the mid-'sixties 40 per cent of the parish school masters held the government certificate.

to be limited in amount and mechanical in kind, regulated in the same way as the market in cotton or molasses. Though Scotland was spared for a decade from the full financial rigours of the code, the mode of examining every child in reading, writing and arithmetic discouraged any extension of the curriculum beyond the rudiments. Teachers' promotion prospects depended on the publicised results, and everything became subordinate to "a mastery of the beggarly elements".

The new code was applied in its full severity to the normal schools.[1] For some time the Privy Council had been perturbed at the numbers of students (estimated at 50 per cent of the women and 40 per cent of the men) who did not take posts in inspected elementary schools.[2] A high proportion had found their way into academies or burgh schools. Others had left the profession for trade, had emigrated, or had gone to a university. Training college authorities repudiated the idea that their students should be absorbed exclusively in elementary education. They pointed out that in Scotland the common school had never discriminated between classes. However, even some of the promoters of Scottish schools felt that the training institutions were aiming too high: in a remonstrance to the Committee of Council, for example, "ladies of high rank" complained that the normal schools provided governesses for private schools and private families rather than mistresses for the poor.[3]

Lowe himself had no understanding of, or sympathy with, Scottish aspirations. Of one deputation he asked, "What do you want to teach in your parochial schools? Would you like your children to learn Quadratic Equations or Latin or Greek?" It is not recorded what his immediate reply was to their answer, "Certainly, that is precisely what they have been in the habit of learning, and what we expect our schoolmasters to be trained

---

[1] There was even some question of dismissing additional students after the beginning of the session in 1863, but eventually it was agreed that future numbers were not to exceed those in training in 1862. *Report of the Education Committee of the General Assembly for increasing the means of Education in Scotland particularly in the Highlands and Islands*, 1863, p 11.

[2] *Report of the Argyll Commission*, vol I, 1865, p 327. (Evidence of R R W Lingen.)

[3] *Report of the Proceedings of the General Assembly of the Free Church of Scotland*, 1860, p 180.

to teach them". Not long afterwards, however, chancing to meet a member of the deputation, he referred to the meeting and commented, "I would as soon ask Parliament to pay a poor man's butcher's bills as to pay for his mathematics".[1]

The Revised Code's definition of a normal school was explicit, "a college for boarding, lodging and instructing candidates for the office of teacher in schools for the labouring classes".[2] A new financial arrangement, introduced in 1864 and designed to come fully into operation in 1868, removed the anomalies of the old system under which the churches had made a profit. The numerous grants, building grants and capitation grants, based on examination results and awarded to lecturers, were to be replaced by retrospective payments to the colleges of £20 in each of five successive years for every man, and £14 for every woman, who had completed a two-year probation period. There was a special arrangement for the transition period, but there was an important proviso that the annual grant was in no case to exceed 75 per cent of college expenditure, which was now to be subject to strict scrutiny by the Privy Council's auditor.[3]

The new regulations brought confusion and anxiety. There were immediate economies. Lecturing staffs were pruned to the absolute minimum. For example, the Free Church College in Glasgow with 170 students was reduced to a staff of four including the Rector. The distinguished science lecturer, John Kerr, who had earlier been short-listed for a Chair at the Queen's University, Belfast, was compelled to teach arithmetic to the children of the practising schools. Even with the economies, however, the college had accumulated a debt of £1,500 by 1869, and was only saved from bankruptcy by the generosity of Free Church supporters.[4] It was at the very onset of the bleak period that Stow died in November 1864. He had continued to serve as Secretary until 1861; though he had been saddened by the deviations from his original ideals, he had had

---

[1] Related by Professor Ramsay (Glasgow University), *Scottish Universities Commission*, 1893, Minutes of Evidence, p 316.
[2] Article 94, Section A.
[3] Article 98.
[4] *Minutes of the Committee of the Glasgow Free Church Normal Seminary*, 26 January 1869.

the satisfaction of seeing his system widely adopted.[1]   The new
code had now introduced an altogether narrower conception of
the teacher's requirements.

THE NEW REGIME

With the abolition of Queen's Scholarships, the Church
authorities had to subsidise as many students as they could out
of their block grants.   They awarded bursaries to men in
preference to women who were less in need.   Under the terms of
the code, all students were required to sign a declaration that
they would complete two years of probationary service in school.
In addition, the college authorities compelled bursary holders
to provide a surety, who promised to repay the money in case
of default.   The retrospective terms of the government grant
gave colleges every incentive to secure the prompt appointment
of their students to inspected schools and to see that they stayed
there.   A strict watch was kept to ensure that no probationer
emigrated or disappeared from the profession without penalty.

As Secretary of the Church of Scotland Education Committee,
Laurie had to track down the defecting teachers.   He confessed
that, in the case of women who married, the situation became
rather delicate.   "You could not really interfere with an event of
that sort without a very good reason," he said, "and I have
had some curious correspondence on that subject with intending
bridegrooms.   Once or twice . . . I have made the man pay for
his wife, and he has sent me a sum to satisfy the authorities."
Premature aspirants to the ministry were a much tougher proposition.   They declined to pay on the legal grounds that they
were not of age when the obligation was signed.   In Laurie's
own words, "all sorts of difficulties were put in the way, and
the only way I could do with those entering the Church was to
say, 'Well, in the Annual Report to the General Assembly, I

---

[1] By both Westminster College (Methodist, 1851) and by Homerton
College (Congregationalist, 1852) from their foundation, and by Cheltenham
(Church of England) after the appointment of John Gill as Master of Method
in 1851.   Gill, a former student of Stow's, wrote a textbook *Systems of
Education* (1876).   He retired in 1888 and was awarded a Civil Pension.   I
am indebted to Mr Trevor Hearl, Principal Lecturer in Education at St Paul's
College, Cheltenham, for drawing my attention to the significance of John
Gill.

shall put down your name as a person who has not fulfilled his obligation and, as you intend to enter the Hall, the Professors there will see that you have broken your obligation.' That, of course, frightened them, and they paid up."[1]

The new code restricted instruction in the training colleges to those subjects which were immediately useful to the elementary school teacher. Physical science, higher mathematics, English literature were no longer rewarded. Instead, learning and repetition from memory of 300 lines of poetry by students of each year (200 lines by women students), additional grammar, mental arithmetic and a course covering "social economy, sanitary precautions and the science of everyday things", took their place. Second-year students, who had previously progressed to advanced work, were now to continue with the same subjects at a slightly higher level. (It says much for the college authorities that, despite financial adversity, they still provided instruction above the required minimum, for men, in such subjects as Latin, science and mathematics and, for women, in French.)

With the emphasis on subject matter, the time devoted to practical teaching was cut, sometimes to one or two hours a week. Simultaneously, the school management course was adapted to conform to the new pattern of inspection in the schools: students were given systematic instruction in the various methods of teaching, "Expository, Interrogatory, Simultaneous, Individual, Mutual and Others". They were also given regular exercises in the drawing up of timetables and the keeping of school registers, so that in the examination they could answer such questions as, "Draw up a specimen of a timetable for a school of 120 scholars conducted by one teacher and two pupil teachers". It was the age of the textbook; James Currie, Rector of the Edinburgh Church of Scotland College, for example, wrote seven textbooks for his students.[2]

In the schools, early results of individual examinations in the "3 Rs" confirmed the suspicion that the advanced teaching of the few had often been at the expense of the majority. Much

---

[1] *Scottish Universities Commission*, 1893, Minutes of Evidence, p 312.
[2] They included "Common School Management", "Infant School Management", "Practical School Grammar", "Practical School Arithmetic", "Elements of Musical Analysis".

more attention was now paid to efficient teaching of the elementary subjects. The new mode of inspection, however, not only revolutionised the work of the schools, it transformed the very atmosphere. With his emphasis on logbooks and registers, on the precise classification of children and on comparison of school with school, the inspector became an inquisitor who was regarded with suspicion and hostility. The old parish dominie had been master in his own domain, the certificated teacher was subject to regular and scrupulous oversight.

There was a sharp fall in the number of recruits to the profession. Under the new regulations, school managers made their own agreements with apprentices and could fix their own terms. Often they confined themselves to temporary agreements and, after a year or two, pupil teachers left their service. Though girls were still available, intelligent boys, who could turn to a variety of openings in industry, rarely looked at teaching. Already by 1865, numbers in training institutions had dropped steeply,[1] and male entrants were so scarce that the Church of Scotland appealed to ministers to bring forward candidates for bursaries even if they had not served as pupil teachers.[2] Not only were women students more numerous, they were altogether more articulate and cultivated than were the men, mostly raw lads from the country who came straight from farm or workshop. With the dearth of men students the Episcopal Church decided to train women rather than men. The surviving males were transferred to Durham, and in 1867 the recently acquired premises at Lochrin House were adapted for a women's college.[3]

Under the new regime, Gaelic-speaking students with their poor command of English were at a great disadvantage. In more prosperous years, the colleges had been able to run the risk of a proportion of failures and had felt it their duty to recruit numbers of Highland students. Indeed, there had sometimes been as many as 50 or 60 in the various colleges. The

[1] To 60 per cent of the 1863 total. By *Minute*, 20 February 1867, the Privy Council awarded bonuses to schools of £5 and £10 depending on the class of entrance examination gained by their well-qualified candidates to normal college.

[2] *Report of the Education Committee of the General Assembly for increasing the means of Education in Scotland particularly in the Highlands and Islands*, 1867, p 26.

[3] *Report of the Committee of Council on Education*, 1865-6, p 481.

Revised Code compelled the authorities to reconsider their position. The Free Church eventually established a fund to enable poor Highlanders to attend special preparatory classes, which would bring them up to the required entrance standard.[1] The Established Church regretfully reduced the numbers of Gaelic-speaking students, though it reserved two bursaries for girls from Highland parishes.[2] On many occasions Laurie urged the Government to make concessions to bilingual students. Ideally he favoured the establishment of a separate college at Inverness (a revival in fact of the former training centre at Raining's School) with a one-year course of training, which would have sufficed to equip Gaelic-speaking students for schools in their own area, but would not have allowed them to compete for the more lucrative positions in the south.[3] At Inverness, training could have been specially directed to the needs of the rural schools.

In violation of Scottish custom, an attempt was made to attract women, who of course could be employed at half the salaries of men, to take charge of some of the small Highland schools. Young women, however, showed some reluctance "to exile themselves to regions in which they are separated by many days' journey from their homes in the Lowlands and settled among a people speaking a strange tongue and with alien habits".[4] Already, under the 1861 Act, women had been appointed as sewing mistresses in the parish schools, but it was one thing to make the provisions and quite another to persuade the parents that sewing was a fit subject for the school. In many areas it was "booklairning" alone which they wanted. They said that "the family could educate to the needle, quite as well as the school".[5]

There was ample testimony to the skill and devotion of certificated women teachers. In the words of one of the inspectors,

[1] *Report of the Committee of Council on Education*, 1870-1, p 420.
[2] *Report of the Education Committee of the General Assembly for increasing the means of Education in Scotland particularly in the Highlands and Islands*, 1868, p 23.
[3] *Third Report of the Committee appointed to inquire into certain questions relating to Education in Scotland*, 1888, p 30 *et seq.*
[4] *Report of the Education Committee of the General Assembly for increasing the means of Education in Scotland particularly in the Highlands and Islands*, 1868, p 45.
[5] *Report of the Committee of Council on Education*, 1863-4, p 240.

"The teaching of the elementary subjects is a task much more congenial to a woman than a brawny man". Some of the men were too ambitious for the work, others too indolent and easy-going, but the mistress with her greater patience and sympathy did not cease making effort because the work was simple.[1] There was general agreement, however, that attendance at normal school was even more essential for women than for men, since, when they taught without training, their lack of system and organisation was "so flagrant and so melancholy to see". Many of the women students paid their own expenses at college. As qualified teachers they could earn a guinea a week, which was "not too much for a schoolmistress who has to support herself, and to endeavour from the beginning of her independence to put by something for failing health and strength".[2]

By 1868, government expenditure on training institutions had fallen to less than half that of the early 'sixties. However, the colleges had adapted themselves to the new situation. By running their practising schools at a profit (the Free Church in Glasgow, for example, had established a new middle-class school charging high fees), by rigorously preparing their students for the certificate examination, and by exercising vigilance over them in their probationary years, they weathered the storm. Very soon they were tapping a new source of revenue by preparing their students for the examinations of the Department of Science and Art at South Kensington. By the late 'sixties and early 'seventies, large numbers of students were taking a great variety of the subjects covered by the Science and Art Department: drawing, geometry, magnetism, physical geography, and animal physiology. Under a system of payment by results a first-class pass was worth £2 and a second-class pass £1.[3]

To safeguard their interests under the new code, training schools employed their own medical officers to examine all candidates before admission and they also showed special awareness of the needs of women students who were prone to

[1] *Report of the Committee of Council on Education*, 1869-70, p 388.
[2] *Report of the Committee of Council on Education*, 1872-3, p 322.
[3] Colleges shared the payments with the lecturers responsible, eg John Kerr (Glasgow Free Church College) sometimes got £130 a year extra. *Minutes of the Committee of the Glasgow Free Church Normal Seminary*, 4 August 1873. (The science, however, was theoretical and was in fact hardly relevant to teachers.)

succumb to overwork and exhaustion. For example, the Glasgow Church of Scotland College tried the experiment of providing a midday meal for women. According to the Report, "A good dinner of soup and meat, boiled roast, mince and steak, with potatoes and vegetables is supplied at less cost than one individually could procure it for at home".[1] By 1872, three of the Presbyterian institutions had boarding houses for those of their female students who could not travel home or live with relations. In Glasgow, Stow's former home in Sauchiehall Street was in use as a boarding house. The "inmates", who each paid £18 a year, were provided with desks in the communal "study" and with dormitory accommodation.[2] The Episcopal College in Edinburgh was exceptional in being entirely self-contained within the 1½ acres of ground enclosed by the high walls of Lochrin House. As a residential institution on the English pattern it was concerned with the pastoral care of students and the nurturing of strong corporate spirit.

The normal school academic year ran from January to December with a break of two months in the summer. In each of the institutions a senior member of the inspectorate was made responsible for the selection of entrants[3] and for the examination at the end of the year. To students and staff he was a well-known figure, sometimes devoting a month in the year to his training college duties. Except for the Shorter Catechism paper, which was specially prepared by a Scottish inspector, the written papers were uniform throughout Britain. In 1866, Dr Morrison, Rector of the Free Church Training College in Glasgow, commented in his Annual Report that for some years past the questions on the Catechism had been "crotchety, peculiar and many of them connected with the Catechism only in the most round-about way". His official complaint apparently had some effect, for the following year he reported that the questions had been "intelligible and . . . confined to the subject specified".[4]

[1] *Report of the Committee of Council on Education*, 1872-3, p 347.
[2] *Minutes of the Committee of the Glasgow Church of Scotland Normal Seminary*, 30 April 1877.
[3] There was a common entrance examination for the normal schools and candidates nominated a particular institution.
[4] The paper had included such questions as: "Explain in the form of a

The conduct of the examinations was only one aspect of the inspector's work, though necessarily he spent a good deal of time hearing the individual students read and recite their lines of poetry, watching them teach and scrutinising their lesson notes. He was also thoroughly acquainted with the day-to-day routine of the college, able to assess the standard of instruction and comment on the general organisation. With their wide knowledge of schools, the inspectors knew what kind of material the colleges had to work with, and they were appreciative of attempts to widen the students' experience and to cultivate their literary taste. They were able to make practical suggestions, and it was on an inspector's recommendation that one college sent its students on regular visits to neighbouring city schools.[1]

PROPOSALS FOR REFORM

On the whole, however, the inspectors were surprisingly uncritical of the curricula imposed by the new code with its lack of encouragement to progressive study and its emphasis on memorising of textbooks and on repetition by heart. John Kerr, HMI[2], was the most outspoken among his colleagues in his disparagement of certain aspects of study and in his positive suggestions for reform. To him the recitation of poetry was "distasteful and harassing . . . more of a school than a college exercise". Kerr who, like Laurie, had a great admiration for the parish teachers in the Dick Bequest counties, deplored the lack of scholarship of many of the certificated teachers, and by 1865 had outlined a scheme for a combined university and normal school course.

Year after year in his reports he returned to the theme which was later supported by several of his fellow inspectors. The existing normal school course, Kerr felt, was too long. "If," he said, "a man of twenty years of age cannot under judicious

---

lesson to girls between 10 and 13 years old, the Fatherhood of God, in connection with the question, 'How did God create man?' and 'What is adoption?' " *Minutes of the Committee of the Glasgow Free Church Normal Seminary*, Annual Reports of 1866 and 1867.

[1] Church of Scotland Normal College, Glasgow, *Report of the Committee of Council on Education*, 1866-7, p 525.

[2] Not to be confused with the Rev John Kerr (see p 63).

F

training learn the art of teaching in months, he will never learn
it." Instead of frittering away time for two successive years on
"minute and, to most minds, evanescent details . . . the majority
of which are soon forgotten or must be got up afresh in the
active exercise of teaching", he should attend university classes
in Latin, Greek and mathematics.[1] Their value would be
intangible, "but no one who has passed through it can be ignorant of the fact that his first year's experience of a university . . .
gives to his whole mental nature an impulse which nothing else
can give in so short a time". The prospect of two sessions at
university would attract to the profession a better class of recruit
who with the stimulus of higher study would bring to the school
a mature and cultivated mind. Thus the intellectual standards
of the old teacher would be combined with the professional skill
of the new.

The Argyll Commission appointed in 1864 to investigate the
schools of Scotland examined the question of teacher training.
Laurie, who submitted evidence, urged that the university
subjects: Latin, Greek and mathematics, including arithmetic,
should form the core of the teacher's study. Normal colleges
would then be restored to their original purpose, the professional training of teachers.[2] (He did not on this occasion refer
to women students, though he had previously recognised the
necessity of retaining training colleges in their existing form as
female institutions.) The general body of evidence was in
favour of combined university and normal school training, "the
one to make the man, the other to make the teacher".[3]   A
fusion of the two elements would appeal to ambitious young
men. Already the Free Church Committee was offering small
university bursaries to those who had distinguished themselves
at normal school. Other certificated teachers were attending
university at their own expense.

[1] *Report of the Committee of Council on Education*, 1867-8, p 408.
[2] *Report of the Argyll Commission*, vol I, 1865, Appendix, p 120.
[3] *Report of the Argyll Commission*, vol II, 1867, p cxlvii. (A plan for
combining university and normal school training was published in vol III,
1868, Appendix p xxxix.) James Currie, Rector of the Established Church
College in Edinburgh, raised practical problems: many of the students were
not equipped for university work, and in a hybrid institution he saw difficulties from "the collision of two different classes of students – the one
favoured, or thinking itself so, the other branded or thought to be so". vol I,
1865, Appendix, p 126.

While the professional skill of the new certificated teacher was generally praised by the investigators, the proficiency of the old type of schoolmaster was more variable. Only half of the parish schoolmasters were judged to be "good" teachers, the rest were assessed as "indifferent" or "bad". There was criticism of the rough and uncouth behaviour of the children under their charge. The masters apparently considered "they had nothing to do with the civilisation of the children, or the formation of their characters, but that their work was done when they heard them say their daily lesson in the classroom".[1]

At his best, however, the university man was an impressive teacher. The Argyll Commission's Report on Burgh Schools referred to the description by an English inspector, D R Fearon, of the masters he had seen in the nine most distinguished middle-class schools of Scotland.[2] Fearon had been struck by the quality of the teaching, by the "scientific and philosophical" manner in which the master handled his textbooks, his subjects and his scholars, by his power of illustration and his knowledge of his pupils. He attributed the natural aptitude of the Scottish scholar for teaching to the demands of the arts course, which compelled him to read and to think, and to the self-discipline of the student, who, during the vacations, took to school work or to private tutoring as a means of support.[3] He described the keen competitiveness of the pupils and the spirit and vitality of the schoolmaster: "In front of this eager animated throng stands the master, gaunt, muscular and time-worn, poorly clad, and plain in manner and speech, but with the dignity of a ruler in his gestures and the fire of an enthusiast in his eye; never sitting down, but standing always in some commanding position before the class; full of movement, vigour and energy; so thoroughly versed in his author or his subject that he seldom requires to look at the textbook, which is open in his left hand, while in his right he holds the chalk or the pointer, ever ready to illustrate from map or blackboard. . . . The whole scene is one of vigorous action and masterly force, forming the greatest possible

---

[1] *Report of the Argyll Commission, Report on the State of Education in the Country Districts of Scotland*, 1866, p 467.

[2] Fearon was acting under instructions of the Taunton Commissioners to investigate the burgh schools of Scotland.

[3] *Report of the Taunton Commission*, vol VI, 1868, p 47.

contrast with the monotonous, unmethodical ill-seconded working of the English teacher."[1]

The Argyll Commission surveyed the schools against a background of contemporary life and prevailing attitudes. The old national system of education was completely outmoded. Not only did the new voluntary schools outnumber the parish schools by three to one, but even they, assisted by government funds, could not cater for the child population of the towns. In the city of Glasgow, for example, only a third of the children of school age were attending school.[2] Similarly glaring were the deficiencies in the Highlands and Islands where, despite multiplicity of effort, education had made so little impression that according to the marriage registers only half the men and a third of the women could write their names.[3] Throughout the country as a whole, the Commissioners discovered that there were over 90,000 children, almost a fifth of the child population, who were not attending any school. Of the 400,000 at school, less than half were at schools subject to government inspection.[4] It was the revelations of the Argyll Commission with its exposure of the extent of the national deficiency which led directly to major reform.

[1] *Report of the Taunton Commission*, vol VI, 1868, p 52.
[2] *Report of the Argyll Commission*, vol III, 1868, p lv.
[3] *Report of the Argyll Commission, Report on the State of Education in the Hebrides*, 1866, p 122.
[4] *Report of the Argyll Commission*, vol II, 1867, table II, p 24.

Chapter 4

RESPONSE TO CHALLENGE, 1872-1900

THE ESTABLISHMENT OF UNIVERSAL SCHOOLING

By the Act of 1872, the old national network was merged in a new system of public schools under popularly elected school boards and controlled by a co-ordinating central authority, the Scotch Education Department. Parish schools were automatically transferred to the new local authorities, and the great majority of voluntary schools were freely handed over. Thus the heterogeneous character of educational machinery gave way to a uniform system of secular administration, which could draw on local rates to supplement government grants to education. Since the new public schools were permitted to give religious instruction according to "use and wont" (ie, the Bible and the Shorter Catechism), the terms public and Presbyterian became synonymous. In effect, a national system replaced the denominational system of the past, and only a small minority of Episcopal and Roman Catholic schools remained apart. In contrast, therefore, to the English compromise measure of 1870, which resulted in a dual system of schools, Scottish legislation achieved a clear-cut transfer to public authorities.

Training colleges were deliberately left outside the scope of the Act. The lack of positive provision for religious education in the schools roused alarm. Indeed some of the most zealous churchmen only accepted the terms on the implied understanding that the training of teachers should be left in the hands of the churches,[1] an anomalous arrangement which apparently perpetuated the sectionalism and party system of the past. In fact, the colleges claimed to be Presbyterian but unsectarian; Free Church students often attended colleges of the Established Church, and, similarly, members of the Church of Scotland

[1] G C M Douglas, *The Scotch Training College,* Erskine, undated pamphlet, p 1.

were found in Free Church institutions. The Rectors of the colleges were always members of the particular denomination, though appointment of other members of staff did not necessarily depend on their religious affiliation. The Established Church and Free Church alike gave prominence to religious instruction within their colleges and published the results of the annual examinations in the Reports of the General Assemblies.

Both Presbyterian Churches were now training teachers for the new public schools. Both had to expand their provision to meet the demands of compulsory education under the 1872 Act. Within a decade, the numbers of inspected schools rose from 2,000 to 3,000 ,while the number of children on roll doubled to reach 400,000.[1] All public schools were required to be in the charge of certificated teachers.[2] Practising teachers were able to qualify without examination, but the training college course offered the best prospects for new entrants to the profession. Large numbers flocked to the colleges which, by 1876, had over 1,000 on roll.

In 1874-5, both Presbyterian Churches had opened small colleges for women in Aberdeen. Laurie himself, with his special interest in the North East, was responsible for the establishment in 1874 of a Church of Scotland College (housed temporarily in a former Baptist chapel)[3] and for the appointment as Rector of Joseph Ogilvie, headmaster of Keith public school. (To the 30 women of the first session, Ogilvie taught single-handed all the required subjects with the exception of drawing, singing and industrial work.) In 1875, a Free Church College in Charlotte Street opened with 38 students under the Rectorship of George Ramage, formerly headmaster of the South Parish Free Church School. Since there was no lack of women students who could pay for themselves, both colleges, housed within a few years in substantial new buildings, were self-supporting.

Meanwhile, large additions were made to the Edinburgh colleges. In 1879, the Church of Scotland transferred men students to a new three-storey building in Chambers Street.[4]

---

[1] *Report of Committee of Council on Education*, 1883-4, p xi.
[2] Section 56 of *Education (Scotland) Act 1872*, 35 and 36 Vic, cap 62.
[3] The West Kirk Sessional School was used as a practising school.
[4] *Report of Committee of Council on Education*, 1878-9, p 298.

Women continued to use the existing building so that, although under the same management and taught by the same staff, the two departments functioned for all practical purposes as two colleges. Even in the practising school, they entered by doors on different levels so that they did not come in contact with each other. Considerable extensions were also made to Moray House – in fact both Churches spent over £8,000 on their Edinburgh colleges – and again the new structure was so designed that the sexes did not meet.[1] The Episcopal Church also prepared to receive larger numbers of students by moving to more spacious premises at Dalry House.[2] There were now nominally seven training institutions in Scotland, but, since men and women were trained separately in all the larger centres, there were actually eleven colleges.

Teachers' salaries, subject to the crude law of demand and supply, rose rapidly. By 1877, newly qualified men were averaging £84.15.0 a year and women £65.13.6. For men there were so many headships available that between 1870 and 1882 the average male salary (exclusive of a house) went up from £102 to £137. By comparison women fared badly; school boards had an aversion to appointing women even to headships of small schools, and the average female salary was scarcely more than half that of the male.[3] The tradition of the dominie died hard and the Principal of Aberdeen University expressed the prevailing prejudice when he spoke of certain local schools having "descended to a female teacher".[4] Yet inspectors were warm in their praise of woman teachers who "having no family cares – were able to give their whole heart and soul" to their work. One of them commented, "the more gentle manners of the female teacher gradually impresses itself upon her pupils and leads to a pleasantness in their conduct which is rarely attained elsewhere."[5]

School boards competed for students from the Presbyterian

[1] *ibid*, p 287.
[2] *Report of Committee of Council on Education*, 1877-8, p 272.
[3] *Report of Committee of Council on Education*, 1878-9, p xviii.
[4] *Scottish Education Inquiry Committee, Minutes of Evidence*, 1887, p 106. (The appointment of a woman to the headship of one of the Dundee board schools was a notable event. *Report of Committee of Council on Education*, 1878-9, p 150).
[5] *Report of Committee of Council on Education*, 1875-6, p 144.

colleges, but they were reluctant to employ those from the Episcopalian college. Indeed, it was the constant complaint of the Episcopalian authorities that their students were boycotted. Since their own schools were few in number, the great majority of their students were therefore compelled to seek jobs in England. "It does not matter what qualifications they have," said the Principal of the Episcopalian college, "it is of no use their applying for a situation under a school board in Scotland. They have tried and tried again, and they have given up in despair trying any longer."[1]   In comparison with other Scottish schools those attached to the Roman Catholic community suffered from a lack of trained teachers.   A few pupil teachers were sent to Mount Pleasant College in Liverpool run by the Sisters of Notre Dame,[2] but the absence of a direct source of supply of teachers was a severe handicap.

Under many parish school boards, the schools of the "Auld Kirk" and of the Free Church were amalgamated.   In the urban areas, however, the school boards were often catering for children who had never been to school before.   As temporary premises, they hired music halls, corn exchanges and even churches, which were soon crowded with children.   School building and the battle for attendance absorbed their main energies during the early years.   Many of the schools, built close to the main thoroughfares, were large two- or three-"deckers", catering for over a thousand children.   Spacious and airy, they offered in contrast to many of the inconvenient, ill-ventilated buildings of the past, all that was necessary for exercise, cleanliness and decency.[3]   At first, many children had to be compelled to come to school by school-board officers who patrolled the streets. Neglectful parents were pursued and prosecuted (sometimes as many as 3,000 a year in Glasgow alone).   Even so absenteeism remained high for many years.   Some boards organised 1d a week schools in order to induce the poorest children to attend, and in times of depression charity dinners were provided for

---

[1] *Scottish Education Inquiry Committee, Minutes of Evidence*, 1887, p 21.
[2] Martha M Skinnider, Catholic Elementary Education in Glasgow 1818-1918, University of Glasgow EdB Thesis, 1964, Appendix D.
[3] The transformation of buildings was such that as early as 1875 a HMI commented that school boards in the Lowlands had done as much for education as was done in the previous 300 years by all agencies. *Report of Committee of Council on Education*, 1875-6, p 151.

those who brought their own bowls and spoons. Similarly, for necessitous children there were gifts of clothing, indelibly stamped with the initials of the school board to prevent their being pawned.

The teachers had to bring order, routine and discipline to bear on unruly hordes of children. With only two breaks in the year, at New Year and in the summer,[1] they laboured with large classes – even pupil teachers were in charge of 70 to 100 children. Whereas, in the smaller areas, both apprentices and teachers were subject to petty interference or the caprice of local factions,[2] under the larger boards they might be chilled and paralysed by the anonymity of administration. The Scotch Education Department encouraged managers to interest themselves in the welfare of young teachers "who being often strangers to the place and living alone in lodgings, without friends and relations, should be the object of their special care." They were urged to remember that "the teacher is a human being who requires friendship and appreciation as much as anyone else."[3]

The "3 Rs" formed the staple of the curriculum, but from early years ex-drill sergeant janitors were engaged to teach boys military drill in order to accustom them to regular movements and instant obedience. (The instructors, however, sometimes forgot they were not on the barrack square and they were "objected to by both teachers and parents for reasons similar to a prejudice against parrots that had been at sea".)[4] Gradually the curriculum expanded; sewing became compulsory for girls and extra inducements were offered for class subjects such as singing, grammar, history and geography. An additional grant was awarded on the quality of discipline and organisation, and inspectors were instructed to note the punctuality and the manners of the children as well as their language, cleanliness, neatness, obedience and truthfulness.[5] Successive codes and

[1] An Easter break did not become customary till the 1890s.
[2] There were instances, for example, of the dismissal of teachers who belonged to the Established Church when the Free Church party won the local school board election. *Report of Committee of Council on Education*, 1879-80, p 112.
[3] *Report of Committee of Council on Education*, 1879-80, p 175.
[4] *Report of Committee of Council on Education*, 1898-9, p 488. Retrospective account. Possibly this background accounts for the fact that the janitor remains a formidable figure in many schools.
[5] Article 19A of the 1873 Code.

regulations endeavoured to bring a new elasticity to teaching. They stressed the need to "promote the development of the general intelligence of the scholars". History and geography were to be taught in such a way as "to awaken the sympathies of the children". As an optional subject for older girls, domestic economy was to cover all aspects of housecraft including budgeting, while other optional subjects were to include elementary science, English literature and a variety of languages.

In all schools, the great occasion of the year was "the Inspection". A former pupil in a village school in Fife in the early 'eighties has recalled that the children "were always told the exact day when the inspector would appear. Great tubbings and scrubbings and washing and pleating of long hair took place the night before. Slates were well-washed and best frocks and shirts were made ready." Sometimes the strain would be too much for the teacher and among the children "it was rumoured in an awful whisper 'she's greetin' ahent the board'."[1]

THE CONCERN FOR STANDARDS

The contemporary challenge was twofold: the taming and humanising of a race of young barbarians and, simultaneously, the preservation of standards associated with the rural past. The first task required teachers to be social rescue workers, missionaries, possessed of both physical stamina and practical efficiency; the second demanded a degree of mental cultivation and scholarship. Since the majority of teachers had come up the hard way as pupil teachers in the schools, they were not customarily lacking in vigour or robustness. During the years of apprenticeship the weakest had gone to the wall; in large schools particularly, as one inspector wrote, "the daily urgency of active work, and the unavoidable pressure quickens the movements and sharpens the wits of pupil teachers"[2]. However, the Scotch Education Department was concerned not only with increasing recruitment but also with raising standards and restoring the links with the universities.

Already, managers received a bonus for every pupil teacher

[1] *To be a Pupil Teacher*, Isabel Law, (Typescript) 1965, p 21.
[2] *Report of Committee of Council on Education*, 1870-1, p 306.

who passed the yearly examinations. (Customarily half the bonus, ie 20s to 30s, was allocated by the managers to the apprentices.) In 1878, the age of indenture was raised to 14, thus shortening the period of service to four years, and the number of apprentices allowed to any one certificated teacher was reduced from four to three.[1] Inspectors were urged to oppose "the appointment of sickly, precocious children as pupil teachers" and to secure that apprentices received a regular course of systematic instruction rather than a "cram" preparation for examination.

There were regrets that in many urban schools apprentices were no longer under the personal superintendence of the head teacher, but became the responsibility of one of the assistant teachers. Often they were not properly looked after. In the words of one report, "their work is not made interesting to them; they are not cheered on, and as a consequence they have no enthusiasm". The payment of apprentices, now left to the discretion of the school boards, was barely sufficient, and the hardship of the pupil teachers was said to be reflected in their "pale and haggard faces and their threadbare garments".[2]

All students accepted by the colleges were now officially Queen's Scholars. With the expansion of the training course to cover new school subjects, the warping influences of the 'sixties were dispelled. Some of the more elementary subjects, such as mental arithmetic, disappeared; others, including history and geography, were confined to the first year. New subjects came in: music – inspected by the celebrated John Hullah – and physical training, in the form of military drill for men and calisthenics for women. Men students could take as many as three science subjects and two languages. (Women were restricted to either a single science subject or one language.) Their training in Latin stood them in good stead in the English grammar examination where their "scholarly confidence" contrasted with the "meagre faltering style" of the English candidates.[3]

Equipment kept pace with innovations in the curriculum. Pianos – the Edinburgh Church of Scotland College had as

---

[1] 1878 Code, Article 70 (g) and (b).
[2] *Report of Committee of Council on Education*, 1878-9, pp 150-1.
[3] *Report of Committee of Council on Education*, 1884-5, p 287. (See Appendix E, IV, pp 244-5, for examples of college timetables.)

many as eight pianos – replaced the old training college harmonium, described by Hullah as "the worst of its class".   Libraries became more important; there were, for example, 3,500 volumes in the Glasgow Church of Scotland College library.[1] Scientific equipment also became more elaborate, and the same college could boast a "museum, furnished with chemical and physical apparatus valued at £450", as well as a set of meteorological instruments housed in the tower.[2]   In 1878, the new extensions to Moray House included the very latest innovation, a model kitchen for practice lessons in cookery.[3]

The term "training college" was now officially used instead of normal school.   Whethei designedly or not, the new terminology coincided with improved standards.   The old title had been appropriate only when the model school was used as the sole place of instruction for teachers.   Gradually, however, the school itself had become more of a demonstration centre to which students resorted now and then.   Indeed, the course of school management, including practical teaching, was only one of fifteen subjects of the training college syllabus, and there were complaints that students spent too little time on the theory and practice of teaching.[4] The time had long passed when students had formed part of the teaching strength of the school. Rather the school was now to training college students what the hospital was to medical students.   In the words of one of the inspectors, "What the clinical lectures are to the one, the criticism lesson and its adjuncts are to the other".[5]

The criticism lesson, with some slight local variations,[6] remained a regular feature of the course.   During the session, a student gave several criticism lessons, each of which was commented on by two or three members of the staff: the Rector, the master of method, possibly one of the subject lecturers, and, of course, by fellow students.   Especially to "the

[1] *Report of Committee of Council on Education*, 1871-2, p 213.
[2] *Church of Scotland Normal College, Minutes of the Committee*, 10 March 1873, MS.   The lecturer in charge of science teaching had recently read a paper to the British Association.
[3] *Report of Committee of Council on Education*, 1878-9, p 290.
[4] *Report of Committee of Council on Education*, 1876-7, p 210.   About a quarter of the time was devoted to this aspect of the curriculum.
[5] *Report of Committee of Council on Education*, 1877-8, p 248.
[6] For example, it was varied sometimes by the expedient of selecting at random another student to conclude the lesson by oral questioning.

young and more sensitive female students", the occasion was a
"severe trial", but so strongly were its advantages upheld that
it remained the basis of practical training. The large practising
school continued to serve all the college needs and the Education Committee of the Church of Scotland quoted with pride
the comment of the inspector, "These schools are the largest in
Scotland, and are conducted with much spirit, skill and success".[1]
If students were introduced to conditions in board schools at
all, it was only on rare and brief visits.

The most significant innovation of the 'seventies was the
opportunity offered to selected students, in the code of 1873, of
attending university classes during the winter sessions. Formerly the occasional normal school student had attended
university classes "on the sly". Now the new concession
opened up the prospect of acquiring the wider culture associated with the university world. Pupil teachers who achieved a
certain standard in classics or mathematics in the entrance
examination could attend two university classes during each of
the two winter sessions of their course of training. The details
of the scheme had been worked out by George Ramsay,
Professor of Humanity at Glasgow University, and John Kerr,
HMI.[2] Male pupil teachers were to be selected for university
after the preliminary examination in the summer. They were
to teach up to November 1st and then to attend university for
three months before the commencement of the training college
session in February, pursuing thereafter a concurrent course at
the two institutions. Since in both Edinburgh and Glasgow, all
four training institutions were within distance of the universities,
it would usually be possible to dovetail attendance at the
university classes, which started at 8.00 am, with the necessary
professional instruction.

The concurrent system, made possible by the low fees of the
Scottish universities and by the non-residential character of the
training colleges, became the distinctive feature of Scottish
teacher training. It represented a reversion to Scottish aspirations which had long been submerged. The new government

[1] *Annual Report of the Education Committee to the General Assembly of the
Church of Scotland*, 1877, p 63.
[2] *Scheme for combining University and Normal School Training for Schoolmasters in Scotland*, 19 February 1873.

requirement that all grant-earning schools should be under certificated teachers now made it essential to supplement the "narrow, professional and confining" curriculum of the training college. It was true that a loophole was still left for the graduate without training who could satisfy the inspector in a test of practical teaching, but such "back door" entrants to the profession were not welcomed by the school boards.

Many of the concurrent students hoped eventually to qualify for a degree. They therefore chose classes which would fulfil the university requirements: Latin, Greek, mathematics, logic, moral philosophy, English and natural philosophy for the MA degree, and, more rarely, biological science, geology and engineering science for the BSc degree. They did not, during the concurrent course, take the usual examinations of the university but they were subject to special tests, the results of which were treated as part of the certificate examinations.

Now, as on previous occasions, the Free Church colleges were the first to seize the new opportunity and, in the early years, they sent twice as many students to university as did the colleges of the Established Church.[1] Until 1877, when the Department assumed partial responsibility, the churches themselves paid the entire university fees, amounting annually to several hundred pounds. They also awarded a few bursaries so that students could stay on at university and graduate. Many students, however, after two years' university work, completed the third year of the degree course at their own expense, or managed to combine their university studies with teaching duties. The Glasgow School Board, for example, permitted teachers in their employment to attend early morning university classes,[2] and from 1886 a number of competitive bursaries were made available from the Glasgow Endowment Fund to enable training college students to spend a third year at the university.[3]

[1] *Report of the Committee of Council on Education*, 1878-9, p 271. Between 1874 and 1878 the Church of Scotland sent 110 students to university compared with 263 from the Free Church. By 1880, the figures were 258 and 455. *Report of Committee of Council on Education*, 1880-1, p 202.
[2] *Scottish Education Inquiry Committee, Minutes of Evidence, 3rd Report*, 1888, p 2.
[3] In accordance with the scheme of the Commissioners appointed under the provision of the *Educational Endowments (Scotland) Act*, 1882.

The trained graduate was much sought after and indeed qualified for the key positions.[1] A senior inspector noted with pride the revival of the democratic tradition of the past. Just as in Napoleonic France the ordinary recruit was said to carry a marshal's baton in his knapsack, so in contemporary Scotland a teacher in the humblest school now had the prospect of "rising to the highest educational position in the land".[2] The concurrent university and college course was the greatest single difference between Scottish and English teacher training. It represented the traditional respect of the Scot for learning and the desire to combine in teachers both breadth of mind and teaching zeal.

UNIVERSITY INTEREST IN TEACHER TRAINING

An important event, though it made little immediate impact on teacher training, was the establishment in 1876 of Chairs of Education at St Andrews and Edinburgh Universities. Professor Pillans had long ago urged the need of systematic professional training in "Didactics", the Science of Education. Indeed towards the end of his life he had offered £5,000 towards the foundation of a Chair of Education at Edinburgh, but when he had approached Lowe, Vice-President of the Committee of Council, he had been told that "there was no Science of Education".[3] He had associated himself with the foundation, in 1847, of the Educational Institute of Scotland which had sought to place the training of teachers on a university footing and had endeavoured to raise funds for Chairs of Education from the teachers themselves.[4]

In recent years Simon S Laurie had become one of the fore-

---

[1] eg Career of John Struthers, 1857-1925. Originally from the parish school in Mearns, Renfrewshire, where he had also served as a pupil teacher, Struthers entered the Established Church College in Glasgow. He took the combined university course and subsequently entered Oxford as an exhibitioner. In 1886 he was appointed to the Scottish Inspectorate. He became Assistant Secretary of the Scotch Education Department in 1900, and Secretary in 1904.

[2] *Report of Committee of Council on Education*, 1876-7, pp 212-13.

[3] D Ross, *Education as a University Subject; its history, present position and prospects*, Maclehose, 1883, p 10.

[4] "The Professional Training of Teachers", William Jolly, *Fortnightly Review*, vol xvi, September 1874, p 359.

most propagandists for education as a university subject. In 1865, he had written in his Report to the Dick Bequest trustees, "It is only through a knowledge of psychology and ethics that the schoolmaster can render to himself an account of what he is doing, and can see to what point his labours are tending. These are the two pillars on which the whole fabric of education rests. I do not mean to say that it is necessary that the teacher should be a philosopher, but it is quite indispensable that he should philosophise. . . . If he does not admit this, he degrades himself from the position of an educated worker, striving by means of intellectual processes to reach certain well-defined moral and intellectual results, to that of a mere retailer of the alphabet, and converts what is a profession . . . into a trade. . . ."[1] Among teachers there were a fortunate few who were endowed with sympathetic insight and sensibility, who by their innate qualities had "a private key with which to unlock the intellects and hearts of their pupils". For the majority, however, the philosophic attitude alone would bring significance to the daily tasks of teaching.

Money for the first university Chairs of Education in Britain came from the bequests of Andrew Bell of monitorial fame.[2] There was apparently some expectation of parliamentary augmentation of the original endowment to include chairs in all the universities.[3] Aberdeen would have welcomed such an extension, but Glasgow made no move. In the meantime, so vehement was the opposition from training college authorities, and so powerful was their influence on Scottish Members of Parliament that the Government abandoned their earlier intentions, leaving the Chairs in St Andrews and Edinburgh so poorly endowed that their occupants had difficulty in making ends meet.[4]

Appointed by the Bell trustees, the first Professors of Educa-

---

[1] *Report to the Trustees of the Dick Bequest*, Constable, 1865, pp 15-17.

[2] The Education Act (1872) had freed a residue fund, intended to encourage his system of education, and the trustees diverted the money (£10,000) to found Chairs of Education in St Andrews and Edinburgh.

[3] "The Universities and the Schools", Sir Joshua Fitch, *Contemporary Review*, vol 29, December 1872.

[4] Church opposition was described in *Report of the Education Committee to the General Assembly of the Church of Scotland*, 1875, p 15; *Report of the Education Committee to the General Assembly of the Free Church*, 1875, pp 17-18.

tion were J M D Meiklejohn in St Andrews and Simon Laurie
in Edinburgh. In their inaugural lectures, both stressed the
philosophic and reflective approach to teaching. In the words of
Meiklejohn, "It is thoughtlessness that stints; it is routine that
withers; it is dullness and deadness of heart that dwarfs the
powers of the soul". Teachers, he said, should ask themselves,
"Has this that I am doing any seed of life in it? Will it grow in
the minds of my pupils?"[1] The Scottish intellect, "naturally
tough", could by training become supple in employing the
Socratic method. In his lecture Laurie made an impassioned
plea for the prospective teacher to be a full member of the university. The attendance of picked students at certain classes
enabled them to do no more than "sniff the academic atmosphere". They had no opportunity to "enjoy all the subtle
intellectual and moral advantages which belong to that serener
air". He outlined the course of study he envisaged in "the ends,
processes and history of Education", a course in which ethics,
history, physiology and psychology were associated with the
practical problems of the school.[2]

Scottish universities, however, did not accept for the MA
degree any courses outside the "sacred seven",[3] and attendance
at education classes was therefore optional. Similarly the
Scotch Education Department did not recognise attendance at
education lectures, and any training college students who went,
did so without official cognisance. Nevertheless, Laurie
probably had Queen's Scholars in mind when he persuaded the
university in 1880 to award the Diploma of Literate in Arts to
students who completed four of the recognised degree courses
together with a fifth, which might be education. The diploma
would be well within their scope and would give definite aim to
their work.[4] In fact it never became popular, for those who were
ambitious enough to proceed to the third year (Queen's Scholars
were only able to attend two university classes each year)

[1] *Inaugural Address*, R M Cameron, 1876, p 11.
[2] *Inaugural Address; The Training of Teachers and Methods of Instruction*,
Kegan Paul, 1882, p 12.
[3] The Seven Liberal Arts, "Lingua, Tropus, Ratio; Numerus, Tonus,
Angulus, Astra" (from the medieval tradition of the trivium and quadrivium). Hexameter quoted in D Ross, *Education as a University Subject*,
p 28.
[4] It was awarded, also from 1880, by Glasgow University.

G

preferred to equip themselves with a degree. Education classes therefore remained an extra, and the fact that Laurie attracted the largest optional class in the university was a tribute to his personal distinction.

Laurie's background was, of course, very different from that of the training college Rectors. His lack of systematic teaching experience did not endear him to powerful officials of the Scotch Education Department who respected professional expertise. Yet his extensive knowledge of schools over a period of twenty years had given him a rich and varied experience. Indeed, for their perceptive insight and practical wisdom, his Reports to the Trustees of the Dick Bequest deserve to rank alongside the much better known inspectoral reports of his contemporary, Matthew Arnold. Both men in very different circumstances brought "sweetness and light" to the schools they visited; both were concerned with the creative task of the teachers in quickening and elevating the intellectual and moral life of their pupils. In his university lectures Laurie did not confine himself to theory, but dealt also with education practice under the titles of "Methodology'" and "Schools and the Teachers".

The establishment of university chairs raised the question of the relation of universities to teacher training. The conditions of service in schools tempted many youths, who in earlier days would have gone straight to university, to enter training college and combine university classes with professional training. Hardest hit financially were the Universities of St Andrews and Aberdeen, which were deprived of an important source of supply of students. In the past, Aberdeen in particular, had been "really a large training institution", and had produced schoolmasters for the whole of the North-East. Now, many boys from the area were taking advantage of concurrent courses at Glasgow or Edinburgh, freely available to promising candidates. Within a decade of the launching of the new scheme, half the men in training were attending a university, and by the end of the century practically all men were combining university courses with professional training.

In 1877, Laurie, as Secretary of the Church of Scotland Education Committee, had proposed an arrangement which would have associated the University of St Andrews (in conjunction with Madras College as practising school) with teacher training.[1] Nothing came of the scheme, but that very year saw the first of a series of attempts by universities to get direct control of an élite of the Queen's Scholars, a request for official recognition of a university diploma in Education to be awarded to Queen's Scholars at the end of a two-year course.[2] The proposal was rejected categorically. The universities, it was said, would not be able to exercise adequate moral supervision over students who were intending to teach; they were not equipped to give either practical training in the art of teaching or instruction in the subjects which were essential for teachers of elementary schools; they could not violate their traditions by insisting on religious instruction, which was univeisally provided in training colleges. Finally, the proposal was declared unacceptable on the grounds that selection by the universities of the élite of the Queen's Scholars would discredit the training institutions. The official view was that the university and the training college each had its own distinct and clearly defined sphere of action, and that the religious, practical and professional training of teachers must remain the special province of the training college.

STUDENT LIFE AND DISCIPLINE

The concurrent university and training college course put considerable strain on the students. Their professors complained that they were too hard pressed by the "drill subjects" of the training college – religious instruction, music, school management, drawing, science, geography, history and so on, and that they were "forever being ground up to pass a multitude of petty cram examinations". With the terrors of the Government schedule ever before them, the colleges did not trust the students to get up work by themselves.[3] During the five-month university session – from November to April – students were hard

[1] His Committee had agreed to pay 50 guineas a year to a master at Madras College (the old burgh school which had benefited from Bell's endowment) who would act as Master of Method to Queen's Scholars attending St Andrews University.
[2] *Report of Committee of Council on Education*, 1877-8, p 85 *et seq.*
[3] *Scottish Education Inquiry Committee, Minutes of Evidence, 2nd Report*, 1887, p 14.

pressed by the variety of their commitments. After April, they could devote themselves exclusively to practical and professional subjects. Already, in the early 'eighties, the training college authorities began to organise tutorials to assist their university students to pass their examinations.[1]

How did the training college students compare with the ordinary run of university entrants? At 18 they were rather older, of course, and in some respects they were better qualified, for they had at least passed a preliminary examination which often raised them above the standard of the junior classes. As the Rector of Moray House, Maurice Paterson, pointed out, they did not, like so many of the university students, have to support themselves by various kinds of private work.[2] The best of them became prizemen, but the great majority, though trained to prepare their work carefully and methodically, achieved only a mediocre standard. As former pupil teachers, accustomed to passing an annual hurdle, they often seemed to their professors to have no real interest in their work beyond the examination.

The university fees, usually four guineas (of which, after 1877, three guineas were reimbursed by the Scotch Education Department), added to the college expenses. The cost of training men students, with the superior staff required by the demands of the science, language and tutorial classes, was far in excess of the cost of training women. Moreover, because of their poor social background all men had need of bursaries. Women, on the other hand, were a great source of income because they could afford to pay fees. Consequently, while the women's colleges at Aberdeen could show annual surpluses, despite their small numbers, elsewhere the mixed training colleges could only just balance their budgets by the expedient of taking in a greater proportion of women than men. The women were directly subsidising the men.

Paid retrospectively for the students they had trained, the college authorities were careful to see that teachers served their probationary two years. In 1887, the Rector of the large

---

[1] *Proceedings of the Free Church General Assembly*, 1883, p 4.
[2] *Scottish Education Inquiry Committee, Minutes of Evidence, 2nd Report*, 1887, p 16.

Glasgow Free Church College, Dr Morrison, told an official committee of inquiry that 99 per cent of his students obtained parchments. Not 1 per cent of the women teachers, he said, got married before two years' service.[1] There were, however, inevitable losses from death and illness even during the college course. The annual medical reports noted the periodic scourges of infection, and recorded the name of the occasional student who had to be sent away with serious illness, consumption or incipient disease of the spine, or who died while still at college.

Despite the marked superiority and polish of the women students, some of them daughters of the manse and the products of Ladies' Adventure schools, they had to grind away at the elementary subjects. Long stretches of their time, both in college and in the evenings, were also absorbed in domestic economy, both practical and theoretical. Practical cookery, given either in a model kitchen or in outside schools of cookery, was a recent innovation. Sewing included practice of the various stitches in needlework, and the cutting out and making of garments in common use – a pair of full-sized drawers, a chemise, two nightdresses (the second more elaborate than the first) and a shirt. In fact, the syllabus covered "the various branches applicable to the family of a working man", including the designing of patterns. Theoretical aspects of domestic economy were learnt with the aid of one of the numerous manuals.[2] In general, the special interest shown by "Scotch girls" in domestic economy was attributed by the examiners to their frugal traditions. Nevertheless, there was criticism of their stitching, their "gathering", "stroking" and "setting in", and of their designs for children's garments, some of which "would fit no child yet born".[3]

Though college hours had been cut to six or seven daily, few colleges allowed any break for meals. Even the Glasgow experiment of the early years of the decade seems to have been abandoned, and the women students like the men snatched their "piece" in the few minutes between classes. It was not surprising that some of them broke down. Indeed overpressure

[1] *ibid*, p 10.
[2] Textbooks included Tegetmeir's *Manual of Domestic Economy*, Laurie's *Household Economy*, Stoker's *Home Comfort*.
[3] *Report of Committee of Council on Education*, 1881-2, pp 288-9.

was not uncommon among female students who, in addition to the burden of memorising, had also to spend a great deal of their time cleaning, cooking, ironing and sewing. The culmination of the year came with the Christmas examination, which, for the second-year students, lasted twenty-seven hours and extended over five days. Many of the women found it a terrifying ordeal. It was particularly unfortunate that the first sitting was in the afternoon for, as one of the Aberdeen Rectors remarked, "the afternoon is the worst part of the day on account of the gaslight".[1]

Lack of rest and recreation and sheer physical neglect sowed the seeds of ill-health among men students. Though the non-residential character of the Scottish colleges suited the native taste much better than the so-called "semi-monastic" English system, it had drawbacks. In the words of one of the inspectors: "Many of the students either from ignorance of the laws of health, or from want of means, rarely enjoy a substantial dinner, and content themselves with a meagre tea instead. In the case of growing lads from the country, accustomed to homely but substantial fare, such a mode of living must gradually sap the foundations of a robust and healthy frame, and seriously endanger even the life of the more feeble." He commented approvingly on the arrangements made at Moray House to give students a midday meal during the annual examination week.[2]

Residence in boarding houses was considered desirable only for the "softer sex". However, the Free Church Colleges in Glasgow and Aberdeen did not have boarding houses at all. The Rector of the Glasgow College considered boarding accommodation unnecessary. The majority of his students, he said, came from Glasgow or travelled by train from surrounding towns. Others stayed in lodgings. "We have had no difficulty with our students, in regard to morals", he remarked, and he attributed the good spirit of the college to the close personal contact between staff and students. The only serious lapse reported in his college occurred when three men students, who had absented themselves from class for two hours, were dis-

---

[1] *Scottish Education Inquiry Committee, Minutes of Evidence, 2nd Report,* 1887, p 117.
[2] *Report of Committee of Council on Education,* 1883-4, pp 208-9.

covered in a local public house.[1] While other Rectors segregated the sexes and expressed a preference for separate institutions, Dr Morrison felt such a move would bring "a distinct
loss of moral power". "Our experience," he said, "is all in
the direction that the mixing of the sexes, is, under proper control,
most healthy."[2]

In contrast, the Rector of the neighbouring Established
Church College, James Leitch, kept a rigid control over his
students. Women, who lived more than twenty miles' train
journey away, had to stay in the boarding house (now equipped
with a library of literature suitable for Sunday reading). Even
requests by students to attend Sunday church with relatives in
the city had to be referred to the committee of managers, and
were only granted reluctantly. In both the Edinburgh and
Glasgow Established Church Colleges men and women were
"told to have no relations with each other". Occasionally in
the Glasgow College, men and women passed each other in the
lobby, but in Edinburgh they were in separate premises.
"Before that," said the Rector, "we used to have more cases
of discipline. . . . They (the men and women) met coming in
and going out."[3]

The strict regime of the Glasgow college – students in the rival
Free Church College described it as "a convict settlement" –
led to a student mutiny in 1877.[4] It all began by the men students letting off detonating crackers in their classes, including
that of the Rector, in protest against the latter's suspension of
bursaries on disciplinary grounds. In what was described in
the Minutes as "The Riot of the 7th June", they met in "tumul-
tuous and disorderly manner" in the staircase and lobby outside
the Rector's room and refused to disperse until he promised
to restore their bursaries. The Rector summoned the lecturers
to his assistance, but they laid down terms before they agreed to
co-operate. At this dramatic point, the Minute Book stops.
In fact the Scotch Education Department intervened and com-

---

[1] *Minutes of Glasgow Free Church Normal College*, 7 September 1885.
[2] *Scottish Education Inquiry Committee, Minutes of Evidence, 2nd Report*,
1887, p 11.
[3] *ibid*, p 20.
[4] The episode is described in *Minute of Church of Scotland Normal College,
Glasgow*, 12 June to 25 June 1877 (manuscript).

pelled the authorities to dismiss the Rector and certain members of staff, and punish the student body.[1]

The new Rector, David Ross, kept the students firmly in hand. A Shetlander by origin, he had formerly taught classics, but as head of Gartsherrie School in Coatbridge he had built up a strong technical side.[2] His appointment in Glasgow carried a comfortable salary of £600 a year, which compared favourably with salaries paid to the Rectors of leading burgh schools and academies.[3] He quickly set to work to transform the institution. He lectured himself, on a variety of subjects, religious knowledge, school management and political economy, and he shared in the work of school supervision, demonstration and criticism lessons. He assembled an able staff, including as science lecturer, David Forsyth, who subsequently earned distinction as headmaster of the famous Leeds Higher Grade School.[4] Very soon the teaching was as efficient as that of the Free Church College. Ross, however, was very different from the genial Dr Morrison. Of the students he said, "We have control over them as to their conduct from the day they come to college. . . . I write to their friends if I do not approve of their conduct and diligence." He visited their lodgings regularly and asked the landladies to report to him. "They are so very anxious to have our students as lodgers," he said, "that I easily know if there is any irregularity."[5]

Ross was especially interested in "the study of education as

[1] Official references to the episode appear in *Reports of Committee of Council on Education*, 1877-8, pp 276, 278: 1878-9, p 297.
[2] A centenary article commemorating Ross's birth appeared in *Scottish Educational Journal*, 29 May 1942, p 332 (unsigned but apparently written by Rev Dr W M Wightman).
[3] In 1874, the Rector of the Edinburgh High School was paid £700, the Rector of the Glasgow High School £512. *Report of the Colebrooke Commission*, vol II, 1874, pp 437, 471.
[4] Forsyth was an extremely able teacher. He lectured in the normal college in geography, grammar, composition, science, reading, penmanship and drawing. He infused his own qualities in the Leeds School which was judged by the Bryce Commission Report of 1895 to be the finest higher grade school in the country. It earned spectacular amounts from the Department of Science and Art under the system of Payment by Results.
[5] *Scottish Education Inquiry Committee, Minutes of Evidence*, 1887, p 33.

a science and an art". Formerly the official school management syllabus had been confined to topics such as registration, classification, timetables, ventilation, school fittings, furniture and apparatus. In 1881, however, the *Principles of Education* were included with Locke's *Thoughts on Education* as recommended reading. There followed the introduction of faculty psychology as part of "Mental Science", and the separation of the theory and practice of education. Each college was required to appoint a special "master of method" to take charge of the practice. Customarily the Rectors themselves assumed responsibility for the theory of education. Ross, in addition to a weekly lecture to all students in school management,[1] gave two courses of lectures each session. He gave forty lectures on logic, psychology and ethics as applied to education, taking for special study Locke's *Thoughts on Education*, Spencer's *Education, Moral, Physical and Intellectual* and Bain's *Education as a Science*. He found those students, who had attended university classes in logic and metaphysics, "showed superior ability in this portion of the subject, and their superiority is found unconsciously to stimulate the mental powers of the rest".[2] He also gave a course of twenty lectures on the history of education, from Luther to Stow.

Ross was a great propagandist for education as a university study. As a leading member of the Educational Institute of Scotland, he supported in 1883 a resolution of that body for the foundation of Chairs in Aberdeen and Glasgow and for the establishment in all the universities of Faculties of Education, which should offer professional degree courses. The existing Chairs, he felt, were merely "excrescences" in the Faculties of Arts, and were too isolated from the practice of education to be effective. With the improvement of training college standards, he looked forward to their affiliation with the universities.[3]

Though still administratively linked with England, Scottish teacher training had in the years since 1872 developed very much on native lines. By the early 'eighties, about 1,000

[1] Based on Fitch's *Lectures on Education*.
[2] *Report of Committee of Council on Education*, 1883-4, p 243.
[3] *Educational News*, 7 April 1883.

students had been through a course of concurrent training, while each year about 150 students (half of the men students) were attending university classes. Gradually, the leaven of university studies was raising the standards of elementary school teachers. In the initial years of the new national system, education had been spread widely but thinly. Now, the concern for standards had revived. The traditional university study was becoming the natural ambition of male teachers, whose intellectual interests were reflected in the advanced work (the "specific subjects" under the code) of the schools.

In a Report written in the mid-'eighties John Kerr, HMI, compared Scottish and English schools. "We have," he said, "less of the repose of manner and absence of effort on the part of the teacher, and less of the politeness and refinement on the part of the pupil. Scotch discipline is not less effective for purposes of work. That it is somewhat wanting in gentleness and finish is probably due to the native ruggedness characteristic of the more northern race."[1] Undoubtedly English influence had brought variety into the curriculum. Subjects like drawing, music, cookery and elementary science had come into the schools and teacher training colleges. There were, however, distinct differences between the two systems. Far less attention was paid in Scotland to the training of infant teachers, and in the schools small children had to be "still as a graveyard", and to spend their days in "profitless drudgery and unutterable misery". The fact that "specific subjects" were widely cultivated among older pupils was evidence of the respect for academic achievement.

Unfortunately, Kerr's comparisons did not extend to teacher training, though on several occasions he condemned the "monastic" character of English institutions, which, he felt, sapped self-reliance. Clearly, however, the differences which he noted in the schools were reflected within the training systems. The temperament and background of the Scottish educator gave him a love of theory rarely found in his English counterpart. His university study of logic and metaphysics had predisposed him to investigate the sciences which bore on education and to search for pedagogic principles, which he could expound to his

[1] *Report of Committee of Council on Education*, 1884-5, p 20.

students.   In contrast, members of staff in English colleges, who lived among their students from morning till night, had far less time and energy to spare for professional study.   They were more concerned with students' welfare, were possibly broader in their sympathies, but they were less intellectual and less interested in seeking a rational basis for practice.

In Scotland there was a deeper sense of professional consciousness.   Already there were strong voices clamouring for professional training in association with the universities, for preparatory discipline and thorough tests of efficiency which should qualify teachers for entry to a register so that teaching could rank with the other professions of medicine, law and theology.[1]

THE NEW "CENTRAL" SYSTEM FOR APPRENTICES

In 1885, the Scotch Education Department became an independent Committee of Council and the chief political office, that of Vice-President, devolved on the Secretary of State for Scotland.   The appointment of Henry Craik,[2] a Scotsman and former senior examiner, as Secretary to the reorganised Department was significant.

Craik's influence was immediately seen in the successive codes which brought a new spontaneity into school work and which helped to raise the quality of teaching.   In 1886, payment by results was abolished in the lower standards, and in 1890 abolished entirely.   Though "specific subjects" continued to be taken by older pupils, all elementary subjects were tested by class examination instead of individual examination.   The partial abolition of fees in 1891, a measure which brought many younger children into the schools, gave a new impetus to kindergarten work and to musical drill.[3]   Indeed, physical

---

[1] eg "The Professional Training of Teachers", William Jolly, HMI, *Fortnightly Review*, vol xvi, September 1874, p 363 *et seq*.

[2] Henry Craik 1846-1927.   Born in Glasgow, Craik went to Glasgow University in 1860 and in 1864 (as a Snell exhibitioner) to Balliol.   In 1870, he was appointed one of the Junior Examiners of the Committee of Council. Later he became Senior Examiner.

[3] It is of interest to note that the abolition of fees brought to an end the practice of children bringing peats to school for fuel.   Circular to School Boards, Circular 160, 19 January 1894.

exercise in one form or other became universal, while among senior pupils, practical subjects – cookery and laundry work for girls and manual work for boys – were given new prominence.[1]

Under the old system, the "3 Rs" had been an end in themselves and children had been taught to perform their tasks with mechanical accuracy. Under the new, the teacher was encouraged to devise individual techniques and to think in terms of developing children's intelligence. The new approach, which required greater flexibility on the part of the teacher, brought up the whole question of apprenticeship to teaching, for the immature pupil teacher, caught up in the drudgery of routine instruction, was often incapable of deviating from drill methods.[2]

In 1889, the Department reduced the size of school which a certificated teacher, aided by one or two pupil teachers, could conduct,[3] while successive codes progressively raised the standards demanded for the pupil teachers in existing subjects and also extended the range of their studies. Already some of the larger school boards had set up central classes for their apprentice teachers. Even in the 'seventies the Glasgow and Govan boards had gathered pupil teachers together for Saturday morning singing classes and, by 1882, Glasgow was running regular evening classes. The new system, which was particularly suited to large centres of population, spread to other areas, including Leith, Dundee and Aberdeen (but not to Edinburgh). Opinion was divided on its merits. Many regarded it as the beginning of a reformed and more efficient method. Others deplored the inevitable loss of personal interest by teachers in the progress of their apprentices.[4] For some teachers had gone beyond the bare requirements of the broadsheet, and at odd hours had given instruction in the "higher branches" of educa-

---

[1] eg Memorandum on Teaching of Cooking in Edinburgh Board Schools, J Struthers, *Report of Committee of Council on Education*, 1889-90, p 290.

[2] John Adams described drill methods. "A writing lesson sometimes began by numbers going up as high as 10, each number indicating a movement towards the final result of making the first ink character in the copy books. Pens had to be held in exactly the same way by all pupils." *Education and the New Teaching*, Hodder and Stoughton, 1919, p 19.

[3] From 100 to 90 (with 1 pupil teacher) from 140 to 120 (with 2 pupil teachers).

[4] In England, similarly, opinion was divided. Matthew Arnold criticised the new system, "It does not compensate for the advantage of being taught by one person". *Cross Commission*, vol I, Minutes of Evidence, 1886, p 188.

tion. The opportunity of qualifying for entrance to university classes had stimulated both teacher and taught, and in some schools it had become a point of honour for a pupil teacher to gain the special university mark.[1]

Under the new central system, pupil teachers were instructed in the evenings by specialists. Often however, they arrived tired and jaded after their day's work. Sometimes they were required to attend Saturday morning classes and always they had to spend long hours in private preparation. An inspector wrote, "Oh, for eight hours a day for these growing boys and girls, but there is no such blessing for them. They must work, work, work. In this worse than Egyptian slavery, there is not a moment for recreation, no time for independent reading. The intellect is starved, the school becomes 'their solar system in which they revolve in a perpetual cycle of parsing and analysis'."[2] A former Aberdeenshire pupil teacher described the "slavery" of apprenticeship:

> "They gyred my feet that ran so fast to please,
> And from mine eyes expelled that glance too wild,
> Now damned be all in schools or factories,
> That take a mean advantage of a child."[3]

Since the country districts could not organise central classes, the rural apprentice was often at a disadvantage in the competitive examination for entrance to training college. A S Neill, for example, has recalled his own unsuccessful attempt, as a pupil teacher in his father's village school, to secure a place in a training college.[4] After the expansion of the 'seventies, the Department had restricted the number of students in training to 860, so that each year apprentices who failed to get places remained in schools as untrained assistants. The more ambitious of them took the certificate examination by home study and duly qualified for the parchment, but they had lost the opportunity of widening their horizons. "The *Wanderjahre* with all that

---

[1] *Report of Committee of Council on Education*, 1889-90, p 292.
[2] *Report of Committee of Council on Education*, 1893-4, p 364.
[3] A A Cormack, *William Cramond, 1844-1907, Schoolmaster at Cullen*, Banff, 1967, pp 27-8.
[4] *Times Educational Supplement*, 6 January 1967.

these bring of animation and experience" had been cut out of their lives.[1]

THE PROBLEM OF THE GAELIC-SPEAKING AREAS

The ex-pupil teachers formed a pool of cheap labour for those remote school areas which could not afford trained teachers.[2] Few young people from the West Highlands and Western Isles were able to gain entry to training college since so many of the schools were either too small to take apprentices or the teachers too ill-equipped to give the necessary instruction. In fact, Gaelic-speaking students were practically excluded from the colleges altogether.

Even before his new appointment, Henry Craik had in 1884 investigated conditions in the Highlands. He had suggested the establishment of specially selected centres for pupil teachers,[3] and in the following years provision was made in towns such as Stornoway and Oban. Those who were able to stay a year or more were brought far enough to make a fair showing in the college entrance examination. However, pupil teachers had to finance themselves and, as the Rector of Oban High School remarked, "in many cases (they) can afford only a few months, long enough to convince them how backward they are (which is of course something) and return to one or other 'side' schools in their neighbourhood".[4] As Secretary to the Education Department, Craik sought to improve the supply of Gaelic-speaking teachers. In 1887, Gaelic was recognised as one of the languages which students could offer at the entrance examination, and subsequently a few scholarships were reserved for Gaelic-speaking students. In order to raise teachers' salaries, extra grants, conditional on good average attendance, were given to Highland schools. Nevertheless trained teachers continued to be scarce, and in the more remote areas educational standards were so lamentable that, in the words of a Highland minister, "it could

---

[1] *Report of Committee of Council on Education*, 1891-2, p 258.
[2] *Report of Committee of Council on Education*, 1879-80, p xviii.
[3] Appendix, *Report of Committee of Council on Education*, 1884-5.
[4] *Disadvantages of pupil teachers in many parts of the Highlands*, James Beattie, unpublished memorandum, December 1899, Scotch Education Department. (The "side" school is described on page 27.)

be said without exaggeration that he knew parishes in which it was a misfortune to be born".[1]

Some of the qualified teachers who served in the area could not speak the native tongue. Indeed occasionally an advertised vacancy attracted a Southron (an Englishman). One such schoolmaster from Birmingham described his experience in a Roman Catholic school in South Uist.[2] As a bachelor he adapted himself to the rugged life, revelling in the open-air pursuits and in the natural beauty of his surroundings. Both in the day school and in his work in adult evening classes he served the community well, but he never learnt to speak Gaelic and depended on successive pupil teachers to instruct the children in their native tongue. Not all teachers were able to settle so happily, especially in the sterner Presbyterian areas. The men sometimes sought solace in drink, while the women became depressed by the sheer tedium and a few unfortunates were even driven to insanity.[3]

THE GROWTH OF SECONDARY EDUCATION

In the absence of systematic provision for secondary education, the pupil-teacher system provided an educational ladder. Yet, though it gave many talented and ambitious boys the chance to proceed to university, it was a poor substitute for secondary education, and compelled the training institution to undertake much of the work of a secondary school. Moreover, the apprenticeship system was wasteful, for many recruits abandoned their course prematurely. "Is there any other profession," asked David Ross, "in which apprentices fail to such an extent in completing their course with credit?"[4]

Some of the surviving parochial schoolmasters maintained high standards. For example, even in the early years of the twentieth century, the village schoolmaster of Cullen in Banffshire taught his older pupils Latin, Greek, French, Euclid,

---

[1] *Report of Committee of Council on Education*, 1903-4, p 275.
[2] F G Rea, *A Schoolmaster in South Uist, Reminiscences of a Hebridean Schoolmaster*, 1890-1930, Routledge, 1964.
[3] John Wilson, *Tales and Travels of a School Inspector*, Jackson Wylie, 1928, p 108.
[4] *Educational News*, vol xviii, 18 November 1893, p 769.

geography and grammar. In the evenings they "attended for higher education at the tail end of a standing row of six pupil teachers around the classroom fire".[1] In many of the public schools, however, the traditional link between primary and secondary education had disappeared. What was now required was a gradation of schools. Though the Argyll Commission in 1868 had recommended the extension and reform of secondary education, it was not until the 'eighties that real progress was made by the diversion of educational endowments[2] and the introduction of state inspection and examination (by means of the Leaving Certificate). Already some of the larger school boards were thrusting into the sphere of secondary education by the provision of higher grade schools,[3] but it was only in the closing years of the century that schools in each area were graded and classified.

Meanwhile, a good deal of the first year of the training course was necessarily devoted to work which should have been covered at school. Examination results were excellent – indeed Matthew Arnold in his evidence to the Cross Commission commented on the superior teaching in Scottish training colleges.[4] Gradually the elementary branches of the college curriculum were pruned (the learning by heart of a prescribed number of lines of poetry, for example, was abolished in 1889). More emphasis was given to disciplinary subjects, Latin for those men who did not attend university classes and French, including for the first time oral French, for women.[5] New subjects came in – elementary dynamics and plane trigonometry for men, together with new options such as navigation and agriculture. With the introduction in 1895 of a half-day system for apprentices, the intellectual attainments of training college entrants went up by leaps and bounds. The higher standards were reflected particularly in the school management syllabus, which emphasised

[1] A A Cormack, *William Cramond 1844-1907, Schoolmaster at Cullen*, p 28.
[2] As a result of the Educational Endowments (Scotland) Act, 1882, under which the Balfour Commission was appointed with certain compulsory powers.
[3] By 1887, Govan School Board had organised 5 Higher Grade Schools, (*Scottish Education Inquiry Commission, 3rd Report*, 1888, pp 166-7.
[4] *Cross Commission*, vol I, Minutes of Evidence, 1886, p 188.
[5] *Report of Committee of Council on Education*, 1896-7, p 439. Their pronunciation was now judged to be "at least recognisable".

faculty psychology and the history of education (based on Quick's *Educational Reformers*), and which was examined only at the end of the second year.

Games had no part in the curriculum of the colleges. It was not only that sites were too restricted and timetables too full; by tradition, recreation was regarded as a waste of school time. However, drill was taught, and sometimes gymnastics. The Aberdeen colleges were outstanding for their physical training, organised by a Major Cruden. John Kerr, HMI, attributed "the absence of headaches and bloodless cheeks" in the female students of Aberdeen to "exercises . . . with clubs and barbells . . . all but perfect in respect of precision and grace of movement".[1] Indeed, Major Cruden became the acknowledged authority on physical education in Scotland. He inspected the drill of other colleges, and he organised, at his own private physical training college in Aberdeen, summer courses for teachers who came from all parts of the country to qualify for his certificate.[2]

In 1889, after years of pressure, the Department offered support (ie, 75 per cent of fees) for a third year at university.[3] Graduation now became a practical possibility for men students and all the colleges systematically followed up the university classes by tutorials. Some allocated mornings for university work, others dovetailed the timetables of college and university. For the students, the dual timetables brought many complications. Dr R R Rusk, writing of his own student days in Glasgow, said that the Free Church College recognised only those university classes which met between 8 and 9 am and after 3 pm. The result was that he had to take his course of study in the reverse order of that advised by the university authorities. There were all sorts of conflicts, for "the training college staffs . . . considered that the training college work should have priority whereas the students tended to regard their university studies as of primary importance".[4] The combined pressure of university and college work caused breakdowns, even among the ablest

---

[1] *Report of Committee of Council on Education*, 1890-1, p 323.
[2] *Report of Committee of Council on Education*, 1898-9, p 488.
[3] Code of 1888, Article 102 (*e*).
[4] *John Adams 1857-1934. Biographical Notes* (typescript), R R Rusk, 1961, p 8.

H

students. In Edinburgh, John Kerr, HMI, was so concerned at the number who "work very hard and feed very poorly" that he raised a subscription list to equip the colleges to provide midday meals. For 6d the students could receive a substantial meal of two courses. In other respects, however, he felt that male students should be left to fend for themselves. "Conventual routine" was no "preparation for future professional success . . . for taking part in the larger life that awaits them outside the classroom".[1]

RENEWED UNIVERSITY EFFORTS TO INCORPORATE
TEACHER TRAINING

The 'eighties brought renewed applications from the universities to participate in teacher training. St Andrews and Aberdeen were hankering, of course, after the financial benefits of teacher training, the £100 retrospective grant for every student who obtained the certificate. It was the authorities of Aberdeen University who first suggested they should organise a male training department.[2] The Department again rejected their request but, in order to check the continual drain of students from the North-East, it conceded that the training colleges in Aberdeen should admit a limited number of men students.[3]

In 1887-8, when the whole question of teacher training was reviewed by an official Committee of Inquiry, the Universities of St Andrews and Aberdeen reiterated their claims to incorporate teacher training departments. The Principal of St Andrews wrote cogently of the suitability to teachers in training of the location of St Andrews, "far from the temptations of large cities, and offering, as it does, the most varied opportunities for outdoor exercise, and for firsthand observation of the most striking phenomena of biology, geology and physical geography", and he referred to the interest the university had taken in the education of women, by initiating courses leading to the

---

[1] *Report of Committee of Council on Education*, 1891-2, pp 323-4.
[2] Correspondence between Aberdeen and St Andrews on their proposals for participation in the training of teachers in *Minutes of Senate of St Andrews*, 1884 and subsequent years. Aberdeen proposed (1884) that students should attend university classes during the winter session, and take the required non-university subjects during a special summer session.
[3] *Report of Committee of Council on Education*, 1884-5, p 93. Numbers were restricted to 44 (in both colleges).

qualification of LLA (Lady Literate in the Arts).[1] He urged that the Professor of Education should be made responsible for a training department.

Alone among the universities, Glasgow had no wish to take any direct part in the training of teachers. Edinburgh, however, was willing to take responsibility for the élite of the teaching profession though the authorities had no desire to see university standards debased by the transfer of large numbers of women students. Laurie was anxious to secure recognition by the Department of the graduate diploma awarded by the University of Edinburgh to students who had successfully completed the education course in the Theory and Practice of Education. (His students – rarely more than 5 or 6 a year – devoted three months to practical training which they received at the Church of Scotland Normal College in Edinburgh.[2]) He suggested that Queen's Scholarships should be individual awards which men could, if they chose, hold at the university. In order that such students might receive a practical training, analogous to that received by medical students in city hospitals, the university would require to use local board schools.[3]

However, the great weight of evidence of the inspectorate and the school boards was in favour of the existing combination of college training and university study. The Glasgow Board, for example, refused to engage graduates who had not been through college. The trained teacher brought to his work qualities which were "not easily acquired, habits of order, discipline and organisation, . . . especially valuable in dealing with the unruly mass of children often found in the large schools of the great cities". Almost two-thirds of their masters had attended or were in process of attending university classes.[4]

---

[1] Letter 20 January 1887, *Scottish Education Inquiry Committee, Minutes of Evidence, 2nd Report*, 1887, Appendix, pp 10-11.
[2] *Scottish Education Inquiry Committee, Minutes of Evidence, 2nd Report*, 1887, p 29. Laurie said, "A man who has got a head on his shoulders and knows something of the principles and methods of education, can very quickly take up all the points of teaching a class and the organisation of a school". Indeed by the Code of 1878, Article 47 (c) the Department admitted as certified teachers graduates who after 3 months' experience could teach satisfactorily in front of a HMI.
[3] *ibid*, p 13.
[4] *ibid*, p 2. Evidence of the Secretary to the Board. Thirty-five assistant teachers in Glasgow schools were attending university in the session 1886-7.

In fact, the Committee of Inquiry declared in favour of the *status quo*: the colleges were doing their work efficiently, they were apparently free from sectarian intolerance – indeed the denominational connexion was said to be "of the mildest and least obtrusive nature", and they enjoyed the confidence of the school boards throughout the country.[1] The State was getting a good financial bargain since teachers were being trained more cheaply than in England (though in fact the proportionate 25 per cent contribution of the churches had now become illusory).[2] On the other hand, the Committee were convinced that the universities could not fulfil all the practical requirements of teachers in training. They could neither guarantee adequate moral and religious training, nor could they provide tutorial assistance or skilled supervision in the practising school. Unlike training college staff, who had intimate knowledge of their students, the professors would not be able to supply the school boards with information on character and personal fitness.[3] Therefore, while they were anxious to secure extension of opportunities of university attendance, members of the Committee felt that the colleges alone could maintain standards of practical training.[4]

Craik was firmly opposed to universities taking a more direct part in teacher training. He expressed his views in 1892 in evidence before the Universities Commission which was considering the relationship of the universities to teacher training. The new university college of Dundee was urging its claim to incorporate a day training college on the same lines as those recently associated with English universities. Despite the fact that Dundee was in the unique position of representing

---

[1] *Scottish Education Inquiry Committee, 2nd Report,* 1888, p viii.
[2] The intricacies of training college finance were elucidated by Craik, *Scottish Universities Commission,* 1893, Minutes of Evidence, p 296. In fact the colleges were allowed to add to the total of their expenses fictitious amounts of £23 for every male and £17 for every female (equivalent to the cost of residence in the English colleges) before calculating the 75 per cent. Colleges also made a profit from their boarding houses and from books sold to students taking university courses.
[3] A S Neill wrote of his experience at university at this period, "I was in Professor George Saintsbury's honours English class in Edinburgh. There were about 10 of us. Just before I graduated George asked me my name: he had not seen me in three years." *Times Educational Supplement,* 6 January 1967.
[4] *Scottish Education Inquiry Committee, 2nd Report,* 1888, p viii *et seq.*

the only large area without a training college, and despite the special plea that the system of mixed classes in the university college would lead to "considerable economy of teaching power as compared with Normal Colleges", Craik resisted the proposal. It would encourage, he said, "a lower grade of students" who would obtain neither a university degree nor adequate professional training: they would "get a mixture of the two, but inferior on both sides". He doubted whether a Professor of Education would have that "minuteness of acquaintance with the practical work of elementary schools" which the Rector of a training college had. He dismissed the suggestion of a university "committee of discipline", which should have oversight of teachers in training; it would, he felt, either mark them off from the rest of the students or, as was more likely, become a mere formality.[1]

Craik's greatest objection, however, was that his Department would not be able to supervise the work of the students effectively. "It would be very difficult for us," he said, "to exercise the same control in the university, or even any committee appointed by the university, which we exercise over the training colleges. They are constantly visited by our inspectors. They are under our supervision as regards their curriculum in every way."[2] He expressed a preference for the separation of the university course from teacher training by the establishment of a postgraduate year at training college, and, though the arrangement seemed illogical, he was in favour of leaving the management of training institutions to the denominations. Indeed he would have welcomed an extension of their activities to Dundee.

In their evidence before the Universities Commission, representatives of Aberdeen, St Andrews and Edinburgh expressed their readiness to take over responsibility for teacher training. Glasgow alone resisted change. In the words of Professor Ramsay, who had long identified himself with education, the alliance between university and training college worked "admirably" and "could not be improved". A dual system of training would, he thought, lead to rivalry between teachers. He

[1] *Scottish Universities Commission*, 1893, Minutes of Evidence, p 298.
[2] *ibid*, p 301.

dismissed the suggestion of a postgraduate course of training.
It could not be compared to the clinical instruction of medical
students for, he said, "when a medical student goes into hospital . . . it is a rise to him to go there; but if a man has been
three years at university, to go back to a training school to learn
to teach the A B C is reversing the process. . . . I think it would
be a painful operation."[1]

However, the Commissioners, in recommending in 1893 the
admission of selected Queen's Scholars to University, had in
mind the special circumstances of Dundee. It was the needs of
Dundee which influenced the Department to revise its policy
two years later. Since the Presbyterians were unmoved by the
current wants of Dundee, the establishment of a training institution on the lines of the new university day colleges in England
offered the only possible solution. A generation had passed since
the transfer of denominational schools to public authorities and
many Presbyterians regarded their training college responsibilities as a tiresome, and sometimes a costly, survival of the
past. With the increase of opportunities for professional promotion, training colleges had become less valuable as nurseries
for the ministry. From time to time, therefore, there were
motions before the General Assembly for winding them up and
handing over the proceeds to some worthy cause, such as the
Aged Ministers' Fund.

QUEEN'S STUDENTSHIPS

It was the inability of the colleges to cater for the needs of
the schools which compelled the Department to give the universities a direct part in teacher training. The reduction in
1889 of the size of classes (to 70 instead of 80 pupils for every
certificated teacher) had brought a deficiency of over 2,000
qualified teachers.[2] Year after year, the colleges were compelled
to turn away good candidates. Many stayed on in their schools
and tried to take the certificate examination externally. In fact,
a third of the certificated teachers were untrained,[3] and each year

---

[1] *Scottish Universities Commission*, 1893, Minutes of Evidence, p 319.
[2] *Report of Committee of Council on Education*, 1893-4, p xx.
[3] Craik quoted the statistics in 1892: 5,200 trained teachers, 2,500 untrained. *Scottish Universities Commission*, 1893, Minutes of Evidence, p 297.

there was a rush from teachers serving in the schools to take the qualification.

In 1895, a new kind of government bursary, the Queen's Studentship (as distinct from the Queen's Scholarship), was established, which enabled the holder to receive professional as well as academic training under university auspices.[1] Local committees based on the universities were to be responsible for the discipline and moral supervision of the Queen's Students and for their practical training in schools approved by the Department. Simultaneously, the Edinburgh University graduate diploma was accepted as a qualification for teaching, so that Laurie's course at last had official recognition. In order to ensure uniformity of standards by the various local committees, HMIs were to be associated with the professors in the examination of Queen's Students.

The universities had now reformed their curriculum and had included Education among subjects qualifying for the MA degree. Lectureships in Education had accordingly been established in Aberdeen in 1893, and in Glasgow in 1894. (The first appointments were part-time and were held by the Rectors of the two Church of Scotland Colleges, Joseph Ogilvie and David Ross.) Other university reforms, designed to improve standards, were the consequence of improvements in secondary education: junior classes were no longer to count for graduation, and entrance to degree courses was restricted to those who had passed the university preliminary examination or who had obtained the Leaving Certificate. Women were also admitted to classes.[2]

The establishment of a dual system of teacher training roused some opposition. For more than half a century teacher training had been undertaken exclusively by the churches. Now for the first time it was to be entrusted also to secular institutions. In the event, however, only St Andrews and Aberdeen established

---

[1] Explained in Circular 174, 4 March 1895, and incorporated in the Code of 1895, Articles 83 and 96. The Circular stated that a normal master must be specially appointed to take charge of the practical teaching. Simultaneously the training college year was changed to run from September to July in order to allow students the full benefit of the university session.

[2] In 1894, 32 training college women attended classes; a year later, 97 did so. *Report of Committee of Council of Education*, 1895-6, p 424. Already women LLAs were being appointed to training college staffs.

local committees at once (in 1896), followed in 1900 by Dundee. Glasgow persisted in its opposition to the scheme which, it was considered, "would bring discredit" on the work of the universities.[1] It was not until 1903 that a local committee was founded in Glasgow.

The new Queen's Studentships were intended primarily for teachers in secondary schools. Under the new system of public grants, a secondary school system was slowly taking shape. The revision of old trusts and the availability of public money for bursaries and for the teaching of scientific subjects had revitalised the "higher class" schools. Meanwhile, the establishment of higher grade schools in the towns and of "central" schools in the countryside were extending opportunities to a wider section of the population.[2] The merit certificate (introduced by the code of 1892) was now the apex of the elementary school career after which, at the age of 13, children were encouraged to stay on for a further three-year course. Under the new order, the educational ladder was accessible to increasing numbers of children, and university graduates both men and women, were required as subject specialists in a variety of schools.

It was not until the concluding years of the century that the new Queen's Students entered the schools in number, and in the meantime the threat of competition spurred the Presbyterian colleges to fresh effort. By 1900, they were training over 1,000 students of whom a half (248 men and 198 women) were attending university.[3] Attracted by the improved prospects, more men came into training, 80 per cent of whom took the concurrent course with graduation as the objective. Women, too, were keen to take advantage of the opportunity of university study.

As pupil teachers, many of the recruits had had the advantage of specialist teaching in central classes where their instruction

---

[1] *The Training of Teachers, Sir George Treveleyan's Circular.* Professor Dickson, pamphlet (privately printed) in University of Glasgow collection, 1895.

[2] In 1900, inspected higher class schools included 32 higher class public schools, 25 endowed schools, 37 schools under private management. *Report of Committee of Council on Education*, 1900-1, p 310.

[3] *Report of Committee of Council on Education*, 1900-1, p 17. Student numbers had until 1895 been limited to 860.

had extended beyond the compulsory subjects to include singing, Swedish drill, Greek, German, dynamics, drawing, geometry and science. Recent regulations had released them from the burden of annual examinations, and had also made it possible for individuals to serve a shortened apprenticeship and to work for the Leaving Certificate, now an accepted alternative to the Queen's Scholarship examination.[1] The results were seen in the superior qualifications of training college students who had matched themselves against senior pupils of secondary schools. The pupil-teacher course thus lost some of the old exclusiveness and isolationism of the past, and pupil teachers themselves, released for part of the school day, became, as one HMI put it, "helpful supernumeraries" rather than constituent members of staff.[2]   Head teachers, however, were critical of the new system. They complained that apprentices took less interest in teaching, that their energies were no longer engaged in the school. Some of them wandered "aimlessly about the room like ghosts on the banks of the Styx. There is no use asking them what subjects or classes they teach. They do not know."[3]

Gradually, the deeper and broader culture associated with university studies raised the ideals and aspirations of teachers. In the 'eighties it had seemed that teaching might become a women's preserve. Salaries had fallen from the peak years of the 'seventies and the profession seemed to have little to offer to ambitious young men. Indeed, with the abolition of fees in 1891, many school boards, on grounds of economy, had deliberately sought out the cheapest teachers. It was the development of secondary education which had transformed the situation and revived the old "stimulus of prospective ascent" associated with teaching in the rural past.

THE ESTABLISHMENT OF A ROMAN CATHOLIC COLLEGE

Roman Catholic and Episcopal schools were a class apart. Roman Catholic inspected schools had increased from 22 to

[1] Code of 1895, Article 70 (b) and (c).
[2] *Report of Committee of Council on Education*, 1893-4, p 303.
[3] *Report of Committee of Council on Education*, 1899-1900, p 518.

176 within twenty years after the 1872 Act (compared with the modest increase in Episcopal schools from 46 to 74).[1] Episcopalians drew on their own training college; Roman Catholics, however, despite the use of facilities in England, had more than two-thirds of their women teachers, and half their men, untrained. While inspectors praised the devotion of school managers, they were critical of the teaching, "mechanical routine that touches neither the intellect nor the heart", and of the concentration on grant-earning dexterity. By their earnestness and perseverance, the teachers had achieved remarkable results in junior classes, but the work of the upper school was beyond them. "It is a deficiency," wrote one inspector, "which no industry of the teachers, no skill of the managers, no stimulus of inspection can remedy; for it arises solely from the intellectual defects of a staff who have not received regular and thorough training."[2]

Eventually Roman Catholic requests for permission to found a training college met with favourable response.[3] Glasgow, with a Catholic population of 150,000, was obviously the most suitable location for a new college, and it was at the request of the Archbishop of Glasgow that four Sisters of Notre Dame came to the city to select a site.[4] Their choice fell on Dowanhill, and in January 1895 the college opened with 21 students. Like the Episcopal College in Edinburgh, Dowanhill was residential with emphasis on corporate life and religious discipline. It was unique in having a woman Principal. The first Principal, Sister Mary of St Wilfred (Mary Adela Lescher), formerly associated with Mount Pleasant, Liverpool, was a woman of great vision. Under her guidance the college was soon flourishing and the original building, described by the Chief Inspector

[1] *Report of Committee of Council on Education*, 1894-5, p xiii.
[2] *Report of Committee of Council on Education*, 1891-2, p 259.
[3] Craik advised the Vice-President of the Committee of Council, "Whatever opinion may be held, or whatever action may be taken, in regard to denominational training colleges, I think it is clearly just that so long as the present system goes on, the Roman Catholics should have the advantage of it". Confidential *Memorandum* (unpublished), 20: 9: 93, Scotch Education Department.
[4] The Scottish Hierarchy had been restored in 1878. The visit of the Notre Dame Sisters and their choosing of a site is described in *Golden Jubilee, 1895-1945. Notre Dame Training College*, pp 1-4.

as of "exceptional excellence" was enlarged to cater for 80 students and to provide a pupil-teacher centre.[1]

Since students came from some of the poorest sections of the community, there was no question of their paying their way as did many of the women students in the Presbyterian colleges.[2] From 1898, selected students attended university classes and by 1900 the college was training postgraduate students. The task was colossal: the building up of standards within a depressed Irish community which was still largely illiterate. From her Liverpool days, Sister Mary of St Wilfred was familiar with the poor background of the Irish immigrants, and with the ghetto-like mentality fostered by life in an intolerant and aggressively Protestant community. For advice she was able to look to the Secretary of the Catholic Poor School Committee, W H Hunnybun, with his considerable experience of English training colleges.

THE END OF AN ERA

The closing years of the century had brought great changes in Scottish education. Elementary schools had been relieved of the last remnants of payment by results, and an educational ladder was now offering new opportunities of secondary education. Elementary education was no longer regarded as an end in itself, but as a basis of further education. The stress was no longer merely on minimum achievements, but on work beyond the standards which should "draw out the interest and stimulate the intelligence of the children and make school life attractive".[3] The emphasis on general culture, on intelligence and thinking power of teachers was reflected in the higher intellectual standards of students. Gradually, the rigours of training college life were tempered by the growth of social life including student clubs, debating and literary societies and musical evenings. The men of Moray House even had their own social "hall" or common room. From the frequent references to enthusiastic reunions of old students, it is clear that there was a strong sense

[1] *Report of Committee of Council on Education*, 1900-1, p 585.
[2] Each paid an entrance fee of £5 which covered all expenses except books.
[3] *Circular 174*, 4 March, p 164.

of loyalty. The Currie Club, for example, flourished for almost forty years and former students from all parts of Scotland came to Edinburgh for the annual meetings.[1]

Within a few months of each other at the turn of the century, there died the two Glasgow Rectors, Thomas Morrison and David Ross, who had done so much to build up standards. Morrison died in harness having been Rector for 47 years (a record which was to be closely matched by Maurice Paterson of Moray House, who retired in 1907 after 45 years' service). A surviving college magazine of 1891, written in beautiful copperplate, gives a vivid picture of student life in the Free Church "Normal". "There is no other training college in Scotland", wrote the editor, "where the ladies and gentlemen are allowed to speak to each other so freely, or where open musical evenings would be permitted without the supervision of the lecturers. Indeed so accustomed are we to getting our own way that we were quite surprised when Dr Morrison objected to our having a dance."[2] With only 80 students in each year, there was "a real family relationship". A great occasion for the students was the annual May picnic, a whole-day affair, when 80 students (each year had a separate excursion) visited Loch Lomond or one of the glens. Dancing to the violin, "parlour tig" (in a barn) and "romping in the hay" were all activities which gave lustre to the day. The Established Church College was referred to as "the other place". "No use to argue which was the better, but many of the Established Church students would admit that the Free was the happier."[3]

In their individual articles the students wrote freely about the foibles and eccentricities of their lecturers. They recognised the scholarship of John Kerr, who, as they rightly judged, would have found a university atmosphere more congenial. Kerr's distinguished scientific papers had already won him election to the Royal Society in 1890, and were to earn him a Royal Medal and a civil pension. At the college, a few of his

[1] *Minutes of the Currie Club*, 1860-1899. Members had been students of the Established Church College, Edinburgh. Funds were raised for a book prize which is still awarded at Moray House.

[2] *Free Church Training College Literary Society Magazine*, 1891, p 97.

[3] From a letter by James Roger, Registrar of the Education Department, Cape Town, 30 September 1948. Mr Roger sent the 1891 edition of the magazine, of which he had been student editor, to Jordanhill College.

students helped him in the cellar laboratory he had equipped at his own expense. To the majority, however, he was "Old John", an absentminded figure whose greatness they dimly apprehended, but whom they frankly admitted to treating shabbily.

The intimacy of life in the colleges was associated with small numbers and church superintendence. For a generation after the disappearance of their own schools the Presbyterian churches had maintained the responsibility of training teachers for public schools. It was an illogical arrangement, a measure of convenience, workable only so long as there were no new demands on denominational resources. By the concluding years of the century, however, there was need of change. The expansion of the whole programme of training had become a matter of national concern and responsibility could no longer rest with volunteers.

Chapter 5

THE NEW PATTERN OF
TEACHER TRAINING, 1900-1921

THE BACKGROUND 1900-6

The revolution in the organisation and spirit of teacher training
in the early years of the twentieth century was the work of John
Struthers. Unlike Craik, whom he later succeeded, Struthers[1]
had come up from the ranks. A former pupil teacher, he had
taken the concurrent course (as a member of the Established
Church College) in Glasgow, and had, after a distinguished
academic career, served in the Scottish inspectorate for twelve
years. Following a brief spell as senior examiner, he became
Craik's assistant at the Scotch Education Department in 1898.

Before the partnership was six months old, elementary education was transformed by an entirely new system of grants.[2]
The former variable grants, based on "promiscuous curricula"
made up of optional subjects, were replaced by an organically
connected curriculum leading to a single comprehensive examination for the Merit Certificate, itself the passport to forms
of post-elementary education. The system of promotion and
inspection became more flexible and a new realism entered the
curriculum with a stress on such subjects as oral English,
drawing from observation and "nature knowledge". Physical
education and, in country districts, rural training were given
special prominence. The aim of education was now "to prepare
the individual for rational enjoyment of his leisure time, as
well as fit him for earning a living".[3]

For the teacher the new regulations offered greater freedom
and greater responsibility. There was no longer an imposed
scheme of work. Instead, the onus was on the schools them-

[1] See p 95, footnote 1.
[2] Code of 1899, Article 19.
[3] Explanatory Memorandum, *Report of Committee of Council on Education*,
1904-5, p 250.

selves to plan their own organisation, classification and gradation of studies, and teachers were encouraged to adopt new methods of approach, to correlate subjects and to devise group work within large classes.[1]   In 1901, the school-leaving age was raised to 14.   A new pattern of post-Merit Certificate education now emerged, geared to the two levels of the public examination: "supplementary courses" (in industrial, commercial, rural and household management) for those who were prepared to stay on to 16 and take the Intermediate Certificate, and "higher class" schools for those aiming at the Leaving Certificate and entrance to the professions.

Meanwhile, the whole system of teacher training was transformed.   Already in 1900, the colleges had been given responsibility for devising their own science courses.   Two years later, the old uniform examination based on a prescribed syllabus gave way to internal examination.[2]   Colleges were thus free to teach according to their own syllabuses (which had to be submitted to the Department for approval), and the final mark, awarded after consultation between college staff and inspector, took into account work throughout the course.   Thus, in the words of one inspector, "the dread of collapse, the staking of one's all on a single throw, on a paper perplexing perhaps, whether from ease or difficulty, are all things of the past".[3]

The old rigid examination system had disappeared, but the Department maintained close supervision of the work of the colleges.   In every subject there was an inspector who looked carefully through the students' examination papers and exercise books, who attended lectures and heard students teach.   At the end of the course the Department issued a list of the students' names with the marks "excellent", "good" or "fair" received by each student in each subject.   The college authorities then prepared the certificate, which was stamped by the Department and despatched to the individual student.   (At the same time university classes attended by students were no longer left to chance or convenience.   Instead, each student

[1] The inspectors noted the reluctance of some teachers to cast aside their former chains and exercise their new freedom. *Report of Committee of Council on Education*, 1903-4, p 273.

[2] *Circular* 329, 30 August 1901.

[3] *Report of Committee of Council on Education*, 1902-3, p 785.

had to choose a well-defined co-ordinated course, classical, modern or scientific, and to follow it through the three years.)

There were changes in the content and method of approach. Laboratory work in science replaced the old textbook courses; oral methods were more generally employed in the teaching of French; manual work was introduced, and drawing from observation and clay modelling became features of the art course. Physical training was now so much in vogue that in some colleges the inspector had to restrain the enthusiasts from devoting more than an hour at a time to it. Lady instructors were now preferred for women's drill which included dumb-bell, bar-bell, hoop and free gymnastics. There was, however, no special clothing worn, and it was not unusual for men to come in heavy boots, coats, waistcoats, braces and collars, and women in high heels and tight corsets.[1]

THE SIGNIFICANCE OF JOHN ADAMS IN SCOTTISH
TEACHER TRAINING

Since the *raison d'être* of training colleges was "to teach how to teach", the subject of education, which now included psychology, ethics, logic, history of education and methodology, was given great prominence. It was commonly the responsibility of the Rector (or Principal) who also kept closely in touch with the practical side. The inspector had especial praise for the "Lady Principal" of Dowanhill who "directs the whole work and generally presides at the criticism lesson".[2] It was an unusual feature of her college that each lecturer was also a mistress of method for her special subject. Elsewhere, method and subject matter were divorced, and the master or mistress of method was confined to the practice of education.

Child study was becoming a feature of the psychology courses in certain colleges, with students applying practical tests to distinguish the varying capacities of children. Outstanding in the field of theory and psychology was John Adams, Rector successively of the Aberdeen and the Glasgow Free Church Colleges. Adams had studied the German literature

---

[1] *Report of Committee of Council on Education*, 1903-4, p 533.
[2] *ibid*, p 522.

on psychology and adapted the Herbartian procedure of exposition and illustration. His *Herbartian Psychology applied to Education* (1897) bore the mark of the experienced teacher who had reflected deeply on what he had learnt in the classroom. As Dr Rusk, one of his former students, says, there was really more of Adams than Herbart in the work.[1] He made the new psychological theory relevant to the practical teacher and he justified one very important part of theory when he said that to teach John Latin, you must know not only Latin but also John. "In Adams' chapters," wrote Sir Michael Sadler, "you feel the teacher's desk, the convenient blackboard, the row of eruptive youth, the eternal and complicated equation in which the factors are John, John Adams and the job in hand."[2]

To his students, Adams emphasised the radical distinction between teaching and education. Teaching he defined as the mere communication of knowledge or the imparting of skill; education, as character building. Those who confined themselves to the narrow conception of teaching, to "knowledge mongering" were "the nine-to-four men . . . they are mostly men", he said, "few women adopt this attitude". They kept to the letter of their contract and disclaimed responsibility for what was done out of school hours or what sort of adults their children turned into. "The nine-to-four men call for Pontius Pilate's basin and wash their hands of the whole out-of-school affair."[3]

Certainly Adams's interest in his students was not confined to the classroom. However, it was as a teacher, as a master of the Socratic method, that he won their respect.[4] The words used by Carlyle to describe the schoolmaster, Adam Hope: "self-delusion, half-knowledge, sham instead of reality could not exist in his presence", could just as appropriately have applied to Adams himself. Dr Rusk recollects his handling of his classes in Glasgow, where students had (and still have) a reputation for rowdiness. A diminutive figure, attired always

[1] R R Rusk, *Biographical notes*, p 26.
[2] Michael Sadler, *Sir John Adams. A Lecture in his Memory*, Oxford University Press, 1935, p 11.
[3] John Adams, *The Teacher's Many Parts*, University of London Press Ltd, 1930, pp 89-90.
[4] Good examples of the method in his *Primer on Teaching with special reference to Sunday school work*, pp 97-9, 101-8.

I

in frock-coat, Adams had great dignity. "He had," says Dr
Rusk, "a disproportionately large head, and he fixed one with
a look of the ancient mariner." "The device he adopted in
getting the maximum out of the men, especially in religious
instruction, was devilish." Of the students of the year he
arranged the thirty men in the front seats of the large hall with
the women behind. A passage was assigned for each meeting
and Adams first called on one of the men. "Socrates was not
more efficient in convicting his fellow citizens in the streets of
Athens of their ignorance than was Adams in the Bible lesson.
When a male student failed to respond to questions, he called
on one of the women students – not always accidentally selected,
as they were always better prepared. It was no wonder that
practically every man in the Glasgow 'Normal' was placed in
the first class at the Church's final examination on Religious
Knowledge, and it was not zeal for biblical exegesis but the
dread of public exposure of my ignorance that made me a
prizeman in Adams's class of Biblical Knowledge."[1]

When nature study was introduced into the curriculum,
Adams arranged for a botanist to take the students on Saturday
morning rambles in the country. Though this ate into students'
spare time, the occasional free excursion to some beauty spot
was a real treat. Dr Rusk recalls, "The high light was a study
of alpine plants when we climbed Ben Lomond, and on the
very top at noon on a lovely June day three cheers were given
for Johnnie Adams who had arranged that the expenses should
be borne on the training college budget".[2]

Adams saw to it that all his men students attended university.
His ideal in teacher training was a "combination of scholarship
and practical skill". He would have liked closer affiliation
between normal school and university, so that the former could
shed much of its teaching function and concentrate on the job
of training. Even in his Aberdeen days, Adams had campaigned
for university evening classes to assist teachers to complete the
degree courses. What he had himself achieved under adverse
conditions (he had both a 1st-class Honours degree in Mental and
Moral Science and a BSc degree) he believed others might do.

[1] R R Rusk, *Biographical notes*, p 16.
[2] *ibid*, pp 16-17.

At the same time he wanted normal school courses to be available to all university students so that in each of three years they could spend their summer sessions in training. The division between the graduate and the certificated teacher – now a real danger – he believed could be avoided by a registration scheme.[1]

Like Stow himself, Adams believed that, though there were a fortunate few who were born teachers, the majority became teachers by training, and for him training included a variety of practice and observation. He was aware of the limitations of the college school. "One school is not enough", he wrote, and urged the need of practice in public schools. Criticism lessons, model lessons, sectional teaching were all part of his scheme. In the criticism lessons he often arranged for the students to take the place of children, and to respond as would pupils of a prescribed age. To some, the method seemed artificial, but Adams claimed that the body of students benefited as much from the exercise as did the teacher. He said, "The educator who cannot project himself into the personality of his pupils has not learnt the alphabet of his profession". Essentially, teacher and children were partners, who must understand and fit into each other.

On the death of David Ross in 1899, Adams was appointed part-time university lecturer in education. Dr Rusk, who was a student under both, has written, "Ross and Adams were opposites. Ross was of an imposing stature, austere and rather forbidding. Students stood in awe of him and approached him only as a last resort. Adams was quite different; a small man, he had a quaint way, rather quizzical and could pass off a joke without betraying the slightest look of humour." His own particular interests in applied psychology and philosophy were reflected in his course of lectures.[2] His exposition of Herbartian theory – with its emphasis on the central position of the teacher and the organisation of a body of knowledge – made a powerful appeal. Indeed, Adams may be said to have exploded the whole faculty doctrine. As a psychologist he called attention to the individual child (his "John" was not *any*

---

[1] Adams writing in *Educational News*, vol XXI, 1 February 1896, pp 77-8.
[2] See Appendix F, II, pp 248-9.

boy; he was a *particular* boy) and he heralded the movement
for individual work.

In 1902, Adams left his dual appointment in Glasgow to
become the first Professor of Education in the University of
London and Principal of the London Day Training College.
A pioneer in the English university field, he had to battle against
empiricists who distrusted educational theory.   England had
bred great amateurs in the field of education, reforming headmasters who were the products of nature, and sensitive and
farsighted scholars like Matthew Arnold himself and Adams's
own contemporaries, Michael Sadler and Edmund Holmes,
heirs to a mellower tradition.   Adams was the Scottish professional, the student of Herbartian literature, whose quest was
for principles and the rejection of the rule of thumb.   Formal
in appearance (he now wore a short velvet jacket), he had "the
animated severity which became the Principal of a Training
College".[1]   Somewhat to the dismay of the authorities, he
proposed – following his custom in Glasgow – to issue in
advance an official announcement that he would give a course
of a hundred lectures during the first session.   They told him
that "that sort of thing" was not customary in England, and
that he must proceed rather differently.[2]

His London students, however, soon came to appreciate his
many qualities, including his sense of humour.   As Ballard,
later a London County Council Inspector, remarked, he was
the first to call their attention to the educational importance
of jokes.   All his jokes were good.   All were original.   Some have
even gained with the passage of time.   We can enjoy today,
for instance, his comment that he read all the current literature
on education in four languages, in English, French, German
and American![3]

THE NEED OF SECONDARY SCHOOL TEACHERS

Close relationships, such as existed between Adams and the
Free Church "normal" students, were a consequence of the

[1] Michael Sadler, *Sir John Adams. A Lecture in his Memory*, p 9.
[2] *Studies and Impressions*, 1902-55 (University of London Institute of
Education), Evans, 1952, p 24.
[3] Quoted by P B Ballard, *British Journal of Educational Psychology*, vol 5,
1935, p 7.

closely-knit community life within the colleges. In contrast, Queen's Students (later King's Students) had little identity as distinct groups and simply merged in the student bodies of the universities. Unlike the day training institutions in England, which were integral parts of the university colleges, the local committees had no buildings of their own and therefore no common centre where students could meet. For practical training, they made use of neighbouring schools whose headmasters served as masters of method. However, when a large number of schools were used, there were difficulties of coordination and supervision. As for the non-university subjects, music, drawing, phonetics, needlework and gymnastics, they were taken by outside teachers who had no close connexion with the students. It was not surprising that the quality of work suffered from lack of unity.

The system of local committees had in fact been devised as a stopgap, an expedient for increasing numbers in training, and, as Craik had foreseen, there was general lack of direction and discipline. Except in Aberdeen, where arrangements were under the control of the energetic convener of the committee, Dr Dey, the system was far from satisfactory. Indeed, Craik's worst prophecies of inadequate supervision were fulfilled when two King's Students had to be expelled from St Andrews in 1901.[1] The appointment by the Dundee committee in 1905 of a Director of Studies (James Malloch, Lecturer in Education at the University College and Headmaster of Blackness Public School) was welcomed by the Department.

In contrast to the diffuse studies and *ad hoc* arrangements of the various local committees, Laurie's course for the Edinburgh University diploma, intended particularly for teachers in secondary schools, was altogether more integrated. Because of his official position, Laurie was able to make use of the facilities of the practising school of the Church of Scotland College and he personally supervised the teaching of his students. His own lectures dealt not only with the fundamentals – the importance of philosophical and historical insight and of psychological

[1] *Memorandum* from "WF" to Henry Craik (unpublished). There is also relevant correspondence between Craik and Professor Meiklejohn, file 122. Scottish Education Department.

foundations – but also with the application of principles to the day-to-day problems of the teacher. The course, covering a single session, was usually taken in the third year, though some students stayed on for three months to complete their period of teaching. The fee was three guineas, with an additional guinea paid to the master of method of the practising school, and two guineas for the diploma itself.[1]

After the admission of women to the university, Laurie's classes were attended by the students of a voluntary institution, St George's Training College for women teachers in secondary and higher schools.[2] Among the students – usually about twenty in each year – were graduates, and holders of the LLA Certificate of St Andrews or of the Oxford or Cambridge Local Examination Certificate. Founded in 1886, the college had originally prepared its students for the Diploma in Education of the University of Cambridge. The venture, inspired by the needs of girls' education, paralleled the earlier efforts of English educationists like Emily Davies and Dorothea Beale.

Highly qualified teachers, men and women, were required in increasing numbers. By 1905, there were 87 secondary schools presenting candidates for the Leaving Certificate examination and 130 higher grade schools aiming at the Intermediate Certificate.[3] Indeed, some of the higher grade schools were staffed and equipped upon a scale which enabled them to give a complete secondary education, similar to that available in the older endowed schools and burgh schools. Industrial counties like Lanarkshire had established (or had up-graded from among the board schools) as many as 30 higher grade schools, while in the rural districts of the North, the most successful of the old parish schools had been designated higher grade schools.

To meet the demand for teachers the colleges had by 1905 increased their numbers to over 1,400. Altogether there were almost 1,750 students in training, including 330 King's Students

---

[1] *Minutes of Evidence taken before the Select Committee on the Teachers' Registration Bill*, 1891, p 82.

[2] The progress of the institution is recorded in the *Annual Reports of the St George's Training College*. The Institution had been founded initially as a Training College. In 1888 it became part of St George's School for Girls.

[3] *Report of Committee of Council on Education*, 1905-6, p 852.

under local committees.   Nevertheless, of the total number of
certificated teachers (80 per cent of the teachers in the country)
only two-thirds had trained and over 4,000 had slipped through
the "back door" of the certificate examination.[1]   It was the
existence of this "back door" route which was continually
deplored.   Already school boards were organising courses for
teachers in the newer subjects of the school curriculum –
drawing, nature study, manual instruction – and some of the
powerful city boards were clamouring for a direct share in the
training of teachers.

Under their existing administration the training colleges had
no hope of closing the gap.   Though the churches had made
great efforts to adapt their buildings by the provision of
laboratories and craftrooms, their resources were quite inadequate to meet current demands for new buildings, including
specialist rooms, gymnasia and well-equipped practising schools.
Various suggestions had been made for the amalgamation of
the dual Presbyterian colleges and the church authorities were
already in close liaison, issuing common prospectuses and
conferring on matters of policy.   They were in fact anxious to
be relieved of the burden of maintaining the colleges, but only
on condition that satisfactory provision was made for religious
instruction.[2]   As far back as the 1880s, David Ross had submitted a plan which would have linked the colleges with the
universities, and would have included among the managers
representatives of both the universities and the school boards.
He had observed that experience would indicate "what portion
of the curriculum could with advantage be relegated to the
university, and what must be retained within the training
college".[3]

Denominational control of teacher training had become completely outmoded.   It was not that the colleges were severely
denominational; members of one Presbyterian Church were to
be found in large numbers in colleges of the other and were
accepted without question.   Rather it was the fact that teacher

[1] *ibid*, p 16.
[2] The United Presbyterians, who had joined with the Free Church, were
particularly anxious to be rid of the training colleges.
[3] David Ross, *Education as a University Subject: its history, present position
and prospects*, p 13.

training, under twentieth-century conditions, was rightly a national concern which should be in the control of authorities more representative of the nation than were the Church committees. For years the churches had been incapable of producing the numbers of teachers required. In fact for years there had been a deadlock: the churches had been unable to undertake large schemes of reconstruction without State support, and the State had felt itself unable to give grants which would increase the value of church property. The difficulty had been eased by the establishment of King's Students' committees in 1895 and, since King's Students had been instructed for the most part in university classes, the necessity of providing additional premises had been avoided. Now, after negotiation with the churches, the difficulty was resolved by the reconstruction of the King's Students' committees.

THE ESTABLISHMENT OF PROVINCIAL COMMITTEES

In 1904, Struthers succeeded Sir Henry Craik as Secretary of the Education Department. Almost immediately, by a Minute of 30 January 1905, the organisation of teacher training was completely remodelled. In each of the four university cities there was to be established a Provincial Committee, responsible for a teacher training centre and for the organisation of courses for practising teachers. The old King's Students' committees had been virtually self-constituted, voluntary associations, composed of representatives of the universities and of the school boards of the university towns. The Provincial Committees were given a definite constitution on a representative basis. They were to include members from all the school boards in the area served by the training centre. In fact, school board representation was the dominant feature of the committees, which also included representatives of the universities themselves, of the local technical and agricultural colleges (later designated Central Institutions), and of the "more important secondary schools". Additional members were to be co-opted from serving teachers and from representatives of the churches. One of the chief inspectors of schools was to sit on each committee as the Department's assessor.[1] Arrangements were made for the transfer of the Presbyterian colleges from the churches on payment of compensation and under guarantees for the continuance of religious instruction. There was also an important provision requiring board schools, and those endowed schools which accepted public grants, to offer facilities for student teaching practice.

With the institution of Provincial Committees the training of teachers was recognised as a direct responsibility of the State. A generation ago the schools had been transferred to popularly elected authorities; now teacher training, which for over sixty years had been under ecclesiastical bodies, passed to secular control. The responsibility which the State had thrust upon the churches had been zealously fulfilled. In the bleak period of the 'sixties, they had from their own resources supported the teaching of subjects above the required minimum. They had encouraged students to go on to university and, after 1875, had from their own funds provided bursaries for an additional year's study. Over the years they had managed the colleges shrewdly and efficiently. The universities, on the other hand, had simply ignored teacher training and their recently awakened interest had been largely pecuniary. They had been slow to escape from the medieval traditions of the *trivium* and *quadrivium*. Subjects of relevance to the teacher, such as history, literature, geography and modern languages, had not counted for the Arts degree.[2] In the past their spokesman had frequently condemned the system of training by bounty, and had implied that the function of the university would be degraded by providing for teachers. As Lyon Playfair had remarked of the universities, "Nothing is more strange than their abandonment of the teaching profession which was their own creation while the older professions were rather the creators of the universities".[3]

[1] The number of members on each Committee was as follows: St Andrews 22, Glasgow 40, Aberdeen 36, Edinburgh 33, Schedule to Minute, 30 January 1905.
[2] Choice of subjects for the Ordinary degree of MA was greatly extended by Ordinance of the Scottish Universities Commission, 1892. Parliamentary Papers, vol LXII, 1892.
[3] Address to Graduates' Association of St Andrews, London, *The Scotsman*, 16 February 1873, Quoted in David Ross, *Education as a University Subject*, p 17.

By 1906, the Presbyterian Churches had reached agreement with the new authorities for the transference of their six colleges in Edinburgh, Glasgow and Aberdeen.[1] Amounts of compensation for college buildings were finally fixed at £10,000 to be paid to the United Free Church (the United Presbyterians had combined with the Free Church in 1900) and £15,000 to the Church of Scotland. Religious instruction in the transferred colleges was to be provided according to "use and wont" at the expense of the churches, representatives of which were to draw up the syllabuses and supervise the teaching. Only the Episcopal college in Edinburgh and the Roman Catholic college in Glasgow remained under denominational management. Indeed the Principal of Dowanhill was anxious to remain outside the Provincial Committee scheme. Racial and religious friction was such that she had good reason to prefer direct dealings with the central Department rather than submit to any form of local control.[2]

THE 1906 REGULATIONS

One year after the establishment of the Provincial Committees the Department issued regulations for the Preliminary Education, Training and Certification of Teachers. With amendments the regulations were operative for almost sixty years. Their general principles were simple: there were to be two stages of preparation for teaching – the junior studentship from 15 to 18 (replacing the former pupil-teacher apprenticeship) followed by the senior studentship in a training institution. Junior students, admitted only after passing the Intermediate Examination, were to receive a secondary education based on an approved curriculum together with "systematic training . . . in the art of teaching each of the Primary School Subjects".[3] Like their predecessors, the pupil teachers, they were to receive maintenance allowances which were to be awarded by county and burgh secondary school committees. At the conclusion

[1] Legal proceedings were completed 1907. The agreement is quoted in the Minutes of each provincial committee, eg, Glasgow Provincial Committee, *Minutes of the Meeting of Sub-Committee*, 14 February 1907.
[2] *Life of Sister Mary of St Wilfred*, by a Sister of Notre Dame, (typescript, p 198).
[3] Chapter II, paras 3-14.

of the course successful candidates gained the Junior Student Certificate, which automatically gave entrance to training centre or college. As secondary school pupils they could also, if they wished, take the Higher Leaving Certificate in subjects of their curriculum.

Of senior students in training there were three categories, described in Chapters III, V and VI of the Regulations. Hence, future generations of students were referred to under the titles "Chapter III", "Chapter V" and "Chapter VI". Chapter III students included ordinary graduates, who took a one-year course. They also included former junior students or those who, in addition to having the Leaving Certificate, had six-months' practical experience in schools. They took, depending on their qualifications, either a two-year course at the training centre or a three-year concurrent course at the centre and neighbouring university, and qualified for a General Certificate, which fitted them to teach primary school subjects. Chapter V students were graduates with honours qualifications in a teaching subject, in English, languages, mathematics, science, history or geography, who took a one-year course of professional training in order to become "teachers of higher subjects" in intermediate and secondary schools. Chapter VI students held diplomas (awarded by a Central Institution) in art, technical subjects, agriculture, commerce, domestic economy or physical training[1] and took a one-year course in order to qualify as "teachers of special subjects". As in the past, teachers were to serve a two-year probationary period before receiving their "parchments". All students were required to teach for two years and had to give surety for the repayment of bursaries.[2]

The new regulations made training essential. After 1915, the external examination leading to the teacher's certificate was to lapse, and thereafter uncertificated teachers were no longer to be recognised as members of school staffs. Thus Scotland was thirty years ahead of England in dealing with the problem

---

[1] Diploma courses covered three years in a central institution, ie, in a Central School of Art, in a College of Agriculture, in a Central Technical College, in a Commercial College, in a College of Domestic Economy.

[2] Chapter IV, para 31, In fact students were pursued or, in the case of emigrants, claims were made on the guarantors.

of the uncertificated teacher. In meticulous detail the regulations differentiated between categories of students and formalised the distinction between grades of teachers. It was a logical system, corresponding to the classification of schools. The pattern of teacher training was thus reorganised to fit the new structure of Scottish education, a simple coherent arrangement based on three examinations – Qualifying (which replaced the Merit Certificate), Intermediate and Leaving, each stage marked by a definite purpose. The examination system, officially controlled, was designed to ensure thoroughness in the foundations of education and at the same time to provide an educational ladder for the able child. The reformed system of teacher training, centrally directed, was geared to the new hierarchy of schools.

THE JUNIOR STUDENT SYSTEM

In 1896, John Adams had described the ideal teacher training. He had written, "From the beginning of his course to the end of it the young teacher should be both pupil and teacher; but at the beginning the pupil element should be almost paramount, at the end the teacher element, and the course of training should be a gradual passage from one pole to the other".[1] The old pupil teachers, however, had had quite the contrary experience. Formerly they had been full-time teachers, and even latterly they had taught half-time. They had in fact been asked to teach before they *knew*, and had learnt to employ techniques of mechanical dexterity which were hard to eradicate. At training college their practical experience had been severely limited, so that as young teachers they frequently relapsed into the antiquated methods they had employed as pupil teachers. The new system ensured that the junior student was a pupil first (up to the age of 15) and that the pupil element was predominant throughout the course.

Junior students were to attend selected secondary schools or higher grade schools, offering a five-year curriculum up to the age of 18.[2] Each selected school (known as a Junior Student

[1] Adams writing in *Educational News*, vol XXI, 1 February 1896, pp 77-8.
[2] *Circular* 389, 24 March 1906.

Centre) was to have a master of method responsible for the practical training, on which students were to spend an increasing amount of time: one period a week in the first year, two periods in the second and three periods in the third year which should also include a brief continuous practice.[1] Requirements for entry to the course ensured that students had already achieved a certain standard of general education. They now embarked on a balanced curriculum of further study, including subjects relevant to their future work as teachers: music, physical education, woodwork or needlework and cookery.

Special grants were made to junior student centres[2] which by 1909 numbered 110 (89 under the direct management of school boards). Some of the urban centres such as Hamilton Academy and Dowanhill School, Glasgow, had over 100 junior students on roll; the majority had between 20 and 50 while a few had less than 10.[3] In the larger centres, where junior students formed separate classes, organisation was simplified; in country districts the system involved complicated time-tabling, duplication of demands on staff and often overpressure on students themselves, who tried to combine the course with additional subjects required for the Leaving Certificate. Indeed, in all the centres, there was a strong temptation to regard the studentship as a preparation for university entrance. Very soon there were complaints of "leakage" from the ranks of junior students of those who, having obtained the Leaving Certificate after two years, entered a university.[4]

In the towns particularly, there were many openings for boys and those who stayed on at school usually preferred to take the ordinary Leaving Certificate course. Some also took the junior student course as a form of insurance. The fact that pupils, who failed the Leaving Certificate, could manage the standard of the more broadly based Junior Student Certificate created the impression that the latter was "simply a safety net"

---

[1] *Circular* 418, 3 May 1909.
[2] Regulations for the Preliminary Education, Training and Certification of Teachers, 9 March 1907. Chapter IX, Article 52 (£8 per annum per student for 3 years).
[3] *Report of Committee of Council on Education*, 1912-13, p S4. The number of junior students in centres ranged from 1 to 242.
[4] *ibid*, p S1. In 1911, out of the 1,223 Junior Students who qualified, only 980 entered teacher training.

on which they could break their fall. Country districts, however, including the North and West of Scotland produced a
healthy supply of recruits. The old pupil-teacher system had
failed here because of the deficiencies of the local schools. The
new scheme, by means of bursaries, maintenance allowances
and hostel accommodation, brought boys and girls to specially
selected centres and gave them the opportunity to go forward
to full training.

The best that could be said of the junior student scheme was
that it helped to redress the inequality between the urban and
rural districts and laid some emphasis on general culture. It
thus offered opportunities previously denied to country pupils
and helped to foster secondary education in many of the selected
schools. In the city centres, however, where the junior students
were a segregated group, there was an unfortunate demarcation
between intending teachers and those destined for other professions. In the words of one of the Fellows of the Educational
Institute of Scotland, "every day they have to rise together
from their desks and be herded apart in order that they may
receive some specialist training, while their fellows continue
their study of the subjects properly pertaining to the higher
course".[1] Critics were not slow to condemn a system which
compelled immature adolescents to decide on a life career, and
pleaded instead for the award of post-intermediate bursaries
"without strings". Indeed the Glasgow and Govan School
Boards discarded the junior student system as early as 1912,
preferring to send their recruits to the training centre by the
alternative route – the Leaving Certificate examination followed
by continuous teaching practice.[2]

The Department, however, laid stress on the special subjects
required of the junior student: music, physical exercises, craft
and domestic economy, which were all systematically inspected.
Indeed, HMIs urged schools to allot more time to games and
dancing, both relevant to the needs of primary schools. They
felt it was unrealistic for large numbers of junior students to

[1] John Smith, *Broken Links in Scottish Education*, Nisbet, 1913, p 139.
[2] John D Wilson, "The Junior Student System", *Studies in the History
of Scottish Education* 1872-1939, ed T R Bone. Publication No 54, Scottish
Council for Research in Education, University of London Press, 1967,
p 214.

aspire to posts in intermediate and secondary schools. They were particularly keen on the preliminary practice teaching which provided a body of experience for subsequent theory, and which gave the intending teachers the confidence "to stand in front of a class without fear and develop a lesson in an orderly manner".[1] Certainly some junior students felt they had gained useful experience. W B Inglis (later to become Director of Studies at Moray House) has recalled his course at Paisley Grammar School: "I wanted to be a teacher from the age of five onwards and felt no hardship as a junior student but rather a sense of taking a step nearer to the chosen goal".[2]

In fact the value of the practical work depended very much on the arrangements at individual centres. In only one area, Edinburgh, was there liaison between the junior student centres and the provincial committee centre. Elsewhere, there was no attempt to secure continuity of method. The master of method, often the headmaster of the centre, or the headmaster of the separate practising school, gave demonstration lessons and supervised teaching practice. In the larger centres, training was rather impersonal and inspectors had to curb the tendency to impart textbook theory rather than to discuss problems arising out of practice.[3] In the smaller centres, the master of method could exert more direct influence on individual students. The consequence was that while some students came to the provincial centres as competent in class management as the old pupil teachers, the majority were much less proficient.

In their nostalgia for the past, many critics of the new regulations forgot the weaknesses of the pupil-teacher system. They ignored the fact that whereas, previously, only the *best* of the pupil teachers had gone to training college, now *all* who obtained the Junior Student Certificate automatically became senior students. As the Director of Studies of the Glasgow Provincial Committee remarked, "under the old system when the conditions were most favourable, that is, when a willing and intelligent pupil was in charge of an intelligent and self-sacrificing headmaster, results were obtained which should not

[1] *Report of Committee of Council on Education*, 1920-1, p 49.
[2] In a letter to the writer.
[3] *Report of Committee of Council on Education*, 1912-13, p S9.

be looked for at the end of the junior student course and which
are not always secured at present even at the end of the course
of full training. But these triumphs were personal. They were
not due to the system. They were obtained in spite of it. And
the cost was too great in the loss of time and of opportunities
for study and in undue mental and physical strain."[1] The old
system had placed emphasis on practical experience at an early
stage, and the function of the college had been very largely
that of the secondary school with only a fraction of the course
devoted to professional training. College students had never
taught in board schools where they would have gained experience under ordinary conditions, and in fact had had no continuous practice at all. As pupil teachers they had gone through
dreary years of practice with next to no theory, as students in
training they had been given theory with little opportunity
(apart from the artificial criticism lesson) for practice.

TRAINING UNDER THE PROVINCIAL COMMITTEES

It was assumed that the majority of senior students would
be capable of taking university courses. The implication
behind the establishment of Provincial Committees in university towns had been that the training centres should concentrate
on purely professional work and that the universities should
undertake the general education of students. Indeed, the
University of Aberdeen was willing to assume responsibility
for all lecture courses, leaving the arrangements for practical
teaching as the sole function of the Provincial Committee. The
proposal was referred to Struthers, who corresponded at length
with representatives both of the Provincial Committee and of
the university.[2] Questions of finance and control both presented difficulties, but in the end Struthers vetoed the suggested
arrangements on the grounds that the Provincial Committee
would "virtually abdicate its function" to university authorities,
who would have no regard for the interests of the students as
intending teachers. He asked, "What reasonable chance is

[1] *Glasgow Provincial Committee Minutes*, Director's Report, April 1913.
[2] Unpublished correspondence of John Struthers with R H N Sellar,
member of the Aberdeen Provincial Committee, and with Professor Hay of
the Aberdeen University Senate, between 14 May 1907 and 19 March 1908,
file 203, Scotch Education Department.

there that the proposed University Committee would ever face fairly and squarely the problem of what kind of training is most desirable for a teacher who is to carry on his life work say in Lewis or among the slum children of a big town? . . . would they not confine their attention to producing a sort of person whose aim would be to turn out pupils for the bursary competition and regard all the rest of his pupils and their future destiny as matters scarcely deserving his serious consideration?   In short if we are to get a broader conception of education instilled among the teachers of the North East of Scotland – a much needed reform – the university is the last agency in the world through which we are likely to obtain it."

He was convinced that the teachers' course would be "stifled" by the university. The university authorities were really only interested in the financial aspect of the arrangement and were most anxious to restrict government inspection "to a mere formality". The differences were too fundamental to admit of compromise. "The truth is," he wrote, "that the professors as a body, walled up in their impenetrable fortress of academic seclusion, are like the Bourbons. They have learnt nothing by experience and forget nothing of their privilege."[1]

The concurrent courses flourished everywhere. Otherwise co-operation between the Provincial Committees and the universities depended a good deal on local conditions and personal relationships. In Edinburgh, for example, some of the two-year Chapter III students attended university classes, which were easily accessible. In Aberdeen, the university lecturers in education and psychology took charge of the work in both institutions,[2] and the Professor of English (though he delegated the lectures to an assistant) took responsibility for his subject in the training centre. Elsewhere, contact was maintained by individuals. In Edinburgh, Professor Darroch, who had succeeded Laurie in 1903, acted as honorary Director of Studies of the training centre during the initial months. In Glasgow, William Boyd, university lecturer in education, gave

---

[1] *ibid.* Letter to R H N Sellar, 24 July 1907.
[2] It was only after the Second World War that the university departments of education and psychology ceased to take responsibility for the work in the centre.

K

courses in the training centre for many years,[1] and similarly in Dundee, lectures were given by C W Valentine, assistant to the Bell Professor of Education at St Andrews. University influence on the Provincial Committees was, however, restricted by the preponderance of school board members. The bureaucracy of the new system was attacked by Principal Donaldson, chairman of the St Andrews committee. He wrote, "The universities have nothing to do with framing or carrying out regulations . . . even the committees are mere machines in the hands of the Department which has the entire control and superintendence of every action of the committee and of their methods of training, prescribing even the mode of hemming and stitching which has to be taught".[2] In fact the Department, which paid the costs of training and maintenance direct to the Provincial Committees, kept them under close supervision and left little to local initiative.

The Department laid down the basic curriculum for professional training: "School and Personal Hygiene (including Physical Exercises), Psychology, Ethics and Logic in their relation to educational theory and practice, Principles of Education and History of educational systems and theories".[3] Those students who took the three-year concurrent course had to select one of several options of university study and follow it throughout. Two-year students took a general course, designed by each college and approved by the Department. One-year students – graduates and certificated (but untrained) teachers – who came in under temporary regulations, simply took professional courses. Each student's work, first assessed by the college, was scrutinised by the inspectors.

During the initial years the Provincial Committees were absorbed in problems of organisation and curricula. In each province a Director of Studies was appointed with overall responsibility for the work of the centre. The Edinburgh and Glasgow Provincial Committees appointed distinguished head-

[1] Hector Hetherington (subsequently Principal of Glasgow University) lectured on ethics for a brief period, *Glasgow Provincial Committee Minutes*, 1911-12, p 143.

[2] "Notes for Speech", MS, undated, in *Donaldson papers*, University of St Andrews.

[3] Article 22 of the Regulations, see note 44.

masters as their Directors of Studies;[1] St Andrews appointed James Malloch (formerly Director of Studies under the Local Committee in Dundee),[2] and Aberdeen appointed the former Rector of the United Free Church Training College, George Smith. Of the other college Rectors, the two veterans, Maurice Paterson and Joseph Ogilvie, had reached retiring age, while in Edinburgh, Alexander Morgan, and in Glasgow, A M Williams and T M Morrison[3] took responsibility for main lecture courses. At the suggestion of the Department, the four provinces formed a joint committee to co-ordinate policy on such matters as curricula and bursary awards. Officials of the Department, and on occasion Struthers himself, conferred with the joint committee on schemes of study.

Until new institutions could be built, the existing colleges had to be adapted and temporary premises acquired for overflow classes. The new group of non-university students at Dundee, for example, was housed in the Technical Institute. Elsewhere much time was lost travelling between scattered buildings. Staffs of the dual institutions (the old Established Church and the United Free Church Training Colleges) had to be unified and the work redistributed on a specialist basis. Everywhere numbers were swollen by the influx of acting teachers who came in for the course of professional training. In all the centres the sheer physical problems of providing accommodation were enormous. Edinburgh was the first to get a new building, on the site of Moray House, in 1913. The other centres had to manage with makeshift accommodation until the post-war years.

Students taking the concurrent courses – about 50 per cent of Chapter III students in the early years – followed a well-defined professional course including educational theory and practice, English, physical training and a choice of several options: drawing, music and needlework. In the winter session

---

[1] John King, headmaster of the Boroughmuir Higher Grade Public School, in Edinburgh, and Donald Macleod, Rector of Hamilton Academy, in Glasgow.

[2] There were two centres – St Andrews and Dundee – each with a separate Director until 1907. (James Malloch in Dundee and John Edgar, Professor of Education, in St Andrews.)

[3] T M Morrison died 1908, A M Williams became sole Principal (under the Director) and Principal Lecturer in Education.

about a third of their time (on average about 8 or 9 hours a week) was spent at university and two-thirds at the training centre, or in school. During the summer session the whole of their time was devoted to the professional course. There was no question of university work dominating their horizon. The usual day, as one former Glasgow student recalls, was "a sort of jigsaw – art at Church Street School, nature study at Stow College, drill at the University gym, methods at a University classroom, criticism lessons and demonstrations mostly at Napiershall School – plus teaching practice. . . . Apart from the university Union there was no community life, though little groups in the various classes became very friendly."[1]

For the non-university students, as they were officially termed, the training centres provided both general and professional courses. Usually the Director of Studies (or the former Principal) lectured on educational theory, while university lecturers were brought in for psychology, ethics and logic. The new regulations demanded a most comprehensive and systematic study of the various aspects of education, covering the nature of human mind (psychology), the best methods of character building (ethics), generalisation based on scientific knowledge and educational experience (logic and principles), and aims and ideals embodied in the work of great educational writers and reformers (history). Indeed, the emphasis of the training course was on the professional subjects. The church colleges of the past had been compelled to spend a disproportionate amount of time on general education. Now, with the greater opportunities of secondary education, the rôle was reversed.

Use of the public schools transformed teaching practice. The former model schools now reduced their enrolment and became experimental or demonstration schools. (Moray House also got a Kindergarten School.) There was no longer any question of their being models "of all a school ought to be". They were simply places where intelligent attempts were made to demonstrate the value of certain lines of work. Students themselves went out into board schools where they could teach normal

[1] Information from Mr James Allison, formerly serving as headmaster of Sandwood Primary School under the Glasgow authority.

classes under normal conditions. Thus for the first time the schools of the neighbourhood were associated with teacher training, and headmasters and staff received payment for their extra responsibilities. With some 3,000 students in training the whole scale of operations had increased and the centres were sometimes compelled to send as many as 30 students to a single school.[1] The amount of teaching was still small, sometimes only one or two weeks of continuous practice throughout the course. The emphasis remained on method lectures, on demonstrations and on criticism lessons.

LIFE AND WORK IN THE CENTRES

The twentieth-century pattern of training was emerging, the large co-educational, "comprehensive" day centre with its classification of students: "Chapter III", "Chapter III with Article 39" (a qualification for teaching a "supplementary" course), "Chapter V" and "Chapter VI". Already in 1908, Glasgow had 1,200 students, Edinburgh 770, Aberdeen 490 and St Andrews and Dundee 280.[2] The intimate days of the church colleges with their 80 students in a year, all known to each other, were memories of the past. Classes were often large (some of the Glasgow classes were over 200) and there was on average one master or mistress of method to every 150 students.[3] In the larger centres the impersonality of instruction (by lecturers, officially "officers" of the Provincial Committees) was not counterbalanced by the warmth of communal life. The churches were not disposed to add to their existing boarding houses and the committees had no power to provide hostels. The Edinburgh Centre continued to provide 6d dinners, while Glasgow supplied only cold snacks which were eaten in a cheerless and uncomfortable room. Almost half the Glasgow students were in lodgings or boarding houses in the city, paying sums of between 3s and 9s a week and, in the great majority of cases, living two or three in a room.[4] Student lodgings were supervised, but apparently students often became

[1] *Minutes of Edinburgh Provincial Committee*, 1910-11, p 79.
[2] *Report of Committee of Council on Education*, 1908-9, p K65.
[3] *ibid*, p K15.
[4] *Minutes of Glasgow Provincial Committee*, 11 February 1910.

so engrossed in their work that they neglected "even the commonest rules of hygiene as regards dietary and periods of study and rest".

Corporate life flourished more vigorously in Dundee, the smallest centre, where the students were all together in the Technical Institute in Small's Wynd. The Dundee students were drawn from a wide area. Indeed, Dundee had some difficulty in recruiting Scottish students, many of whom preferred to go to one of the larger cities, and for years it took in a number of English and Welsh students. The Director of Studies, James Malloch, knew his students personally. He lectured to them, and supervised a good deal of the teaching practice – indeed the surviving reports on students are written in his hand. The concurrent course worked particularly well in Dundee where, because both university college and training centre were relatively new, there were no prejudices or inhibitions to be lived down. Malloch put great stress on the social side of training centre life. He recollected how little Moray House had done for him as a student,[1] and he and his wife were keen to foster community spirit. It was no coincidence that Dundee was the first centre to acquire a new hostel, Mayfield, which was opened for women students in 1912. As in the small colleges of the past, the students of Dundee had their picnics when "skipping, rounders, mixed football and tig were indulged in", with waltzes and reels in the open at the end of the day.[2]

The demand for specialist teachers was all the time growing with the expansion of post-primary education and, in particular, with the growth of higher grade schools. In the country as a whole, in 1913 one child in every six or seven who left primary school embarked on a course of higher education. As the junior student course declined in popularity and more students went direct to university, numbers in the postgraduate (Chapter V) course for teachers of "higher subjects" increased. By 1913, there were over 200 graduates in training.[3]

In the past the great majority of intending teachers who aspired to university education had enrolled in the concurrent

[1] *Scottish Educational Journal*, 8 April 1922.
[2] *Dundee Training College*, 1906-56, p 13.
[3] *Report of Committee of Council on Education*, 1914-15, p R48.

course because it had offered assistance throughout the three years. It was the new Arts Ordinances of the universities of 1908 and the subsequent introduction of the university summer session – a period previously devoted to intensive professional training – which made the old arrangement impracticable, and which finally, in 1912, compelled the authorities to extend the concurrent course to four years. The distinction now was between the concurrent course, which offered financial assistance during the four-year period, and the degree course, for which the student must win a bursary or find his own means of support, followed by postgraduate training. The relative merits of the two schemes were the subject of controversy. The supporters of concurrent training claimed that the continuity of professional work both developed students' personal qualities and gave point and purpose to academic study; the opponents stressed the danger of divided allegiance and of dissipation of students' energies. In fact the popularity of the concurrent and postgraduate courses varied at the different centres and depended largely on the proximity of the university and training centre. Almost all students in Edinburgh and Dundee took the concurrent course while in Glasgow and Aberdeen the postgraduate students were more numerous.

By the First World War, Scotland had achieved a qualified profession. Of the 20,000 certificated teachers in the country, 75 per cent were trained teachers.[1] The uncertificated assistant belonged to the past. By now the junior student system was yielding fewer recruits and the training centres were drawing their entrants from other sources. The premature segregation of junior students and the additional burdens their course imposed when combined with study for the Leaving Certificate, had made it extremely distasteful. Among the junior student centres, even those schools which owed the origin of their secondary departments to the 1906 Regulations, had come to regard the Leaving Certificate and the Bursary Competition as the sole tests of success. Moreover, the extension of the concurrent course to four years had reduced the need for the preliminary training of teachers. In 1917, the Joint Committee of the Provincial Committees urged the Department to abolish the

[1] *ibid*, p A32.

system so that students could come up to the centres with a uniform qualification, the Leaving Certificate.[1] However, the Department was reluctant to abandon preliminary training which "gives at a comparatively early age a definite focus of paedagogic interest" and "has afforded to some of the best teachers .. an interesting share in the work of preparing others for their profession". As an experiment in 1919, it agreed to admit to the training centres entrants who held the Leaving Certificate, but who were without preliminary training, on condition that, in addition to the normal two-year certificate course, they should devote an extra term to practical teaching.[2]

For the non-university students the academic, as distinct from professional, studies were intended not to give a wider background knowledge but "to enable them (the students) to make analysis and synthesis of each school subject so as to bring out clearly their value and limitations for the mental and moral training of the children".[3] The core of their curriculum consisted of professional subjects including logic and ethics, studies which, traditionally associated with the arts degree, were considered culturally enriching in themselves. Under the early Provincial Committees it had been assumed that the universities would provide specialist instruction in psychology, logic and ethics. However, there were so many unsatisfactory lecture courses given by "young university lecturers, who whatever their academic attainments have no experienced knowledge of the real needs of intending teachers"[4] that very soon the Department discouraged the practice and urged that the work should be done by staff of the centres.

The study of psychology was given special prominence throughout the course. The new Edinburgh centre, for example, was equipped with a laboratory for practical work in psychology. Professor Darroch undertook responsibility for "experimental psychology", and he had himself in 1906 (as acting Director of Studies) secured the appointment by the

[1] Quoted in *Minutes of the Edinburgh Provincial Committee*, 16 June 1917.
[2] *Report of Committee of Council on Education*, 1919-20, p 110, *et seq.*
[3] Expressed at the Joint Committee, *Minutes of Aberdeen Provincial Committee*, 18 February 1913.
[4] Quoted in the Director's Report, *Minutes of the Glasgow Provincial Committee*, April 1910.

Provincial Committee of James Drever as Lecturer in Psychology.[1] When the centres eventually acquired their buildings, special rooms were assigned to individual branches of education, and duly labelled in large letters: "Ethics", "Logic", "Psychology", "Education". While psychology was related to child study, much of the work in ethics and logic remained at an academic level. From time to time, the principal lecturers were brought together by the senior chief inspector and urged to make the subjects relevant to practice. Lecturers were encouraged, for example, not to dwell overlong on the metaphysics or the history of ethics, but to stress the influence of moral tradition. "Not knowledge, not skill, so much as a missionary spirit is what the Training College should seek to communicate; and in no secular subject does this spirit find articulate expression so naturally as in Ethics", commented the inspector of training colleges.[2]

Education as a study had at last been accorded the prestige so often demanded. The emphasis on pedagogy, on the art of teaching studied in relation to philosophy and psychology, had already made Scottish teacher training distinctive. Education, interpreted as a search for ultimate purposes and an understanding of intellectual processes, was a demanding subject. It presupposed, on the part of students, a good general education and an ability to think and, on the part of staff, a genius for relating theory and practice. Under conditions of mass teaching where one or other of these conditions was missing, the systematic treatment of abstract subjects might bear little relation to the practical training. At its best, the study of education encouraged depth and independence of mind; at its worst it impinged neither on thought nor on practice.

ESTABLISHMENT OF DUNFERMLINE COLLEGE OF PHYSICAL
TRAINING AND HYGIENE

Under the Provincial Committees, hygiene and physical training were given new status. Though students previously

[1] The story of the appointment is told by James Drever junior in an obituary of his father. *British Journal of Educational Psychology*, vol XXI, pt I, February 1951.
[2] *Report of Committee of Council on Education*, 1920-21, p H21.

had been required to learn "the laws of health as applied to school premises, scholars and teachers", their study had been confined to textbooks. At the school level "drill masters", still identified with army instructors, had been a class apart from ordinary staff, though in the separate infant departments mistresses had frequently taught a form of musical drill. Instruction on hygiene in schools had been confined to the occasional lectures on the dangers of drunkenness, given under the title of "Physiology in its Relation to Temperance".

It was the revelations of poor physique among the volunteers for the Boer War which first drew attention to the neglect of children's bodies as distinct from their minds. With the appointment in 1902 of a Royal Commission to inquire into the provision for physical training in Scotland, the whole question of physical fitness assumed new significance. The response was seen in the publication of an official syllabus of physical exercises in 1904, in the establishment of medical inspection in 1908, and in the institution of "special schools". Meanwhile, school hygiene courses for intending teachers became much more practical. Students were taught by means of clinical visits to recognise abnormalities such as rickets, ringworm, scabies, adenoids and anaemia. They were also encouraged to take note of signs of incipient infection and of defective sight or hearing in children.[1]

The Swedish system of physical training was now coming into vogue. A new college at Dunfermline, based on the Swedish system, had replaced Colonel (formerly Major) Cruden's college at Aberdeen as the centre of physical training.[2] Struthers himself had taken the lead in transforming a small experimental venture into a national College of Physical Training and Hygiene. The ancient burgh of Dunfermline, Carnegie's birth place, had in 1902 received from the multi-millionaire a trust fund of $2,500,000 (bringing in an annual

[1] *Report of Committee of Council on Education*, 1906-7, p 668. (Inserted in surviving Glasgow board school log books are leaflets sent to parents warning them of the signs, for example, of measles "which cause more deaths than scarlet fever". Leaflet issued by the Glasgow School Board, 1897.)

[2] I am indebted to Mr Ian Thomson of the Scottish School of Physical Education for permitting me to use his typescript account based on the *Minutes of the Carnegie Dunfermline Trust*.

revenue of £25,000) to be used to bring "more of sweetness and light" into the lives of the townsfolk. The trustees decided to build new baths and a gymnasium, and to associate with the latter a qualified instructor of physical training who should teach in the schools. It was Struthers who had pressed the trustees to extend their enterprise. Emboldened by Carnegie's own advice, "Remember you are pioneers and do not be afraid of making mistakes", they had responded in 1905 by admitting men and women students of physical training.

In fact it was as a women's college that the institution flourished. The few men who trained found the drill-sergeant image so powerful a deterrent to their acceptance in the schools that they were compelled to seek jobs in England or abroad. Women came in increasing numbers, however, and found a warmer welcome in schools. In order to secure recognition for the professional training (under Chapter VI of the Regulations), the college associated itself with the Provincial Committee of St Andrews and, from 1909, under the official status of Central Institution, received financial support from the Department. The college prospered as a centre for women's training, but it was not until after the return of ex-servicemen in 1919 that the male side of the institution revived.[1]

In order to give expert help in the schools some of the school boards appointed superintendents of physical training. The Provincial Committees meanwhile established classes for serving teachers in various centres. Gradually the old military drill disappeared and a number of larger schools began to boast Swedish apparatus – beams and wall bars – and to lay much more emphasis on games. The new trends, however, conflicted with the austere traditions of the past: when one inspector inquired of an infant mistress what games the children played, he was told that "they played no games there; and the tone of voice in which the reply was made and the expression which accompanied it could not have been more rebuking if I had asked her if she taught her children to pick pockets".[2]

The three smaller teacher training institutions functioned

---

[1] With one-year courses for students who already possessed the general certificate.
[2] *Report of the Committee of Council on Education*, 1907-8, p 393.

separately from the large centres. Indeed, the Edinburgh
Episcopal College only survived with difficulty, since the
requirement of the Junior Student Certificate as an entrance
qualification excluded English applicants. A temporary
concession by the Department enabled the college to continue,
but so numerous were the English recruits (in 1911, for example,
16 of the 27 new entrants were from England) and so precarious
was the financial position of the college, that it was on the brink
of closure when the wartime demand for women teachers
transformed the situation.[1]

The fortunes of the Glasgow Roman Catholic College were
very different. Already by 1910, it had 200 students, drawn
very largely from the West of Scotland, but including also a
number of Irish girls. The college kept abreast of all the newest
developments. Extensions to the existing buildings gave the
students a drill hall (the college actually appointed a physical
instructress before the large Glasgow centre[2]), an art room and
a science laboratory, destined to become famous under the
direction of Sister Monica.[3] The inspectors had high praise for
the quality of instruction and the proficiency of the practical
work. They noted the pastoral care of the students whose
"quiet refined tone used in teaching" they attributed to the
personal example of the Sisters.[4]

St George's College in Edinburgh had been recognised for
training teachers for the Chapter V qualification. The students
attended university lectures, and after 1913 some of them
entered the new diploma course conducted by Professor
Darroch. The old diploma course, which had disappeared with
the new Regulations, had combined theory and practice. The
new diploma course, open to graduates or graduands taking the
four-year concurrent course, was combined with practical
training taken at Moray House or St George's. Relations
between the university department and Moray House were

[1] Confidential Report "The Episcopal Training College", file 218(2),
SED. (By 1919, it had 75 students, the largest number in its history.
Report of Committee of Council on Education, 1919-20, p 31.)
[2] *Report of Committee of Council on Education*, 1908-9, p K21.
[3] A sister of Professor Sir Hugh S Taylor, FRS, Sister Monica, a
biologist, was lecturer at the college, 1901-46. Awarded Hon Degree of
LLD by University of Glasgow, 1953.
[4] *Report of Committee of Council on Education*, 1913-14, p R17.

very close. As in Dundee, the proximity of the two institutions made the concurrent course popular. In the words of the Principal, Alexander Morgan, the college was "practically an extra-mural school of the university".[1]

Indeed its facilities were far superior to those at the University. Professor Darroch himself had been largely responsible for the incorporation in the new building of a psychological laboratory, which he used for child study and experimental methods with diploma students, and later with students proceeding beyond the diploma to a new degree, that of Bachelor of Education. Instituted in 1917, the Edinburgh BEd degree ranked as an honours degree in Education and Psychology, as did the EdB of Glasgow and Aberdeen, which were intended similarly for students who had taken university diploma courses.[2] Over the years these degrees were to attract students, including experienced teachers, who were interested in special fields: in child guidance, administration and educational psychology.

GENERAL ASSESSMENT OF REFORMS

Under the Provincial Committees, the organisation of teacher training had become representative of public interest. Within a general framework and subject to the supervision of the Department, centres had freedom to devise their own syllabuses of study and to assess their own students. Working under immense physical difficulties – Edinburgh alone had a new building before 1919 – they were sending 1,300 qualified teachers into the schools each year. Not only had the entire scale of teacher training been transformed, the centres were also providing throughout their areas numerous in-service courses (as they were subsequently to be called) to equip teachers for the different grades of post-primary work and for the great variety of "supplementary" subjects. The summer school courses at St Andrews catering particularly for secondary school teachers

---

[1] *Makers of Scottish Education*, Longmans, 1929, p 213.
[2] The study of education and psychology was the basis of courses which covered at least two postgraduate years. (In Edinburgh the diploma was followed by one year of full-time study: in Glasgow and Aberdeen by two years part-time study.) St Andrews had a diploma course from 1928, but no degree course until after the Second World War.

were exceptionally popular and attracted a wide clientèle. Lecturers included some of the most eminent educationists of the day such as John Adams, Cyril Burt and Percy Nunn. Indeed, the venture was Britain's nearest approach to the North American summer school.

Altogether, teacher training had received a great impulse. The problem of the uncertificated teacher had been tackled efficiently and apparently for all time. The immediate post-war years had seen the last of the uncertificated teachers from the Highlands and Islands – some of them middle-aged and even elderly – completing their college courses alongside the youngsters. By 1920, unqualified teachers formed only 1 per cent of Scotland's teaching force. Simultaneously, career prospects in secondary education (combined with pension rights)[1] were attracting well-qualified graduates into the profession. Already by 1915, the proportion of graduates entering teacher training had reached a sixth of the total. By contrast Chapter VI courses except in domestic economy and in educational handwork (which was organised entirely within the centres) attracted relatively few students.

Standards had risen all round. All students were better educated than their predecessors, the ex-pupil teachers. The great majority of men and a considerable number of women attended the university. Indeed in no country in Europe had primary school teachers such opportunities of higher education as they had in Scotland. Inspectors referred to recent recruits as being "less under the dominion of routine and tradition than their predecessors". They had a "broader outlook" and "wider culture".[2] Above all, they were open-minded and willing to learn, and did not regard themselves as "finished products". Alas, their spirit of adventure was all too often suppressed by the narrow outlook of the older teachers, and by physical conditions in large urban schools; their humanity shrivelled up and their enthusiasm waned. As one of the inspectors wrote of the young teacher, "Spending his days in the foul air of a dingy schoolroom in the middle of a foggy,

---

[1] Extended to secondary school teachers under the 1908 (*Scotland*) Education Act.
[2] *Report of Committee of Council on Education*, 1912-13, pp C18-19.

smoke-begrimed town with sixty boys and girls to know and teach individually – if he can – his efforts to improve too often suffocated by an unsympathetic headmaster, or left to die out from mere lack of encouragement, it is not to be wondered at that he sometimes loses the elasticity and the keenness which makes it possible to take a long view".[1] Despite the new developments in experimental psychology and child study, the persistence of traditional attitudes hindered the advance of new methods in schools.

A system of teacher training had been devised which was rational and efficient. All students with the necessary qualifications were given entry, all categories of students were trained under the same regulations and within the one centre. It was a system in which the sections of teachers in training corresponded to the classification of schools, and in which uniformity of standards was achieved by central control. As "comprehensive" institutions, the training centres avoided some of the strains and tensions associated with a more obviously hierarchical system, though as day colleges their contribution to personal development was necessarily restricted. In the past, neither the highest ranks of the profession (in higher class schools) nor the lowest (the ex-pupil teachers) had been trained. The old system had been partial and inadequate. The new one was all-embracing.

[1] *Report of Committee of Council on Education*, 1913-14, p B16.

Chapter 6

THE INTER-WAR PERIOD

The demand for education is always cumulative – education breeds the desire for more. During the war years, however, there was unprecedented enthusiasm for education. War wages brought higher standards of living and encouraged educational aspirations among wider sections of the community. Between 1914 and 1919, attendance at intermediate (formerly higher grade) and secondary schools increased by 25 per cent to 59,000.

This wartime enthusiasm found expression in the 1918 (Scotland) Act with its provision for additional types of schools (Nursery and Day Continuation Schools) and for the raising of the school leaving age to 15 "after a day appointed". Administratively it replaced almost 1,000 school boards by 38 county and burgh authorities, *ad hoc* educational bodies charged with the responsibility of providing places in intermediate or secondary schools for all pupils who showed "promise of profiting".[1]

Foremost among the problems of educational reconstruction was the need to provide sufficient teachers, for it was estimated that altogether an additional 6,000 to 7,000 would be required in order to cater for the new age ranges and to keep pace with growing demands.[2] Accordingly, in 1919, there was established a national salary scale differentiating between the various qualifications and discriminating in favour of teachers with graduate qualifications.[3] It was, however, a national minimum scale and many authorities paid more than the minimum. In 1920, overall responsibility for teacher training was given to a

[1] Section 6(1) (*a*).
[2] *Education (Scotland) Reports*, etc., 1919-20, p H4.
[3] See Appendix D, I, p 235.

new authority, the National Committee for the Training of Teachers.

Established to co-ordinate the work of the Provincial Committees, the National Committee consisted of representatives of all the education authorities which, under the 1918 Act, were required to contribute towards the expenses of teacher training in proportion to the number of qualified teachers in their service.[1] Simultaneously, local authorities, rather than the Provincial Committees, became responsible for maintenance allowances to students in training. The new system recognised the strong financial interests which the education authorities now had in teacher training. From their very foundation, the Provincial Committees had felt the need of regular consultation. The new National Committee was much more than a consultative body. While some of the duties assumed were taken over from the provinces, others were delegated by the central department. In fact the establishment of the National Committee represented a measure of decentralisation in the control of teacher training.

The real work of the National Committee, a large unwieldy body which met only once a year, devolved on a small active Central Executive Committee under the same chairman as the National Committee and including also the chairmen of the Provincial Committees as well as representatives of the teaching profession and the Church.[2] There was thus a three-tier administrative arrangement: Provincial Committees were in charge of the management of training centres and were also authorised to conduct classes for practising teachers; the National Committee (acting through the Central Executive Committee) had general responsibility for teacher training including the control of finance, buildings and staffing, student numbers and types of courses; and the Department had the

[1] Education (Scotland) Act, 1918, Section 9(3).
[2] The National Committee had forty-five members, representatives of the education authorities. The Central Executive Committee consisted of: the chairman of the National Committee, the chairmen of the Provincial Committees and (later) the chairmen of the Committees of Management, ten members elected from the National Committee, two members appointed from teachers' representatives on Provincial Committees and one representative of the Education Committee of the Church of Scotland on a Provincial Committee. The Secretary of State was represented by Assessors at all meetings of all committees.

L

final decision on policy and the ultimate control of expenditure. It was a simple structure in which the local authorities had majority representation and other interests – the Church, teaching profession, universities, central institutions – only a minor voice.[1]

Appropriate arrangements were made for the transfer of the remaining denominational colleges to the National Committee. (Denominational schools had already, under the 1918 Act, been transferred to the local authorities.) The denominations undertook to be responsible for the buildings, including extensions, repairs and rates, while expenses connected with the actual training of students were to be met by the National Committee. A Committee of Management, composed of equal numbers of representatives of the particular denomination on the one hand, and of the National and Provincial Committee on the other, was to be responsible for the affairs of each college.[2] The older denominational institutions, the Edinburgh Episcopal College at Dalry House and the Roman Catholic College at Downhill, Glasgow, were transferred in 1920. A newly established Roman Catholic College, Craiglockhart, conducted by the Society of the Sacred Heart, was transferred in 1922.

Originally known as St Margaret's, the college had opened in 1918 in Moray Place, Edinburgh, to cater for Catholic girls from the East of Scotland, and in 1920 it had moved to larger residential premises (including a demonstration boarding school) on the outskirts of the city at Craiglockhart. Always a smaller college than Dowanhill, since it drew on a sparser Catholic population, it similarly emphasised corporate religious life. The association with St Margaret was perpetuated in the college coat of arms – the buckle – and the motto, given by Queen Margaret to the Leslie family, "Grip fast".[3] Under the terms of transfer, the Principal of each of the denominational

[1] Ministers of religion were frequently members of the Provincial Committees as representatives of education authorities, eg, in 1931-2, one-third of the Aberdeen Provincial Committee were ministers.

[2] There were to be five denominational representatives, three from the Provincial Committee and two elected by the National Committee.

[3] The story is told in each edition of the college magazine, *The Buckle*. Queen Margaret, riding behind Bartholomew Leslie across a swollen river, was urged to "Grip fast". "Gin the buckle bide", she replied. The buckle did bide and King Malcolm in reward gave to Bartholomew and his heirs a coat of arms representing three buckles and the motto "Grip fast".

colleges was to be a member of the particular denomination (at Dowanhill also a member of the Congregation of Notre Dame, and at Craiglockhart of the Society of the Sacred Heart).

In 1921, both St George's Training Department and Dunfermline College were also transferred to the National Committee. St George's had over 40 students, many of them training for the Froebel, or the Chapter V, qualification. Dunfermline had only 56 students, all of them women, though in the immediate post-war years it had organised one-year courses for men. The increasing demand by the schools for qualified men and women clearly indicated an extension in the scope of its work. In 1922, a significant change in the Regulations opened new prospects for teachers of physical training.[1] By taking an additional year's course, they could also qualify for the Teacher's General Certificate, and provide themselves with alternative employment in middle life.

The entire system of teacher training was now under common administration. The key administrative post was that of Executive Officer to the Central Executive Committee, held until 1926 by James Malloch, the former Director of Studies at Dundee. He and Professor Darroch, chairman of the Committee (by virtue of his position on the Edinburgh Education Committee) until his sudden death in 1924, were largely responsible for shaping policy in the early years. In effect, the Provincial Committees and Committees of Management had given up many of their independent powers to the new central committee. The staffs of the centres, for example, were now regarded as a single unit, and questions of transfer and promotion of lecturers were decided by a single body. Similarly, the initiation of new courses and the collation of syllabuses of instruction and of prospectuses, were undertaken by the Central Executive Committee. The new body decided at once to establish a course for teachers of the blind (at Moray House) and made arrangements to send to Manchester University students training to teach the deaf.[2] It agreed to combine

---

[1] *Regulations* 1922. Article 15 (*d*).

[2] In fact, the earliest provision for handicapped children in Britain had been made in Scotland. The first school for the deaf was founded in 1760 and the first school for the blind, 1793. Both were private ventures in Edinburgh.

with the Glasgow Education Committee in providing courses for teachers of mentally defective children.[1]

NEW PREMISES AND NEW IDEAS

The advent of the new administration coincided with a complete transformation of the material conditions of training, the fruition of previous plans.   The new buildings at Aberdeen and Dundee, the former on the site of the old United Free Church Training College in St Andrew Street, and the latter in close proximity to the University College, both commandeered during the war, were now available.   In Glasgow, the Provincial Committee had long debated the relative merits of various sites.   Eventually in 1913, with great foresight as it proved, it had purchased 60 acres at Jordanhill, in order to build a college for 1,200 students, a demonstration school and a hostel.   With operations suspended during wartime the college was not finally completed until 1922, when inflationary prices had brought the total costs up to £300,000.[2]   The centres were now fully equipped, with the exception of Moray House which did not get its main demonstration school until 1931. Each had a library, a gymnasium and changing rooms, a dining and assembly hall, subject rooms and even separate "'crit" rooms.   Altogether, the centres and colleges were able to cater for over 3,000 students.[3]

As one former member of the Aberdeen staff recalls, "The immediate post-war years were full of interest.   We had staff conferences in which we discussed with avidity the new ideas that were floating around – new ways of teaching Art from Vienna, the implications of Freud on education, Soviet developments – throwing out often ideas that I hear the young members of staff bringing up today (1967) as desirable and imminent.   The men returned from the war, brought a dynamic liveliness (and

[1] The course (held twice annually) was begun at Jordanhill in 1923, with Mr D Kennedy-Fraser in charge.
[2] Students were in fact using the building during the 1921-2 session.   It was not officially opened till November 1922, by the Chairman of the Provincial Committee, the Rt Rev Dr John Smith, Moderator of the General Assembly of the Church of Scotland.
[3] Moray House had been built for 700 students, Aberdeen for 450 and Dundee for 300.

a few problems) into our midst . . ."[1] There was great emphasis
on psychology and on the application of scientific methods to
educational problems. Indeed, psychology, including experimental psychology, seemed to have displaced philosophy as the
core of the professional curriculum.[2] Dr Rusk's *Introduction
to Experimental Education*,[3] one of the earliest books in the
field, was based on his lectures at Dundee. Dr Rusk recalls
the well-equipped laboratory in Dundee in which he used to
illustrate aspects of child development and the learning process.
He taught by class experiment and demonstration. On mental
testing, for example, he included Binet tests, which were put
on lantern slides. He also sent to the USA for sets of puzzles
relevant to various aspects of learning. "The criticism of a
head of one of the St Andrews colleges was that surely a pencil
and notebook were all that was needed for lecturing on psychology!"[4]

It was the age of the New Education Fellowship, an inter-
national movement[5] whose British members in 1920 had
launched the publication, *The New Era*. William Boyd,
lecturer in charge of education at Glasgow University and
until 1923 part-time lecturer at Jordanhill, was one of the
leading members. A great visionary, Boyd was dedicated to
the child-centred approach to education and sought by means
of public lectures on such reformers as Montessori and Decroly
to publicise different aspects of New Education.

Boyd founded in 1926 the first child guidance clinic in
Britain, though he himself preferred the term centre, which

[1] Letter from Dr Nan Shepherd (lecturer in Aberdeen 1915-56) to the
writer.
[2] There was some concern lest, with the popularity of Freud, students
should develop a morbidity. *Memorandum on Lecturers' Conference* (typescript) 1928, p 2.
[3] Published 1912, one year before E L Thorndike's *Educational Psychology* (*The Journal of Experimental Pedagogy*, predecessor of the *British Journal
of Educational Psychology*, was founded in 1910).
[4] From a letter to the writer.
[5] *The Story of the New Education*, William Boyd and Wyatt Rawson,
Heinemann, 1965, p 79. Summer schools were held at St Andrews under
the direction of Professor William McClelland and Neil Snodgrass. (One
of the founder members described the ideals of the movement, "We hoped
for a new and better youth, able to find the right balance between continuity
and freedom, patriotism and internationalism, faith and criticism". *Professional Education as a Humane Study*, Robert Ulich, Macmillan, New York,
1956, p 121.)

had no association with medicine or ill-health. Here generations of students were able to study children, and some of the
former EdB students undertook specific training for work in
clinics.[1] Boyd in Glasgow – like Drever in Edinburgh – pion-
eered many of the techniques in the diagnosis and treatment
of children who were maladjusted to life or learning. Two
teacher-training institutions – the Dundee Centre and Notre
Dame College – were also directly associated with clinics. The
foundation of the Notre Dame clinic in 1931 was due largely
to the inspiration of Dr Rusk[2] (then at Jordanhill). Under the
direction of Sister Marie Hilda, who had studied Dr Rusk's
methods in experimental psychology, the clinic became widely
renowned.

After the long years of dispersal, the 'twenties brought
opportunities of social and cultural life. New hostels for
women students brought the number of women in residence up
to a quarter of the total. Designed specially for the purpose,
they were very different from the Victorian boarding houses
and incorporated such luxuries as study bedrooms and service
lifts.[3] Within the centres themselves mid-day lunches were
provided at a charge of a shilling a day. Student-elected bodies,
which had achieved only precarious status in the past, were
now officially recognised under the title of Student Representative Councils. Student magazines, dramatic clubs and choral
societies were indicative of a healthier community feeling. In
Aberdeen, the men founded a modern drama club, and had the
distinction of being mentioned in *The Observer* for their production of Synge's "Playboy of the Western World" with
Scottish accents! There was also, in the early post-war years
in Aberdeen, an Open Air Club which explored the surrounding
countryside on foot.

Compulsory games came in during the 'twenties. Dundee
already had pitches at Mayfield before the war, but the other

[1] By 1935, the clinic was dealing with 150 children a year at a cost of £10.
"Preaching and Practice", William Boyd, *New Era in Home and School*,
vol 16, no 7, July-August 1935, p 192.
[2] Tribute is paid to Dr Rusk's inspiration in *Golden Jubilee, 1895-1945*,
Notre Dame Training College, p 12.
[3] Service lifts were incorporated in the two Aberdeen hostels at Hilton
and Clifton, completed 1927. Minutes, 14 May 1927, *Report of Central
Executive Committee*, 1926-7. (The hostels cost £50,000.)

centres could make little provision until they moved to more spacious sites or acquired land adjoining new hostels. There-after, physical education took on a wider aspect. Emancipated womanhood had no qualms about wearing gymslips and instead of being confined to the old "exercises of the Swedish system, games for gymnasia and playground", students now had Scottish and English country dancing, Scandinavian folk dancing, and a variety of indoor and outdoor games.[1]

Even the early 'twenties, however, brought the chill winds of economic recession. In fact the new types of schools, nursery schools and day continuation schools, never materialised, and the date for the raising of the school leaving age was postponed indefinitely. The National Committee found itself with student places to spare and seriously considered closing the Dundee Centre in order to curtail expenses. Built for 300, the college had in 1920-1 only 119 students and the cost per head was more than twice the average elsewhere.[2] There was a proposal to transfer women students from Dunfermline to Dundee, and another to withdraw the small numbers of honours graduates (which were expensive to cater for) to one of the larger centres.

Indeed the training of Chapter V students was felt to be one of the least satisfactory aspects of the entire teacher-training system. There was complete lack of uniformity among the centres. In some Provinces, staff took complete charge; elsewhere the work was shared with specialist staff in the schools. The difficulties of Dundee were resolved by general reorganisation which made possible the reduction of staff. By agreement with the university college it was arranged that non-university students should take their academic subjects in the arts or science classes of the university. Simultaneously, by co-operation with the education authority, members of the professional staff were to be employed part-time in local schools.[3] In 1925 – again as a means of saving money – the Directorship of the Training Centre was combined with the Bell Chair of Education in St Andrews in the person of William

[1] *Handbook for Students*, Aberdeen Training Centre, 1928, p 62.
[2] The present Position and Prospects of St Andrews and Dundee Training Centre, 1924. *Report of Central Executive Committee*, 1923-4, p 58 *et seq.* (The cost per student at Dundee was £154 a year.)
[3] *Report of Central Executive Committee*, 1924-5, p 11.

McClelland, who had been successively Director of Education in Wigtownshire and Lecturer in Education in the Universities of Aberdeen and Edinburgh. A similar arrangement was made in Edinburgh with the appointment – also in 1925 – of Godfrey Thomson, Professor of Education at the University of Newcastle, to the combined post of Professor of the University and Director of Studies at Moray House.

Already, threat of unemployment had begun to dominate student horizons. The "Geddes axe" economies in school staffing had curtailed the demand for teachers, while the general depression and housing shortage had effectively reduced the "wastage rate" among women members of the profession. The combined effect of the 1914-18 death toll and of the pro- longed post-war slump was to make teaching almost synony- mous with celibacy so far as women were concerned. England, which had customarily welcomed Scottish teachers, could not absorb its own products and the National Committee urged outgoing students to apply overseas.[1] During bleak years when the Committee found itself obliged to cut back expendi- ture and increase fees, it was embarrassed by a flood of recruits who turned to teaching as a safe pensionable job. Graduate salary scales were especially attractive, and by 1926, two-thirds of the annual output of graduates in arts and science of the Scottish universities were training to teach.[2]

THE 1924 REGULATIONS

Changes in school organisation had already brought reper- cussions in teacher training. In 1923, post-primary education had been entirely remodelled.[3] Higher grade schools and sup- plementary courses had both disappeared, the former being absorbed in the secondary schools system, the latter being replaced by new "advanced divisions" in elementary schools. Instead, on the basis of a qualifying examination (now conducted by education authorities), children went either to a secondary school and pursued a five-year academic course for the Leaving

[1] *Report of Central Executive Committee*, 1922-3, p 10.
[2] *Education (Scotland) Reports etc*, 1926-7, p C13.
[3] Changes outlined in Circular 44, and brought into effect by the 1923 *Day School Code and Regulations for Secondary Schools*.

Certificate examination or to an advanced division of an elementary school where they took the day school certificate. The old supplementary courses had encouraged practical instruction, but their success had been limited especially in rural schools, which had not been able to offer a range of subjects. Under the new scheme local authorities were encouraged to develop central schools offering a variety of advanced division courses taught by specialist teachers. Implicit in the thinking was the idea of a "clear cut" at the age of 12, so that all chilren would get at least two years of post-primary education. The advanced division in Scotland was, like the central school in England, the *Mittelschule* in Germany and the *école primaire supérieure* in France, an attempt to evolve variety in the educational provision for the adolescent age group.

In 1924, there were significant amendments to the Regulations for the Training of Teachers. In the first place, the junior student system, devised in the first decade of the century as a special passport into teacher training, was abolished. Perhaps the surprising thing was that the system had persisted so long, for the "wastage" rates had always been high (indeed in the latter years only 60 per cent of the original entrants had completed the course). Secondly, the new Regulations differentiated between women and men; while the Leaving Certificate became the minimum entrance qualification for women, men were no longer permitted to come direct from school. Either they must be graduates taking a course (of one year and a term) under Chapter III (the Teacher's General Certificate) or under Chapter V (now renamed the Teacher's Special Certificate), or they must be holders of a diploma of a central institution training under Chapter VI (the Teacher's Technical Certificate).

The junior student curriculum at last disappeared. In some respects, however, preliminary training was more strongly entrenched than before, since it was now compulsory for all girls seeking admission to the two-year training college course.[1]

[1] Article 13 (*a*), *Statutory Rules and Orders*, 1924. In the past, Article 15 had provided a loophole. Circular 62, 7 February 1924, defined the Leaving Certificate course which was to include English and another language, mathematics and science. Successful candidates had to pass two subjects: English and either mathematics or science or a language at higher level, and two other subjects: either mathematics or science or a language at a lower level.

Therefore, though they did not have to decide to teach at the premature age of 15, many girls preferred to combine their preliminary training with the Leaving Certificate course rather than, as was now permitted, defer it to a final year at school after completing the Leaving Certificate.

The official requirement of graduation for men was scarcely more than a recognition of accomplished fact.   Indeed, spokesmen of the powerful teachers' union, the Educational Institute of Scotland, which had been pressing for graduation for all teachers, were bitterly disappointed at what they considered half measures.   They urged the Department to break down the segregation, which had for so long cut off teachers in training from those preparing for other professions, by the establishment of degree courses within Faculties of Education of the universities.[1]   The very term "non-graduate", used of teachers in a country which had long venerated a university qualification, automatically gave two-year trained women a low status.   Indeed, graduation for all became a recurrent theme at annual congresses and one, which with the growing unemployment rate among teachers, seemed within prospect of realisation. With the increase in the number of girls now going direct to university from school the training centres were becoming predominantly postgraduate institutions.   Indeed, throughout the 'twenties, the number of students entering arts faculties increased steadily.   In 1900, there had been less than 1,000; by 1927, there were 1,800, of whom the great majority looked to teaching.

The revised Regulations were related to the new organisation of schools.   After 1923, only first- and second-class honours degrees were recognised for training under Chapter V of the Regulations.   Even so the majority of well-qualified graduates preferred to work for both the General and the Special Certificate (Chapters III and V).[2]   With the scarcity of secondary school posts the General Certificate was for many students a form of insurance; for others, who chose to teach in areas like Glasgow where the authority insisted on all newly-qualified teachers going into primary schools, it was a necessity.   Ordin-

---

[1] "Plea for a Professional Degree", *The Scotsman*, 9 December 1927.
[2] 70 per cent in 1925-6.   *Education (Scotland) Reports etc*, 1925-6, p A30.

ary graduates trained, as did non-graduate women, for the General Certificate, but they could in addition obtain recognition (under Article 39) to teach subjects to advanced divisions in post-primary schools or, under certain circumstances, to classes in secondary schools. Students with qualifications in art, domestic science, music, educational handwork, physical education, agricultural or commercial subjects trained under Chapter VI of the Regulations for a Teacher's Technical Certificate covering all types of post-primary work. In fact, apart from housecraft, there were few practical courses in the advanced division centres and most children found the academic fare so unappetising and indigestible that they did not stay on to take the Day School Certificate.

UNEMPLOYMENT AND THE DEMAND FOR A GRADUATE PROFESSION

By 1931, unemployment among teachers had become so acute that the National Committee decided to limit entrants to teacher training. Even the decrease in the maximum size of class from 60 to 50 in 1928 had done little to alleviate the situation and, within two years, classes in excess of the new maximum had been eliminated.[1] Already, in 1929, the Episcopal College had finally closed as a result of the ban on students from outside Scotland, although Dalry House continued to be used as a hostel for Episcopal students at the Edinburgh Centre until 1934. The demand for Roman Catholic teachers was such, however, that neither Notre Dame nor Craiglockhart was affected by the emergency restrictions.

Arrangements were made to admit to the centres in October 1932 only 1,000 students training under Chapters III and V of the Regulations (800 graduates and 200 non-graduates) and, on the evidence of the work of the first term, to "axe" 10 per cent of them by Christmas.[2] By a rigorous selection procedure therefore 140 graduates were refused entry to courses at the beginning of the new session. However, since there were only 168 non-graduate applicants for the 200 places, it was decided

---

[1] *Education (Scotland) Reports etc*, 1932-3, p A11.
[2] *Report of Central Executive Committee*, 1931-2, p 5.

not to reduce total numbers at the end of the first term. Instead, the National Committee took steps to discourage even pupils at the school level from thinking of teaching as a career. They were concerned that intending aspirants for the profession should be stopped before they embarked on a university course.[1] Even the necessity of limiting the flow of honours as well as ordinary graduates had become a practical issue.

The combination of the high unemployment rate and of the 10 per cent salary cut (introduced in 1931 and not fully restored until 1935) had the desired effect of restraining candidates. By the middle 'thirties the graduate boom was over. Even in 1935 there were only 718 graduates for the 800 places offered and two years later there were only 565.[2] Simultaneously, the concurrent courses had practically disappeared. Looking back, older members of the profession have regretted that the opportunity of realising the ideal of a graduate profession was lost in the 'thirties. Deterred by the bleak prospects in schools, graduates sought employment elsewhere. The drift away from teaching in the lean years has never been reversed.

Survival of the non-graduate courses has been attributed to those education authorities which, whether for educational or economic reasons, preferred to appoint two-year trained women, rather than graduates, to posts in primary schools. It was not only local administrators, however, who felt that the possession of a degree was not essential for all teachers. Inspectors stressed the need of a diversity of routes into the profession: teachers of art and housecraft, for example, did not take a university course; nor was intensive academic study necessarily the most suitable preparation for teachers of young children.[3] The same conclusion was reached by the Advisory Council on Education (established under the Education (Scotland) Act, 1918),[4] which, after investigation, reported in 1935 in favour of a four-year course of training for women teachers of primary children with emphasis on practical work in schools rather than a university degree course. The training authorities

[1] *Report of Central Executive Committee, 1932-3*, p 8.
[2] *Report of Central Executive Committee, 1937-8*, Appendix, p 6.
[3] *Education (Scotland) Reports etc, 1926-7*, D4; 1928-9, p D6-7.
[4] *Report of Advisory Council to Scottish Education Department as to the Training of the Woman Primary School Teacher*, 1935.

themselves were divided on the issue. Glasgow, the largest and most powerful of the Provincial Committees, came out strongly in favour of a graduate profession. The National Committee, however, decided to support the recommendations of the Advisory Council.[1]

ASPECTS OF LIFE AND WORK

After 1931, many non-graduate women students took advantage of new regulations, which permitted them to enter training centre (or college) with Leaving Certificate qualifications at the age of 17 and take a three-year course.[2] Others who had taken their preliminary training at school entered at the age of 18 on a two-year course. Postgraduate students, by the same regulations, took a three- or four-term course, depending on whether they had undergone a course of preliminary training at school. Perhaps the survival of preliminary training seems the strangest feature of the 1931 Regulations. It can be explained only on economic grounds, for it was cheaper to keep students at the local centres for an extra year than to make universal provision for three-year courses at the provincial centres. Nevertheless, long before its final demise in 1949, the preliminary training year had become an anomalous feature in the general pattern of teacher training in which there were now two main categories: the three-year course for non-graduate women (by contrast the three-year course in England dates only from 1960) and the four-term course for graduates and diploma holders.

Many of the recruits who had come straight from school had been overtaught. They came in limp from the intensive study for the Leaving Certificate and starved of broader culture. In the smaller centres and in the colleges, staff were able to establish personal relations with the students. On the basis of a

---

[1] *Report of Central Executive Committee*, 1935-6, p 8.
[2] *Statutory Rules and Orders*, 1931, Article 25 (*a*). Women who took a one-year preliminary training at school (which, according to Article 3, had now to be after the Leaving Certificate examination) entered on the second year of the three-year course. Non-graduate women might (and, for example, in Edinburgh frequently did) attend university classes. By Article 15 (*a*) concurrent training was extended to men, who could not, however, receive a Teacher's Certificate until they had obtained a degree or diploma.

house system at Craiglockhart, for example, there were a variety of activities and excursions. At Dundee, the Director of Studies, Professor McClelland, put great emphasis on the students' social experience and on their contacts with the outside world. He regretted the loss of the English and Welsh recruits who had brought their own distinctive contributions to college life.[1] During the early 1930s he encouraged students to participate in relief schemes in the city, then a depressed area, by working with children and youth. He believed that first-hand acquaintance with living conditions would give them a deeper understanding of children's problems and difficulties and would enrich their teaching. Students, he felt, were too often treated as children instead of being encouraged to express their own views and being given responsibilities which would enable them to mature.[2] Of Professor McClelland's many qualities, his students remembered and appreciated most his personal interest, his concern for their welfare and his practical assistance in helping them to secure jobs in the dark days of the 'thirties.[3]

The fostering of a community spirit was a much more difficult task in the larger centres where Directors of Studies were heavily burdened with administration. At the time of restriction on entrants, George Burnett at Jordanhill personally interviewed 729 graduate applicants for admission.[4] The separation of theory (and indeed of the branches of theory) from practice ("Method") encouraged specialised research, but it deprived students of that close personal contact with staff which was possible in smaller colleges and which was the most distinctive feature of the English system of teacher training. The danger was of anonymity, of students by day moving from room to room in a barrack-like building and returning home at night to cram lecture notes. Indeed many graduate students had experienced little better at university. One teacher recollecting his student days at Glasgow University in the 1930s has said that

[1] Result of the restriction on "outwith" entrants. Report of Director of Studies, *Minutes of St Andrews Provincial Committee*, October 1928, p 149.
[2] "Social Aspects of the Teacher's Preparation", William McClelland, *New Era in Home and School*, April 1936, p 13.
[3] *Dundee Training College*, 1906-56, p 23. Also information from former students.
[4] *The New Dominie*, Memorial Number, 1940, p 4.

he and his contemporaries attended classes by day "and went back to Renfrewshire or Ayrshire in the evening. As for partaking of the whole body of university life, they hardly tasted it."[1] There were students who had never had a personal conversation with a member of the university staff during their whole course.[2]

For prospective teachers, the training centre atmosphere at its worst was hardly conducive to the growth of desirable personal qualities. Rather the system put a premium on mass production, on turning out teachers who had dutifully memorised lecture notes, but who had no time or opportunity to explore the byways of learning or cultivate qualities of independent thought. Students heard a great deal about "free activity", but freedom remained "a doctrine commended to them rather than a way of life practised".[3]

The Department's Regulations, amended in 1924 and again in 1931, laid down requirements of professional training. General Certificate students had to take: physical training, the principles of teaching including psychology, ethics and logic "in their direct bearing upon the work of the teacher", school management (covering discipline, organisation and general method), methods of teaching primary school subjects and practical teaching. Responsibility for approval of syllabuses still rested with HMIs who inspected the students' work and from time to time attended lectures. The award of the probationary certificate depended not only on examinations but on a detailed record kept throughout the course of each student's "ability and promise of success as a teacher during training".

In practice there was much more in the way of consultation with HMIs than inspection. Lecturers in the various aspects of education met the Senior Chief Inspector to discuss the content of the course. Over the years much of the old formal logic was pruned or linked with psychology, while ethics was largely merged into educational theory.[4] For a period of ten

---

[1] *Higher Education, Evidence*, Part I, vol F, Cmnd 2154-XI, 1060.
[2] *Higher Education, Evidence*, Part I, vol C, Cmnd 2154-VIII, 996.
[3] "Growing Points in Scottish Education", William Boyd, *New Era in Home and School*, July-August 1935, p 177.
[4] See Appendix G, I, pp 251-4, Aberdeen Syllabuses.

years, 1924 to 1934, there was an interesting experiment of conjoint examination papers in education and psychology for all training centres and colleges. A composite paper in each subject was devised, from questions previously submitted, at a meeting of all the principal lecturers under the chairmanship of the Senior Chief Inspector. Each institution then printed the paper, conducted the examination and marked the scripts which were subsequently submitted to the inspectors as external moderators. Apparently the procedure had been adopted in response to the demand for the reintroduction of a uniform external examination from older teachers, who feared a lowering of standards. However, publication of the papers in education and psychology was sufficient to quell all murmurings from the profession. Indeed, the papers themselves, though they naturally reflect current topics of the day, stand the test of time remarkably well.[1] The system of common papers was abandoned with the appointment of a new Senior Chief Inspector, who "with a natural humility assumed he was not competent to chair meetings of specialists on subjects of which he had no expert acquaintance".[2] Accordingly the training institutions reverted to the previous practice of setting internal papers.

In the demonstration schools, students were able to observe the new approaches to teaching – the play way, the Dalton plan, Montessori methods and project work. (At Moray House there was a special Montessori course, and at Notre Dame the Montessori system was particularly favoured.) In the largest centre, however, it was only possible to give students one day a year in the college school, which was so different in atmosphere from the ordinary run of schools where students were sent on regular practice. As one student remarked in her "Observation Notes", "The first thing which struck me on entering the infant room was the freedom with which the children expressed themselves, and the correctness of their speech. The room was bright, large and well ventilated, prettily decorated, and more like a nursery than an ordinary classroom."[3] It was to the

[1] See Appendix G, II, pp 255-7. Examination papers.
[2] From a letter by Dr R R Rusk to the writer.
[3] *Glasgow Provincial Committee, Student's Diary*, 1927-8, Marion Mac-Corquodale.

student another world from her own practice school with its poor physical setting, its drill methods of instruction and ill-kempt children.

The demonstration and the criticism lesson (popularly known as "the crit") were still extensively used. The persistence of the public criticism lesson is perhaps surprising, and there were some who doubted its value. As one HMI put it, "However salutary it may be for the victim, it cannot greatly profit the audience unless the performer is of more than average ability".[1] Apart from the introductory term of practical teaching for those who had come direct from school without preliminary training, the course for non-graduate women followed a similar pattern during each of the two or three years. In addition to the professional subjects and practical teaching, students studied the content and method of each of the primary school subjects.[2] The emphasis of the training was thus almost entirely vocational, based on the general principle that any subject to be taught in the primary school should be a subject of study throughout the college course. The arrangement reflected the commonly held view of the teacher as "a repository of information" rather than a person of breadth and culture. In general, instruction was rarely above the secondary-school level. The assumption was that students on entry had a reasonable grasp of subject matter and that the main function of the training centre was to give instruction in teaching technique.[3]

For graduates and non-graduates alike, it seems clear that in most institutions, educational theory and psychology were, under the able teachers of the period, the most demanding and stimulating courses and played an important part in the personal education of the students. Nevertheless, the barriers which separated theory from practice meant that new ideas were

---

[1] *Education (Scotland) Reports etc*, 1926-7, p D13.

[2] *The Regulations* (1924 and 1931) were explicit in their separation of professional training from general education. Only after the professional requirements had been met, might the training course provide for "the revisal or the development of the students' knowledge of the subjects of general education". (Section 23.)

[3] A large proportion of the staffs were masters or mistresses of method, eg, 10 out of a staff of 25 in Aberdeen in 1925-6. *Report of the Central Executive Committee*, 1925-6, pp x-xi.

M

rarely applied, but remained simply an academic exercise. The isolation even of education and psychology, taught in different classes by different lecturers, deterred students from thinking of a problem as a whole or relating it to their work in the classroom. Consequently there was little interpenetration of theory and practice.

DEVELOPMENTS IN THE INDIVIDUAL CENTRES

There were exceptional developments in individual centres. In 1931, male physical education students were transferred from Dunfermline to Glasgow, where a new Scottish School of Physical Education was integrated in Jordanhill. Both the Glasgow and Edinburgh centres made special provision for the Gaelic-speaking students and gave instruction in the technique of teaching Gaelic. Aberdeen provided for non-graduates a choice of cultural subjects: English, French, biology and Gaelic. English, based on group reading and discussion, became an enriching feature not only of the General Certificate course, but also of the various branches of the Technical Certificate course, domestic science, art, music and handwork.[1]

From 1933, Edinburgh offered a one-year nursery school course, but the nursery school movement made so little headway in Scotland that few students attended the course in the inter-war years.[2] There was rather poor response also for the one-year infant school course offered by centres. Most women preferred to obtain the necessary qualification for infant mistresses (the endorsement of the General Certificate) by attending classes on Saturday mornings or during the vacation.

A special feature of the period was the rural school courses. Because half the schools in Scotland were one- or two-teacher country schools, there was real need to relate training to the rural context and give students experience in handling a composite class. In Aberdeen, almost all the non-graduate men training for the General Certificate up to 1926, joined the rural course which included practical mathematics, surveying and

---

[1] Information from *Student Handbooks* of the period.
[2] There were only 44 students in a decade. In the whole of Scotland in 1940 there were only 34 nursery schools and 10 nursery classes. *Summary Report*, (*SED*), 1939-40, p 13.

rural science, taken in conjunction with the College of Agriculture. Many of them became head teachers, others, peripatetic teachers of rural science. In the late 'twenties, Aberdeen created within the demonstration school a little *rus in urbe*, a unit which, staffed with teachers experienced in rural work, reproduced conditions of a country school. (Moray House similarly had a two-teacher "rural" unit within the organisation of the demonstration school.) Dundee, on the other hand, sent students to selected schools in the neighbourhood. Practical rural science was done in the laboratory and in the greenhouses and gardens at Mayfield, and a theoretical course was given by a member of the staff of the Edinburgh and East of Scotland College of Agriculture.

The decline in the numbers of students taking the concurrent course and the surge of graduates into the centres compelled authorities to reconsider the organisation of the postgraduate course. In 1926, the Glasgow authorities were forced by sheer pressure of numbers to divide the graduates in two sections, spending alternately a month in schools and a month in college, an early example of the "Box and Cox" arrangement. Such continuity of teaching was a novelty, but to the schools themselves a welcome venture, since it offered the most natural conditions of practice. The lecturers, however, expressed their disappointment that the students did not continue their college reading or craft work nor assimilate the subject matter of their lectures during the month "out".[1]

At Dundee, Professor McClelland was a keen exponent of the concurrent course which continued to be a strong feature there. He considered a postgraduate course of 30 or 40 weeks wholly inadequate for the process of reorientation which students needed to experience. "It is," he said, "surely the stupidest way of training teachers that the mind of man can devise." In contrast, the concurrent course offered many advantages. It got students into the classroom three years earlier, before they had "lost the plasticity upon which the successful mastery of the art of teaching depends". It gave members of staff the opportunity to get to know the students

[1] *Scheme for the teaching of graduates, Directors' report on the experience of the session, 1926-7* (typescript).

and to guide them in their choice of university classes and it gave to the centres continuity of student life and tradition.[1]

Everywhere the curriculum of the postgraduate course was grossly overcrowded, partly because students felt that in order to obtain employment they must gain as many additional qualifications as possible. The majority of honours graduates, therefore, combined the courses for the General and the Special Certificate. A minority, often those with aspirations for administrative posts, took both the university diploma – the first part of the degree course in education – and the Special Certificate. Similarly, ordinary graduates aimed at a double qualification by combining Article 39 subjects with the General Certificate course. The graduate timetable, frequently averaging 300 hours a term (about 11 weeks) listed a formidable array of lectures on aspects of educational theory, methods of teaching primary and secondary school subjects, as well as several practical courses – handwork, drawing and needlework. Overloaded courses left little time for reflection. Of the two larger centres, Edinburgh made a great effort to break down graduate numbers into discussion groups, and students in schools were encouraged to study individual children.

Philosophy and psychology were very much to the fore. In philosophy, Rusk's *Doctrines of the Great Educators* (1918) and *Philosophical Bases of Education* (1928) gave students insight into the influences of the past. In psychology, the emphasis moved after the early 'twenties from psycho-analysis to mental testing, as a method of assessing and classifying children. The old "standards" had registered attainment, the new objective tests distinguished between intelligence, attainment and aptitude. Both the Professor-Directors, Godfrey Thomson and William McClelland, mathematicians by training, applied scientific method to educational research. (In the late 'thirties, P E Vernon was also working on similar lines in Glasgow.)[2] McClelland's investigations related to the prognostic value of examinations, Thomson's to the principles on which mental

---

[1] Report of the Director of Studies, October 1932, *Minutes of St Andrews Provincial Committee*, 1932-3.

[2] P E Vernon, head of the psychology department at the Glasgow centre 1935-8 and subsequently head of the university department.

tests should be conducted and standardised. Both looked for a humane system of guidance in schools; both believed that the application of new techniques of statistical measurement and interpretation were highly relevant. In fact psychology, in its various branches, had adopted the methods of applied science, and the researches of James Drever, now head of the psychology department of the University of Edinburgh, in the industrial field were paralleled by those of Thomson and McClelland in the field of education.

All three men were closely connected with the Scottish Council for Research in Education, an organisation founded in 1928 by the combined effort of the Educational Institute of Scotland and the local authorities. In 1930, Dr Rusk became the first Director of the Council, a position which he held in conjunction with his principal lectureship in Education at Jordanhill. During its early years the Council, working on an extremely modest budget, sponsored a variety of investigations. It conducted, for example, a nation-wide Mental Survey in 1932 (and again in 1947), and it was responsible for such publications as *Studies in Reading*,[1] a series associated with the names of W B Inglis and P E Vernon, which had a direct influence on the reform of school readers and methods of teaching reading.

Thomson was intimately involved in the two Mental Surveys, in which every 11-year-old child in the country was tested. With his great gifts as a teacher and researcher, he was able to inspire students and give them insight into the powers and limitations of research. Under him, Room 70 in Moray House became famous as the centre of experimental and statistical investigation in which successive teams of young men and women, students for the degree of Bachelor of Education, were engaged. Their work in practical testing and mental measurement became famous throughout the world, and the Moray House intelligence and attainment tests were widely adopted in Britain as the basis of selection for secondary education. The "11+" was the product of the age, the result of the shortage of places in selective secondary schools. Without the work of

---

[1] Vols I and II published 1948 and 1956 (Scottish Council for Research in Education, Publications Nos XXVI, XXXIV).

Thomson it would have been a worse kind of "11+".[1] He had himself risen from the ranks as a "scholarship boy" and, as one of his former students wrote, "Most of his work in large-scale intelligence surveys developed out of a desire to give an equal educational chance to children in different classes of society and in different districts".[2] The practical implications of his work, however, extended beyond selection to guidance, teaching materials and method.

At the Dundee centre, McClelland's major project, started in 1935, and based on the school careers of over 3,000 children in the city, became the central research interest of the whole college. Students were introduced to the plan of research so that they understood how their own contribution fitted into the whole. McClelland himself described the project: "Its general headquarters, the Inquiry Room, was a meeting place for students from all sections who were co-operating in the work. It had a real research atmosphere, and no one could associate with the students in it without feeling that the project was an enriching influence in the life of the college."[3] Published in 1942 – a year after McClelland himself had left Dundee to become Executive Officer to the National Committee for the Training of Teachers – under the title *Selection for Secondary Education*, the work became the basis for allocating pupils to courses of secondary instruction throughout Scotland.

In Glasgow, Boyd was not so directly connected with teacher training as were Thomson and McClelland. Nevertheless, through his postgraduate students and his child guidance centre, his influence was widely felt. Like so many Scottish educationists he had a broad range of interests, and he combined the scholarly detachment of the philosopher – his famous *History of Western Education* was first published in 1921 – with a realism based on his own experience. He was a practical

[1] Sir James J Robertson, "Godfrey Thomson", Godfrey Thomson Lecture, Moray House, 1964, p 7. The "11+" was, of course, English terminology. In fact Thomson was opposed to the principle of educational segregation and favoured the comprehensive high school. "The contribution to Education of Sir Godfrey Thomson", P E Vernon, *British Journal of Educational Studies*, vol X, no 2, May 1962, p 128.

[2] "Sir Godfrey Thomson 1881-1955", John Sutherland, *British Journal of Educational Psychology*, vol XXV, part II, June 1955, pp 65-6.

[3] *Selection for Secondary Education*, Scottish Council for Research in Education, Publication No XIX, University of London Press, 1942, p xiii.

psychologist in his use of mental and achievement tests in the analysis of maladjustment. It was, however, particularly in his interpretation of education, in his plea for the school as a democracy and for the nurture of individual differences that Boyd was ahead of his time. He wrote, "The disciplined school with demands and controls all issuing from the adult teacher can only train boys and girls for subjection and dependence".[1]

His work with the underprivileged gave him a concern for wider social service. He was the inspiration behind the establishment of children's libraries which still flourish in the less favoured areas of Glasgow, and he helped to organise, during the depression years, the Clydebank Mutual Service Association, which provided a diversity of interests for the large numbers of unemployed craftsmen and labourers. Former students recollect Boyd's illumination of contemporary educational issues by reference to his work in Clydebank.

Postgraduate students working for the degree in education were most numerous in Edinburgh. Here the close links between the University Department and Moray House gave rise to a great school of education, which deployed a common staff in teaching and research and from which there came a steady stream of Bachelors of Education, trained educationists who made their mark in the teachers' centres, in educational guidance and in administration. In previous generations, aspiring teachers had gone abroad to further their professional education. Adams had gone to Ziller in Leipzig and, in the first decade of the twentieth century, Rusk had studied under Rein at Jena. Now the Scottish universities were sending out a cadre of professionals trained in scientific and philosophic disciplines. As heads of departments Thomson, McClelland and Boyd in education, and Drever, Thouless, Vernon and Knight in psychology had built high reputations.[2] When Thomson retired from the Chair of Education in Edinburgh in

[1] Ed William Boyd, *The Challenge of Leisure*, New Education Fellowship, 1936, p 52.
[2] Thouless and Knight were heads of the psychology departments of Glasgow and Aberdeen respectively. Glasgow University established a chair of psychology in 1947 and a chair of education in 1949. Aberdeen University established a chair of psychology in 1946 and a chair of education in 1961.

1951, he was able to count among former BEd students
thirteen professors and heads of colleges.[1]

ACHIEVEMENTS OF THE PERIOD

Postgraduate training dominated the work of the training
centres in the inter-war period. The clamour for graduate
teachers was an expression of what Boyd called "the extreme
intellectuality of Scottish schools". Teachers of practical subjects were less in demand. Indeed, many children never had
the opportunity of taking a more practical course in an advanced
division simply because they could not get over the hurdle of
the qualifying examination; condemned to repeat an unsavoury
academic curriculum they left school with a permanent dis-
taste for education. Of teachers in training under Chapter VI
of the Regulations, housecraft students were by far the most
numerous. Handwork students in the 'thirties included a
number of older men from overseas, planters and engineers
who had lost their jobs in the slump and who returned to
qualify for less precarious work. Openings for men teachers
of physical education encouraged some graduates to take additional training at Dunfermline or, after 1931, at the Scottish
School of Physical Education at Jordanhill. As late as 1939, a
Student Handbook was recommending the commercial course
as offering a "new field for unemployed trained teachers".[2]

Despite economic gloom, the inter-war period had brought
striking changes in Scottish teacher training. First, the administration had been unified so that there was now one simple,
homogeneous, planned structure. Secondly, material conditions of training had been completely transformed with the
completion of new centres, demonstration schools and hostels.
Thirdly, there had been all-round improvement in academic
standards and the provision of a variety of new courses.

Within the distinctive systems of English and Scottish
education there was no single feature so divergent as teacher
training. The few co-educational, multi-purpose day centres

[1] "Theory and Practice in Scotland", W B Inglis, *Times Educational
Supplement*, 1 December 1967.
[2] *Student Handbook*, Jordanhill Centre, 1939-40, p 51.

of Scotland contrasted with the heterogeneous English pattern: 22 university departments (formerly day training colleges) for the minority of students who were training for secondary schools and, for the rest, 83 small, single-sex, residential colleges owned by the churches or by the local education authorities. Quite apart from the administrative simplicity, the Scottish system was in many respects superior with its well-equipped physical "plant", its high proportion of graduate students and its specialist staff including some of the most eminent scholars in their particular fields. The benefits of transfer to secular authority in a previous generation were plainly visible in the extensive modern buildings and generous staff salaries. Certainly the Scottish centres did not suffer as severely as did the English training colleges from "the trail of cheapness" which had characterised the elementary school system of the past.

Nevertheless, there were disadvantages in a system where institutions drew largely on defined local areas, where opportunities for deepening social and cultural experience were limited, and where respect for academic standards was such that non-graduate students were condemned to inferiority. While the Scot might regard the English training system as untidy, uneconomic and inefficient, the Englishman might well consider the Scottish system, with its divorce of theory and practice, academic and impersonal. Yet by reason of the many anomalies within the English pattern, England still had large numbers of uncertificated teachers – one-fifth of the staff of public elementary schools and one-quarter of all graduates.[1] In Scotland, in contrast, a coherently planned system had secured not merely a trained profession, but one in which the graduate element was almost half, and in which types of training corresponded to particular, specialised functions within the schools.

[1] *Teachers and Youth Leaders* (McNair Report), 1944, pp 10-11.

Chapter 7

EXPANSION AND REORGANISATION
SINCE 1945

POST-WAR REPLANNING

The Second World War marked the end of a relatively static era in Scottish education, one which was associated with the drabness of the depression years, cuts in expenditure, contraction in the school population and unemployment among teachers. The outbreak of the war had postponed the raising of the school leaving age to 15, though already education for the 12+ age-group was given under a common code in junior and senior secondary schools. However, whereas the Hadow Report in England encouraged teachers to think in terms of a new type of secondary education for the average child, the Scottish Code implied merely an extension of the traditional secondary course for all children.

It was the European aspect of Scottish education, its academic nature, centrally controlled examination system and powerful inspectorate which struck an English educationist newly appointed to a teacher training centre. It was, he noted, male dominated and, at the post-primary level, apparently untouched by agitation for Hadow reforms which were under way in England. Even on the primary schools, the advances in psychology and child study had made astonishingly little impact, and the traditional emphasis was still on formal learning.[1]

William Boyd had similarly commented on the conservatism of the teachers. They were, he said, "a fine group, but canny, very canny". The absence of experiment he attributed to a variety of causes: to the temperament of the Scot "who wants to move forward but take no risks", to the late age of pro-

[1] Typescript of talk by H P Wood, "Modern Trends in the Organisation of Scottish Education".

motion of teachers to headship and to a system of inspection
which "is educationally sterile because the inspectors have
come to the schools as outsiders with powers that paralyse
originality".[1]   His colleague at Glasgow University, P E
Vernon, was struck, as were many English observers, by "the
appalling efficiency of Scottish teaching methods".[2]

Wartime denuded the training institutions of their male
students. Though only one college was evacuated – Dunfermline College which was accommodated in Aberdeen – the
problems of evacuation bore indirectly on the centres and on the
other colleges which were compelled to send students far
afield on teaching practice. One of the most eventful developments of wartime was the launching of the Youth Service under
the direction of the Scottish Youth Leadership Association,
founded in 1941. The Association was keen to link the preparation of Youth Leaders with teacher training, and the early
courses were provided under the combined auspices of Moray
House and Edinburgh University. After the lapse of the
the government-sponsored scheme, Moray House assumed
responsibility for future courses, a move which was promoted
by Dr W B Inglis, Depute Director under Sir Godfrey Thomson, whom he succeeded in 1951. Dr Inglis, a founder member
of the Scottish Youth Leadership Association, had long experience of social welfare. For him, the extension of the college
into this particular field was part of forward planning, designed
to assist the building up of a strong sociology department which
should undertake the training of social workers, and should also
provide basic courses in sociology (ranking with those in philosophy and psychology) for all teachers in training.

Already, in the middle of war, men's minds had turned to
the future. A new Education Act was planned, and, simultaneously, the Advisory Council on Education considered future
policy, including the recruitment into teaching of men and
women newly demobilised from the forces. In the event, the
Council recommended their absorption into the existing centres

[1] "Growing Points in Scottish Education", *New Era in Home and School*,
vol 16, no 7, July-August 1935, p 176.
[2] "A Comparative Study of Educational Attainments in England and
Scotland". *British Journal of Educational Psychology*, vol XXV, part III,
November 1955, p 195.

and colleges, which with 1,000 empty places were thought to
have ample reserves of accommodation.[1]   The veterans were
thus merged into the general student population and the opportunity was lost of establishing new institutions which could have
been specially adapted to the needs of mature students and
which later could have been utilised as permanent colleges.[2]
Despite the native predilection for a few large colleges it is
difficult not to regret the decision.   In fact the continuing
"baby boom" was to confound all the population experts and
was to result in an unprecedented demand for teachers which
the training institutions were simply not equipped to meet.
In particular, Jordanhill, whose numbers were to rise to over
3,000, bore the brunt of expansion and was compelled to work
under conditions of intense overcrowding until the establishment of new colleges in 1964.

   Altogether, over 4,000 teachers qualified under the Emergency Training Scheme,[3] which in 1951 was superseded by a
Special Recruitment Scheme offering financial assistance to
suitable men and women from other occupations who were
prepared to train as teachers.   The Education (Scotland) Act
of 1945, which made provision for the raising of the school
leaving age to 15 and for the establishment of junior colleges,
obviously implied a need for more teachers.   Simultaneously,
salary scales, uniform for the first time throughout Scotland,
were designed to make the profession more attractive.[4]   In fact,
continuing inflation was to require their regular revision and
was to be the cause of unrest, particularly among a section of
male teachers.

   As part of the long-range educational planning, the Advisory
Council published in 1946 a Report on the Training of Teachers[5]

   [1] Report of the Advisory Council on Education in Scotland, *Teachers,
Supply Recruitment and Training in the period immediately following the War*,
1944, Cmd 6501, Appendix 12.
   [2] The exceptions were two Emergency Centres for training specialists
(men and women) in physical education.   (English Emergency Colleges
introduced innovations, eg, discussion techniques and continuous assessment.)
   [3] *Report of the Central Executive Committee*, 1951-2, p 4.
   [4] Teachers' Salaries (Scotland) Regulations, 1945.   See Appendix D, I,
p 235.
   [5] Report of the Advisory Council on Education in Scotland, *Training of
Teachers*, Cmd 6723.   (Other Reports of the Advisory Council: *Primary
Education*, Cmd 6973, 1946, *Secondary Education*, Cmd 7005, 1947.)

which, like the 1944 McNair Report in England, considered the present system and made proposals for reform. It stressed the need to foster the personal qualities of students so that as young teachers they would not easily be deflected from experiment by "the distrust of superiors or the cynicism of disillusioned colleagues". Students should be able to see theory related to practice; they should also have the opportunity to mature as persons so that they could make their own judgments. A wider basis of recruitment and longer periods of training, followed by in-service courses, were among the recommendations of the Council. McClelland is generally credited with the writing of the Report which came out strongly in favour of concurrent training.[1]

McClelland was probably also responsible for the proposed Institutes of Education which should be focal points for research and further training. The institutes, however, were not to be associated, as were the English institutes, with the universities, a move which "would tend to create a bias towards the academic as opposed to the professional side of training", and a preference was expressed for *ad hoc* authorities.[2] In the end nothing came of the proposal, for an institute composed of two colleges, or even of a single constituent college, was clearly impracticable, and major administrative reorganisation was postponed for a decade.

However, new courses suggested in the Advisory Council's Report were introduced within the next few years. There were, for example, courses for teachers of physically-handicapped children and for teachers of speech and drama as well as a variety of courses in religious education. With the expansion of teacher training it had become necessary to review the old arrangement with the Church of Scotland. Instead of the Church providing a Director of Religious Education at each centre, it was agreed in 1947 that lecturers, now to include women as well as men, should be appointed and paid on the same basis as other members of staff.[3] At the same time, facilities were given to other denominations to instruct their students.

[1] *ibid*, pp 18-19.   [2] *ibid*, p 59 *et seq.*
[3] *Report of the Central Executive Committee*, 1946-7, p 15.

Meanwhile, centres and colleges were under constant pressure to take in more recruits. Both the population explosion and high "wastage" rates among women teachers, a consequence of earlier marriage, combined to create an acute shortage of school staffs. In pre-war years, spinsters had been the mainstay of the profession.[1] By the 'fifties, the majority of women were marrying within a few years of qualifying and often leaving the profession so that, despite the considerable increase of female recruits, the number of single women within the profession was diminishing.

Initially, the Special Recruitment Scheme, launched in 1951, met with modest response.[2] Despite the fact that it made no concessions either on conditions of entry to training (though selected candidates could be assisted to acquire necessary qualifications) or on length of training, there was still some feeling within the profession that mature students were "dilutees" and accordingly they were not always welcomed in the schools during periods of teaching practice.[3] Estimates of future requirements regularly fell short of actuality. In 1957, it was officially estimated that the country would be 3,000 teachers short by 1961. In fact by that date, the situation was so acute that there were 2,000 uncertificated teachers in the schools, and the shortage of qualified teachers for 1966, was then estimated at 5,000.[4] It was at this point that a great national campaign was launched to persuade married women to return to service in order to relieve the shortage in primary schools.

In secondary schools there were disturbing deficiencies of staff, particularly in modern languages, mathematics and science. Even before the war the numbers of graduates entering teach-

[1] eg, annual wastage rate of women teachers 1935-8 had been 4.5 per cent. *Teachers, Supply Recruitment and Training in the Period immediately following the War*, 1944, Cmd 6501, Appendix 12. By comparison, of those who completed training 1959-63 over 40 per cent married, and 25 per cent left teaching by 1963. *Education in Scotland in 1963*, p 71.

[2] Between 1952 and 1961, 2,693 completed their training. *Education in Scotland in 1961*, p 73.

[3] Notre Dame College, *Triennial Report* 1958-61, p 7.

[4] *Education in Scotland in 1961*, p 12. Uncertificated teachers included a number of teachers with English qualifications, eg, two-year trained teachers. (By 1966, there were 3,000 uncertificated teachers in the schools.) *Education in Scotland in 1966*, p 66.

ing had fallen. In the post-war years, posts in industry and commerce, in the scientific and civil services had absorbed increasing numbers of graduates direct from the university. Indeed, in their efforts to recruit staff, employers exercised their arts of salesmanship early in the undergraduate career. A few graduates might eventually find their way back into teaching by the Special Recruitment Scheme, but the sombre fact was that by the middle 'fifties, graduate entrants to teacher training numbered only 500 a year, a mere 40 per cent of the numbers being recruited a quarter of a century before. Even the ordinary arts degree was no longer regarded primarily as a teacher's degree.

Already the Regulations of 1948 had reduced the postgraduate course to one year (and had thus effectively killed the concurrent course). Ten years later, as an emergency measure, the specialist teacher's course (under Chapter V) was temporarily reduced to two terms. The days when Chapter V students had taken a dual course to enable them to teach in both primary and secondary schools were long past. Indeed, the emphasis in the training of ordinary graduates was on secondary work, so far as the regulations of the General Certificate permitted.

Many graduates looked for a more adventurous career than teaching. Some undoubtedly were repelled by the image of the training institution, a place associated with regimentation and close supervision. Though possibly no more critical of the content of their courses than were graduates in England, they resented the physical transition to an institution associated with the restrictive atmosphere of a school.[1] By 1962, men entering teacher training had shrunk to 17 per cent of the total intake, and a strong body of opinion was pressing for the payment of salaries during training as the only effective means of attracting able graduates into the profession.

---

[1] *Higher Education, Evidence*, part 1, vol C, Cmnd 2154-VIII, pp 884-5. Evidence of Scottish Union of Students. Sir Philip Morris, a member of the Robbins Committee, also commented – "The colleges have to deal with seventeen-year-old girls who are manifestly not suited to a fully adult form of institution and also with people who have had four years in the free-and-easy atmosphere of the university". *Higher Education, Evidence*, part 1, vol C, Cmnd 2154-VIII, p 1064.

Girl entrants straight from school came to train in ever-increasing numbers in the 'fifties. There were moves to extend their general education by encouraging the study of one or two selected subjects at a deeper level. (At the same time seminars and specialist study groups were introduced for honours graduates). Preparation for work in rural schools had traditionally been the distinctive feature of the Aberdeen centre. Rural courses, including teaching experience in country schools, were also developed at the Edinburgh and Glasgow centres, while for Gaelic-speaking students there was special provision to encourage them to teach young children of the outlying areas in the language of the home. The emphasis, however, was still on the subject approach to learning and on training children in mechanical skills. There was even official concern lest the kindlier discipline of the schools would jeopardise standards: in the words of the Scottish Education Department's Report for 1953, "Schooling by fear has largely disappeared in favour of schooling through persuasion or interest. Against this positive gain, however, there must be set a decline in the habit of hard work, even where the tradition was strongest."[1]

For the majority of students "activity methods" and "the integrated day" remained textbook phrases, divorced from experience. In part, the formality of work in primary schools was a consequence of the particular system of promotion employed by many authorities, the appointment to primary headships of male graduates whose teaching experience had been confined to secondary schools. The tradition of the dominie and the mystique of the degree demanded that the head be a university man, even though his previous knowledge of junior children might be limited to a brief part of his now distant training course and his future ambitions fixed on promotion within the secondary sphere.

The bookish tradition had similarly impeded the provision of a varied curriculum for senior children. Professional conservatism, bureaucratic regulations and the prestige of examinations, all combined to restrict curricula to a diet which was both irrelevant and distasteful to many. Those who failed successive tests simply slipped downstream. It was a system

[1] *Education in Scotland in 1953*, p 17.

Free Church Training College

Glasgow, June 30th. 1900

It is hereby Certified that Mr. Robert R. Rusk was enrolled a student of this College on the 25th. day of Dec. 1898

He has finished his full course of Training at this date.

At the Queen's Scholarship Examination he passed in the First Class ranking ... on the Merit List for Scotland and ... on the Merit List for this College.

At the Certificate Examination at the end of the First Year he gained a place in the First Class.

At the Certificate Examination at the end of the Second Year he gained a place in the First Class.

In the Religious Knowledge Examination he was classed as under:

Entrance Examination	First Class
At end of First Year	First Class
At end of Second Year	First Class
His attendance has been	Regular
His conduct has been	Exemplary

Mr. Rusk's standing and progress in the various subjects of the College Curriculum are indicated by the marks in the subjoined list.

(The marks employed are in descending order. E.. E.G.. G.. F.G.. F.. F.M.. M.)

READING	Greek E.G.	Drawing	Music
READING G	FRENCH		
PENMANSHIP E	GERMAN	FREEHAND E	THEORY
ARITHMETIC	LATIN	GEOMETRY E	SINGING
ENGLISH E.G	MATHEMATICS	MODEL E	INSTRUMENTAL
SCHOOL MANAGEMENT	DYNAMICS G	LIGHT & SHADE	Drill
POLITICAL ECONOMY E	PHYSIOGRAPHY E.G	BLACKBOARD E	

The marks given in the Practical Work of Teaching are:

For tact and skill	E.G.
For Discipline	E.G.

John Adams M.A.B.Sc.&c Rector

Jno. Kerr, LL.D, F.R.S.

Thos. Morrison, M.A.

Archibald J. Hood D.S.

William Almond M.A. B.A

James Gallin, A.M., &c &c

Hector Kay B.D.; B.D. &c

Robert G. Moore R.A.

Louis Labovius F.E.I.S.

5   *Teacher's certificate awarded to R R Rusk, 1900*

6   *Hamilton College of Education Hall of Residence*

which catered for the academically gifted, but which under-valued those whose talents lay elsewhere.

Despite their preoccupation with numbers the training centres were concerned also with analysis and forward thinking. John Sutherland, principal lecturer in education at Moray House, made a study of students admitted under the emergency scheme.[1] In the field of special education a number of publications by the Advisory Council were based on work in the centres. The report *Pupils handicapped by Speech Disorders* (1951) was based on the work of Dr Anne H McAllister, head of the speech department at Jordanhill. Reports on pupils handicapped by other particular disabilities and a final report on *The Administration of Education for Handicapped Children* (1952) were generally ascribed to Dr Inglis, Convener of the Advisory Council's Committee.

THE ESTABLISHMENT OF THE SCOTTISH COUNCIL FOR THE TRAINING OF TEACHERS

Full-scale discussions on the proposals for administrative overhaul of teacher training, outlined in 1946, were strangely delayed until the middle 'fifties. As Executive Officer of the National Committee for the Training of Teachers since 1941, McClelland had exercised a decisive influence within the training system. He had been responsible, for example, for the institution of a Committee of Directors and Assessors, a body which was to be given legal standing under the succeeding administration. He had also developed inter-college liaison through conferences of lecturers in academic and professional subjects. The reorganisation, which coincided with McClelland's retirement, brought devolution of responsibilities.[2]

Preliminary draft proposals had elicited response from the interested parties. (In the circumstances it was perhaps not surprising that the suggestion by three of the four universities that they should undertake the whole of the professional

---

[1] "A survey of students admitted to train as teachers in Scotland under the post-war emergency scheme". *British Journal of Educational Psychology*, vol XXV, part II, June 1955, p 78 *et seq*.
[2] Based on Circular 375, *Draft of the Teachers (Training Authorities) (Scotland) Regulations*, 14 February 1958.

N

training of graduates was never considered as a practical possibility.[1]) Under the new structure, the Secretary of State retained ultimate control of teacher training, but the National Committee, which had exercised direct and extensive powers over centres and colleges, was replaced in 1959 by a co-ordinating and advisory body, the Scottish Council for the Training of Teachers. As a corollary, a greater measure of autonomy was given to the training institutions, now to be called colleges of education, under their Principals (formerly designated Directors of Studies). The Provincial Committees and Committees of Management were succeeded by governing bodies more widely representative of educational interests and including, as did the Scottish Council itself, a large proportion of members of the profession.[2] Each governing body was to award its own diplomas and certificates, bearing the arms of the college. Within the colleges the appointment of staff, apart from the Principal, was to be an internal affair, and organisation of courses was to be the responsibility of Boards of Studies. In effect, each college was freer to develop its own individual character. In place of inspection by HMIs, unobtrusive though this had become, the colleges were now given responsibility for devising their own syllabuses and for arranging their own forms of assessment. Boards of Studies, which enabled members of staff to express their views on academic policy, gave a degree of self-government.

The greater independence afforded by the new administrative arrangements was long overdue. Training centres and colleges in the past had never really ranked as part of the system of higher education. They had been forward-looking in many of the courses they had launched and had contributed research of the highest order. At the worst, however, their authori-

[1] Mentioned in "Teacher Training in Scotland", John Pilley, *Universities Quarterly*, vol 12, no 3, May 1958, p 286.
[2] Each governing body included 6 teachers and 3 university representatives out of a total of 22 or 23 members. The Scottish Council for the Training of Teachers was to consist of 25 members of whom 7 were chairmen of governing bodies and of the remainder the majority were to be nominees of the governing bodies. The 7 Principals were to attend the meetings of the Scottish Council as Assessors, ie, they could speak but had no voting powers. Members were to be disqualified after the age of 70. It was at this point that many of the elderly clerical members – often representatives of the education authorities – disappeared.

tarianism and inbreeding had fostered a narrowness of outlook and a sense of complacency. Lecturers from further afield were frequently dismayed by the restricted experience of many of their colleagues whose entire educational careers had been confined to a particular area.[1] Nor did they find the hierarchical structures of the teaching institutions conducive to proper academic relationships. Perhaps the greatest need of centres and colleges was to recruit more widely, to encourage fresh thinking and to make use of the new opportunities for research.

With their new autonomy, the four large colleges were able to assume many of the functions which in England were associated with Institutes of Education. They extended their range of activities to cover further education and a great variety of in-service courses. Their annual graduation ceremonies for the presentation of certificates and diplomas,[2] which in the past had been distributed by post, gave a dignified conclusion to the academic year. They were not, however, able to offer experienced teachers the incentive of full-time study for diplomas and higher degrees. (The dissolution of the posts of Professor-Director in St Andrews and Edinburgh in 1951 had broken the closest links between universities and teacher training centres.) Nor were they able to provide for local teachers much needed library and conference facilities. Indeed their premises, which by pre-First World War standards had represented the very latest in design and layout, were now out of date and overcrowded.

Accommodation was the most pressing problem. By 1959, the number of students was approaching 5,000 (the greatest increase was in girls who, having passed the necessary school-leaving examinations, were automatically accepted),[3] and

[1] Dr Rusk himself had been disturbed by this feature at Jordanhill (mentioned in discussion with the writer whose experience in the 'sixties was similar).

[2] Women in the three-year course now worked for a diploma and were known as diploma students rather than by the old disparaging term, non-graduates, with its associations of inferiority.

[3] Many of the girls possessed the "Attestation of Fitness", ie, the necessary academic qualifications for entrance to university. "Many deliberately avoided university because they want to work in a primary school". Evidence of Association of Directors of Education in Scotland. *Higher Education*, part 1, vol 3, Cmnd 2154-VIII, p 1065.

colleges were catering for almost twice the student populations they had been built for. Their structures were designed for formal methods of instruction, and their lofty classrooms and cumbersome furniture discouraged more flexible groupings. Without additional buildings they had difficulty in finding space for the "hardware" required by educational technology and in providing library and common room facilities. Overwhelming numbers and lack of space made it impossible in some colleges to offer the majority of students anything but a standard compulsory course. With a low staff-student ratio (it was 17.1 in 1959-60),[1] the organisation of numerous parallel classes entailed wearisome repetition of subject matter by members of staff.

Even during this period of unprecedented strain the colleges took the lead in a great national drive for a reform of teaching methods in schools. In primary education, for example, the new interest in the teaching of arithmetic was due very largely to the many in-service courses on the Cuisenaire method, organised by the colleges. In secondary education, the general adoption of new syllabuses in the sciences and mathematics was made possible only by a crash programme of college courses, making use of progressive teachers, university lecturers and college staff. The success of the drive – it is claimed, for example, that 90 per cent of Scottish schools changed over to the new mathematics in three years – was made possible by the efforts of the colleges with their specialist staffs working within a highly centralised educational system. Resistance to change in pupil-teacher relationships, however, made it much more difficult to promote interest in new forms of class organisation.

NEW COLLEGES AND NEW REGULATIONS

Temporary alleviation to accommodation problems was provided by a proliferation of supplementary huts. Finally, in 1960, the Scottish Council for the Training of Teachers under the chairmanship of Sir James J Robertson recommended a large-scale expansion – namely, the erection of a new residential

[1] *Higher Education*, Appendix 3, Cmnd-III, p 102.

college for 900 women at Hamilton and the rebuilding of
Dunfermline College of Physical Education (since 1950, back
in its wartime home at Aberdeen)[1], on a new site in Edinburgh,
and of Notre Dame College, Glasgow, on the outskirts of the
city. The decision to build a new single-purpose college
roused considerable controversy. The idea of a single-sex
college was alien to Scottish tradition, and fears were expressed
for the status of an institution which catered only for non-
graduate women.[2] Because of the early loss of women to the
profession, the Principal of Jordanhill College, Mr (later Sir)
Henry Wood, was of the opinion that the money could be more
usefully spent in offering new types of courses for men students.[3]
However, despite the growing competition for university places
and the consequent exclusion of well-qualified men candidates,
professional opinion still remained strongly opposed to the
most obvious source of recruitment, the admission of non-
graduate men to a three-year training college course.

While plans for the new Hamilton college were unavoidably
delayed, the need of additional accommodation was such that
a crash programme was launched in 1963 for the establishment
of two women's colleges. Envisaged originally as overspill
colleges for Jordanhill, the principalships, temporary appointments in the first place and, as such, confined to women candidates, were advertised only within the Scottish training
system.[4] In the event, the new institutions, Craigie College in
Ayr and Callendar Park College in Falkirk, were completed in
nine months. Opened in October 1964, each had its full
complement of 600 women students two years later. It was in
1966 that the long-planned college at Hamilton, built with its
"hostel village" including a spectacular hexagonal tower block,
was ready to admit students.

The construction of the new colleges, erected at a cost of over

---

[1] On the recommendation of the Report of the Scottish Advisory Council
which proposed inclusion of general courses and removal to a cultural centre,
Training of Teachers, 1946, p 80.

[2] *Minutes of the Scottish Council for the Training of Teachers*, 4 November
1960.

[3] "Teacher Training in England and Scotland", *Advancement of Science*,
March 1964, p 514.

[4] Posts advertised within the existing colleges, June 1963. Appointments
were to be for four years in the first instance. The limit was removed in May
1964.

£3 million, had been entirely the responsibility of the Council (through its Building Committee), a remarkable achievement for amateurs. The colleges were the first to be built in Scotland for over 40 years and, outside the denominational sector, the first new foundations since the beginning of the century. In several respects they represented a break with tradition. They were sited in pleasant parkland areas outside the main centres of population; they were at the outset single-sex institutions and they were designed to give large numbers of students the amenities of residence. Because of the special circumstances of the foundations at Ayr and Falkirk, two of the three principal-ships had gone to women. On the retirement of the first Principal of Callendar Park College in 1969, however, a male successor was appointed.

In 1966, Dunfermline College occupied its new buildings at Cramond, overlooking the Firth of Forth and within sight of the original Carnegie Institution. The location of the college within the city of Edinburgh would, it was felt, aid recruitment of staff and students and enable it to extend its influence. The structure itself reflected the modern conception of physical education as interpreted by Rudolf Laban, with emphasis on the creation, observation and analysis of movement.[1] It was the first college, not only in Scotland but in Britain, to be purpose-built for women teachers of physical education. In the meantime major building extensions, already completed at Jordanhill, Moray House, Dundee, and Craiglockhart, had relieved the worst congestion in these colleges. Work had begun on the new Notre Dame site and a completely new building was projected for the Aberdeen College. After frustrating delays, the Scottish Council for the Training of Teachers had made very considerable additions to the physical "plant". A good deal of initiative had come from the Com-

---

[1] In contrast to the former emphasis on correctness and precision of style. The development of women's physical education in Britain has been described by Ida M Webb, "Women's Physical Education in Great Britain, 1800-1966", unpublished MEd thesis, University of Leicester, 1967. Men's and women's courses are very different. The emphasis of men's courses at the Scottish School of Physical Education, Jordanhill, is on games and athletics and improvement of techniques. Women's courses stress move-ment education, including "movement literacy" ("motif writing" and "kinetography").

mittee of Principals which had assisted the Council to adjust to the realities of the situation.

Delegates from the Council were among the several Scottish deputations whose members in 1961-2 gave evidence before the Robbins Committee investigating Higher Education in Britain. The Committee noted the distinctive features of the Scottish system of teacher training, namely, the dominance of the four multi-purpose colleges of education – "near-university institutions in their own right" – catering for 85 per cent of the teachers in training, the exclusion of the universities from the field, the lower age of entry of the majority of Scottish recruits, who had not experienced the "rapid maturing" of the English sixth-former, and the determination of the main body of teachers, as expressed by the Educational Institute of Scotland, to control training and entrance to the profession.[1]

Some of the evidence led members of the Committee to express concern lest veneration for the "glorious achievements of the past" should inhibit present-day thinking.[2] In their Report they distinguished between the systems of teacher training in England and Scotland. While they recommended University Schools of Education for England, their proposals for Scotland were altogether more cautious. They suggested closer collaboration between colleges and universities only in certain limited respects. In particular, they proposed that students in colleges of education should be able to work for a degree of Bachelor of Education awarded by the neighbouring university.

A professional degree at university level had long been the objective of the Educational Institute of Scotland. In the 'sixties it had an additional appeal since, with the increasing competition for university places, it was likely to attract men of ability who might otherwise have been lost to teaching. In co-operation with the neighbouring colleges of education, new four-year BEd degree courses (the old BEd and EdB have been renamed MEd) were launched by Aberdeen University in 1965, by the Universities of Edinburgh and Glasgow in 1966

[1] *Higher Education*, Appendix 2 (A) Cmnd 2154-11, Part 2, Section 2, p 79 *et seq.*
[2] Words of the Chairman, *Higher Education, Evidence*, part one, vol F, Cmnd 2154-XI, 1054.

and by Dundee University in 1968. Apart from a compulsory core of professional study, the courses vary considerably in content and arrangement.[1] In general – Dundee is the exception – they are modelled on the traditional ordinary degree structure of the Scottish arts faculty, with its seven courses each equivalent to one year of study, and are divided into three parts, consisting of professional subjects, academic subjects, and "methods" and practical subjects. (As an extension of its flexible degree structure Dundee was the first university to offer practising non-graduate teachers the opportunity – subject to certain conditions – of obtaining graduate qualification by means of a course of full-time study.) The danger, strongest in those areas where the work is divided between university and college, is of lack of fusion and of an excessively academic pattern. The challenge lies in the stimulus which degree work will give to the staffs of the colleges and in the opportunities for co-operation between universities and colleges.

With the shortage of places in the arts faculties of the universities, the new degree course will attract able candidates (candidates must satisfy the formal university entrance requirements). There will be students with a strong vocational urge who will prefer it to a university arts degree followed by postgraduate training, and there may be some who will be attracted by the dual qualification for primary and secondary education, permissible under certain BEd regulations. It is unfortunate, however, that, apart from Dundee, where all students take the first two years of the diploma course, regulations require selection of students before entry to college and offer no loophole to late developers to join the course.

The introduction of the new degree has not been without divisive effects within the colleges. Among members of staffs there may well be some sense of discrimination between those, who, by virtue of teaching the academic and professional subjects of the BEd degree courses, are accorded university recognition, and the rest of the lecturers. Among students

[1] All the teaching for the Aberdeen BEd is undertaken by members of the college staff. In Edinburgh, Glasgow and Dundee, the teaching is shared between college and university.

there is certainly a feeling, already marked because of the traditional prestige attached to postgraduate courses, of degrees of citizenship. The universities take no responsibility for the practical training of the BEd students which is the concern solely of the colleges. At the conclusion of the four-year course the student receives two documents: the BEd degree awarded by the authority of the Senate of the university, and the Teacher's Certificate awarded by the authority of the governing body of the college. Among the universities there are differences in the credit given for the new degree. Glasgow and Aberdeen do not accept it as fully equivalent to the university Diploma in Education for entry to MEd courses.[1]

Nothing has yet come of the proposal, favoured by the colleges, for courses leading to Associateships[2] (similar to the Associateships of the former Central Institutions, the Royal College of Science and Technology in Glasgow and the Heriot-Watt College in Edinburgh). The Associateship would have attracted men as well as women. As an internal qualification it could have avoided some of the dangers of fragmentation and neglect of practical and aesthetic subjects, inherent in certain of the BEd syllabuses. It might well have provided a bridge between primary and secondary education, by equipping teachers for that age-group known south of the border as the middle school.

In 1965, new Regulations for the Training of Teachers abolished the system of "Chapters" devised 60 years before. In the past, rigid classification had ensured high standards and uniformity of qualification but, even with the successive amendments, the old Regulations had been too complex and inelastic to cover adequately the developments of post-war years, in particular, the provision of universal secondary education and the growth of further education. Moreover, their emphasis on definition and segregation according to academic achievement had encouraged vested interests and

----

[1] "The Study of Education in Scotland", S D Nisbet, *Scottish Educational Studies*, vol I, no 1, June 1967, p 15.

[2] Draft proposals were submitted by the sub-committee of Principals, *Minutes of the Scottish Council for the Training of Teachers*, 2 December 1964. Throughout the discussions, opposition had come from the teacher members.

cliques within the profession. Differentiation, according to a single criterion, had ignored other qualities vital to the teacher. It had led to a neglect of the non-academic pupil wholly at variance with current thinking embodied in the Report *From School to Further Education* (the Brunton Report), and in the English Report *Half our Future* (the Newsom Report).[1] It was out of keeping with the spirit behind comprehensive reorganisation, that of the growing sense of egalitarianism which rejected a dual system of secondary education.[2]

Under simplified Regulations (10 Chapters and 78 Articles were now reduced to 13 Regulations and 4 Schedules) the Teacher's Certificate was to be awarded for work in one of three fields, primary, secondary and further education. Graduates were to devote the whole of their training year either to primary or secondary school work, and those qualified in the non-academic subjects (who formerly came under Chapter VI of the Regulations) could choose to train either for secondary or for further education. In practice, however, training remained separate for the different categories of students who went into secondary schools, ie, for honours and for ordinary graduates as well as for those qualified in practical subjects. The new forms of primary and secondary certificate have been welcomed for their implicit promise of improved quality. However, some concern has been expressed at the possible threat of professional mobility, since it is no longer possible for ordinary graduates to qualify both for primary and secondary work in a single session.[3]

THE GENERAL TEACHING COUNCIL FOR SCOTLAND

Teachers had long lamented their low status and had looked with considerable envy on the medical profession whose high

[1] Both published in 1963. The Brunton Report proposed that vocational interests should be the core of the curriculum in the final years at school. The Newsom Report gave certain prominence to the vocational impulse.

[2] *Circular* 600, 27 October 1965, urged education authorities to reorganise secondary education on comprehensive lines.

[3] Especially voiced by men students who have been concerned about future prospects of promotion to headships of primary schools. It has been customary for the colleges to organise in-service courses for "promoted" teachers. Conversion courses are suggested for those changing to a different type of school.

prestige was bound up with the degree of self-government exercised by the General Medical Council. Already, in 1963, the Wheatley Committee[1] had proposed a similar Teachers' Council, a significant proportion of whose members should be elected by the teachers themselves. The Council should control entrance to the profession by means of a Register, should exercise disciplinary powers and general oversight of training and should take over from the Scottish Council for the Training of Teachers responsibility for advising the Secretary of State on matters of policy.

Since 1963 the administrative framework of teacher training has undergone changes in both England and Scotland. In England it has, in accordance with the recommendations of the Robbins Report, become more closely associated with the universities by the foundation of Schools of Education. In Scotland, it has been linked more directly with the teaching profession by means of a General Teaching Council, a body very largely representative of the teachers themselves.[2] Indeed, the Council is unique in the world in the responsibility which has been given to the teaching profession. In its executive capacity, it keeps a register of qualified teachers,[3] takes responsibility for the probationary period of teaching, controls exceptional admission to the register and exercises powers of discipline. In its advisory capacity, it can influence the nature and content of training, though it is confidently expected that its powers of visitation will be used diplomatically.

Elected in 1966, the new Council in the following year replaced the Scottish Council for the Training of Teachers as

---

[1] *The Teaching Profession in Scotland, Arrangements for the Award and Withdrawal of Certificates of Competency to Teach*, 1963, Cmnd 2066.

[2] Established by the Teaching Council (Scotland) Act, 1965, 20 of the 44 members were to be elected by the teachers, 5 were to represent the colleges (4 to be elected by the Principals), 15 were to represent the local authority associations, the universities, the central institutions and the churches. There were also to be 4 nominees of the Secretary of State. Circular No 1, issued by the Council in 1966, defined the disciplinary powers of the new body which were to be confined to cases involving criminal offences or infamous conduct in any professional respect.

[3] Only registered teachers – including conditionally registered teachers (certain uncertificated teachers who are given a limited time to gain full qualifications) can now be legally employed in primary schools. The Council has also secured a measure of control over the temporary employment of unqualified teachers in secondary schools.

the body responsible for advising the Secretary of State on policy. At its very birth it established its independence and ability to resist pressure groups, by recommending the admission of men to non-graduate training for primary teachers.[1] The General Teaching Council has shown promise of establishing itself as a body above sectional interests. It has overcome the worst of its teething problems and offers hope of a unified profession, self-governed and self-controlled. Naturally, the Scottish development has roused keen interest elsewhere and already in England the Secretary of State for Education and Science has outlined proposals for a similar organisation.

On the dissolution of the Scottish Council for the Training of Teachers, the colleges assumed a new independence. Under the terms of reconstitution the Principal of each college became ex-officio vice-chairman of the governing body which now included a larger proportion of teachers and, for the first time, a proportion of elected members of staff.[2] With the new devolution, colleges have become virtually autonomous and make their own arrangements for mutual consultation.

THE NEW PATTERN OF TEACHER TRAINING

Today, the variety and experiment in teacher training reflect the ferment in the world of education generally. By happy chance the launching of the new colleges for teachers of young children coincided with the publication of the report *Primary Education in Scotland*.[3] Already in primary schools a strong movement of curricular reform had brought a re-interpretation of craft work, physical education, speech and drama, as well as the introduction of mathematics, science and a modern language. The Report gave new impetus to the movement and served to turn a searchlight on many of the traditional practices. Its recommendations on approach to curriculum, on

---

[1] *Minutes of General Teaching Council*, 9 November 1966. The decision was contrary to the policy of the Educational Institute of Scotland, the main teachers' union.

[2] Draft Statutory Instruments. The Teachers (Colleges of Education) (Scotland) Regulations, 1966.

[3] Produced by a working party including HMIs, teachers and college lecturers, 1964.

more flexible school organisation and on freedom and initiative of teachers stimulated discussion at a diversity of levels.

In the field of primary education the new colleges have distinct advantages. They have no entrenched interests to combat and no defined hierarchy of students. As single-purpose institutions, they can devote their energies to a particular sector. From their foundation they have laid stress on integration of studies and on students' personal education. They have eliminated the old "crit lesson" together with all that term implies of staff-student relationships. As well as skills they have been concerned to develop appropriate attitudes towards learning and to encourage willingness to experiment and to evaluate different approaches to school organisation and teaching methods. Co-operation between schools and colleges is close. Two of the colleges in particular invite regular inter-change of students and teachers. By arranging in-service courses to coincide with students' final teaching practice they release teachers from the schools. Since 1967, the colleges have expanded their recruitment to include non-graduate men.

Of the older colleges, the smallest, St George's – a survival from a former era – closed in 1939. The denominational colleges, however, have expanded in response to the requirements of Roman Catholic schools. Under the Scottish Council for the Training of Teachers they acquired new buildings paid for entirely out of public money, a major extension at Craiglockhart and an entirely new college at Bearsden, which was completed in 1967. The arrangement is a natural sequel to the famous "Scottish solution" to the problem of denominational schools, which permits local authorities to provide new buildings as they are required.[1] Currently, the number of Roman Catholic women in training is almost 1,400 and Notre Dame College has also opened its doors to non-graduate men. Expansion and the impulse of the times have brought changes. Residence, which a few years ago was rigorously insisted upon, is no longer a condition of entry. The guarded domestic discipline of the past, reminiscent in some respects of girls'

[1] 1918 Act Education (Scotland) 8 and 9 Geo 5c 48, Clause 18, Sub-section 8. (The extension at Craiglockhart College was built on land belonging to the Order of the Sacred Heart.)

finishing schools, has given way to greater freedom more in keeping with students' future responsibilities. Building on the academic traditions laid by its great foundress, Notre Dame College plans to present students for the BEd degree. As a smaller college, Craiglockhart prefers to concentrate on the variety of preparation required for primary school teaching.

The large multi-purpose colleges have had to face a complexity of problems arising from developments in different sectors of education. They have responded to the improved standard of non-graduate entrants (based on the broad Scottish Certificate of Education) by the provision of optional courses, of studies in depth designed to offer intellectual challenge and stimulus; they have experimented in primary schools with different forms of group teaching and they have been concerned to cater for the needs of the rural teachers. For those who seek a qualification in secondary and further education, much of the old "methods" work has been transformed in response to recent curriculum development in the schools (the introduction of new subjects and of new syllabuses)[1] and by means of new techniques (audio-visual and audio-lingual aids and programmed learning). Meanwhile sociology, one of the seminal studies of our time, has come to rank with psychology. For students, accustomed only to the formal learning situation, the subject has brought new perspectives, an awareness of the multitude of outside influences which affect education, and of the wider rôle of the teacher as a guide, counsellor and social worker.

Despite massive expansion, attempts have been made to establish closer relationships with students. By means of "focus days" or "introductory weeks" the purpose of college courses has been explained. Larger lecture groups have frequently been broken down for discussion, for the personal dialogue without which a college becomes a mass production factory, in Newman's terms, a "foundry" or a "mint". However, high student-staff ratios have persisted, and the provision

---

[1] New subjects include modern studies and sub-division of older subjects now accepted as separate subjects in the Scottish Certificate of Education O grade examination, eg, biology, 5 branches of technical subjects, 2 branches of homecraft and 3 branches of commerce. There are new syllabuses in the science subjects and in mathematics.

of individual staff rooms, which would have encouraged genuine tutorial relationships, has been slow to materialise.

No aspect of Scottish teacher training is so striking as the overt separation of theory and practice. In 1946, the Advisory Council urged the need for an integrated programme of professional studies, but still in the larger colleges, education, psychology and "methods" (including teaching practice), are organised in separate departments.[1] The divorce is complete for those graduates who, by choosing to work for the university diploma, attend different institutions for the theoretical and practical parts of their course. In the colleges the level of academic study is high but, because those who lecture on education and psychology do not see their students in the classroom and may never enter classrooms at all, theory is confined to general principles and too rarely impinges on practice.

Naturally the staffs of the larger institutions reflect the diversity of the work. The great majority are recruited from the schools. Indeed during the post-war years a proportion came on secondment from schools, a scheme which, though admirable in theory, has had to be modified. Differential salary scales, the attraction of work with graduate students and opportunities for research have brought in men and women of high calibre. With expanding opportunities some have moved quickly to more senior positions in other colleges or to appointments in universities or the inspectorate. Staff mobility has brought problems, but the infusion of new blood has brought vitality and fresh ideas.

In the past, traffic of staff between England and Scotland was very largely one way.[2] Of recent years exceptions to the general trend have become more numerous, and the widening source of recruitment to Scottish colleges has helped to modify the traditional inbreeding. It is noteworthy, however, that two of the most distinguished heads of colleges, Sir Godfrey

---

[1] Persistence of traditional arrangements has been explained as follows – "Divisions which are built into the administrative structure of a large college and the career structure of its staff are formidable factors to reckon with". "The Study of Education in Scotland", S D Nisbet, *Scottish Educational Studies*, vol I, no 1, June 1967, p 10. "Methods" Departments may be very large, eg, there are 47 members of staff in the Jordanhill department.

[2] Scots who moved south included E J R Eaglesham, Ben Morris, Charlotte Fleming.

Thomson, a former Director of Studies at Moray House and Sir Henry Wood, Principal since 1949 of Jordanhill, came from south of the border. Northumbrians by origin, both came with experience of teacher training in English universities. A more recent appointment to a Principalship, that of Dr Douglas M McIntosh to Moray House, is unusual in a different sense in that he was formerly Director of Education for Fife.[1]

With their highly qualified specialist staffs, the older colleges have a great diversity of activities, and each has its own particular interests and fields of research. Sited in what Patrick Geddes called "the respective regional capitals of East and West Scotland", Moray House and Jordanhill are distinctive not only for their size (Jordanhill with nearly 3,000 students is the largest teachers' college in the Commonwealth) but also for the range of courses they offer. In fact, each is a complex of colleges, rather than a single college.

Moray House has had for many years a high intake of Commonwealth students for whom it has provided courses in the teaching of English as a foreign language. As a direct consequence of its overseas connexions and of its work in applied linguistics, it has set up a Centre for Information on the Teaching of English, part of the general movement for reform based on local development centres. Its sociology department, established with great foresight in the early post-war years, caters for a wide range of social services. For school leavers who intend to enter social work, it offers a generic two-year course followed by specialist programmes in the final year. In 1969, the college became the national centre for training teachers of the deaf and partially deaf. (Hitherto teachers of the deaf had received their training in England.)

The college maintains its tradition of research. Under the direction of the Principal, Dr McIntosh, a study group is in process of investigating aspects of organisation and management in secondary schools. Other current projects, include survey

---

[1] Dr McIntosh had assisted McClelland in his investigation of selection for secondary education. He has described a later investigation of allocation in Fife in *Educational Guidance and the Pool of Ability*, University of London Press, London, 1959. Outstanding for his many contributions in the field of educational research, Dr McIntosh has been, since 1960, President of the Scottish Council for Research in Education.

and experiment in programmed learning. Already the college has built up a large library of programmes from many countries and has organised a Learning Resources Centre. Over fifty members of staff are recognised by the University of Edinburgh as lecturers in the BEd course. Further evidence of close liaison between the two institutions was the arrangement, in 1968, whereby the college became responsible for the university postgraduate diploma course.

Like Moray House, Jordanhill with its variety of courses seems well set to become a multi-vocational college. In-service training, in which all the colleges participate, has been most highly developed here. Even during the period of intense overcrowding of the early 'sixties, the college built up an impressive programme of in-service courses, part of the campaign for curricular reform. Currently, some 6,000 teachers a year attend courses organised by the college. Recent developments – the provision of residential accommodation and the appointment of full-time tutors who follow up their courses by work with teachers in schools – are intended to strengthen the contribution in this field. By the siting on the campus of the Scottish School of Physical Education (now housed in new, well-equipped buildings), the college has long been associated with the training of men specialists of physical education. Since 1956 it has had a Department of Further Education (now upgraded to a School of Further Education), and it has also more recently undertaken the training of speech therapists in its Department (now School) of Speech and Drama. With its scope of activities it is able to offer graduates in training, optional courses in librarianship, television, programmed learning and youth work.

Jordanhill made a notable contribution towards staffing the new colleges. Initially the principals of all three colleges, together with a large number of senior staff, were appointed from Jordanhill. Naturally, ties of affection are strong. Staffs of the new institutions recollect the generous help given in the early stages. They recall the realism implicit in the advice of the Principal of Jordanhill – his encouragement to strike out on their own and do for primary education what the multi-purpose colleges could not be expected to attempt.

o

Among the old established colleges, Dundee and Aberdeen have extended the range of their responsibilities. Both colleges, for example, offer a three-year course leading to a teaching qualification in music. Dundee has done pioneer work in the field of closed-circuit television – here as elsewhere closed-circuit television is being used to an increasing extent in the preparation of teachers. It has also become the national centre for experimental work in the initial teaching alphabet. Aberdeen College has sponsored investigation into programmed learning, and has been associated with a follow-up survey of teachers in their early years in the profession.[1] It has also been the first college to launch its own journal, *Education in the North*.

Autonomy and self-government will liberalise the colleges and give them the incentive to self-scrutiny. As Professor K R Popper has said – "The secret of intellectual excellence is the spirit of criticism".[2] Criticism has not been sufficiently welcomed in the past. The present affords opportunity to analyse aims, to plan courses *as wholes*, and to consider the nature of staff-student relationships. Within the colleges, thought and energy are being directed to restructuring pro-grammes. Already, curricular innovations in the schools have made their impact. The use of closed-circuit television and tape recordings and the employment of simulation techniques have helped to give students vicarious experience of teaching situations and enabled them to relate theory and practice. Abandonment of the time-honoured lecture system comes hard. Nevertheless, there is a readiness to examine college practices in communication, assessment and supervision.

Rapid expansion has brought social as well as organisational problems. Jordanhill with almost 3,000 students is by far the largest college; Moray House and Aberdeen have 1,600 each, and Dundee nearly 1,200. With their strong departmental structures the danger is of fragmentation, of staff and students alike identifying themselves with a section or sub-section rather than the whole. Sheer size and complexity of organisa-

---

[1] R P Clark and J D Nisbet, "The First Two Years of Training", prepared by Aberdeen College of Education and Aberdeen University Department of Education, September 1963.
[2] *The Open Society and its Enemies*, Routledge, 1945, p 118.

tion require the re-examination of the whole question of relationships, of modes of contact and consultation.[1]

A vital injection into teacher training came with the opening in 1967 of Stirling University, the first completely new university foundation (as distinct from the Universities of Strathclyde and Heriot-Watt, formerly central institutions) in Scotland for 400 years. Alone among the universities, Stirling takes direct responsibility for teacher training by a combination of professional and academic education and plans to make educational research a prominent feature of its activities. The scheme, not unrelated to combined courses in the post-war English universities of Keele and Sussex, has been thought out in terms of Scottish requirements. It enables a student to take an education course as part of the honours or general degree (an honours degree course combined with education will cover 4½ sessions, nine semesters, and the general degree course, 3½ sessions, seven semesters). The new concurrent course has been approved (subject to periodic review) by the General Teaching Council though, as a departure from traditional Scottish practice, it has not escaped criticism. Nevertheless, it represents a striking innovation, a chance to place education on a parity with other professional studies and to root it firmly in research. Close partnership with the schools will bring incentive unique in the context of Scottish university studies.

THE PRESENT

Changes in teacher training in the 'sixties have transformed the old Scottish system, erected in the first decade of the century. The emergent scene is one of healthy variety. Indeed in Scotland, as in England, the national pattern is less distinctive than in the past. The end of the traditional isolation of teachers in training, welcome though it would be, lies far away. Nevertheless, university incursion into the field and the broadening of the scope of the work of colleges to include various aspects of social service may well be auguries for the future.

[1] A staff-student consultative committee has been established in Aberdeen College in 1969. "Student Participation", N Jackson and H Paterson, *Times Educational Supplement (Scotland)*, 12 Sept 1969, p 34.

Meanwhile, faced with the necessity of catering for the raising of the school leaving age to 16 and for the expansion of day-release courses for school leavers,[1] energies will be absorbed in manning the schools and colleges of further education with men and women who can appreciate and foster a variety of aptitudes. New aspects of professional training in counselling and educational technology must be provided, together with expansion of management courses for Headteachers and Principals. Dual-rôle training for teacher-social workers and teacher-youth leaders may well become a prominent feature in the future.

Pressure of new knowledge and changing techniques will demand large-scale retraining programmes. Indeed, the expansion of in-service work with the employment of full-time tutors and the provision of attractive residential accommodation is well launched. In order to meet the need of teachers to keep abreast of new developments and the need to offset dangers of isolation of those teaching in remoter areas, future facilities must include day-release. Certainly, initial training can no longer be thought of in terms of equipping a teacher for a life-time's work, and "immersion" courses, together with "conversion" courses for those who wish to adapt themselves to a different field of service, must become an essential part of the provision.

Above all, the colleges of education must draw strength from the quality of research. In the inter-war years the pioneering studies on intelligence and intelligence testing, based on Moray House and Dundee, were related to the needs and assumptions of that period. Today, the concepts of differentiation and selection, to which that psychological research was related, have been modified. Yet amid the current fashion for change with its effervescence of ideas, the spirit of rigorous investigation is required. Today, research workers seek to collaborate with teachers in the examination and appraisal of experiments in curricula and organisation at home, as well as in the study of relevant developments elsewhere. It is in this active relationship with the schools, in the pooling of effort and the

[1] In consequence of the Industrial Training Act, 1964. The abolition of pre-training and the expansion of in-service training is the current programme for teachers of further education. *Future Recruitment and Training of Teachers for Further Education in Scotland*, 1965.

process of rethinking and evaluating that those engaged in teacher-education can give a dynamic lead. By encouraging in their students an interest in research they can help to change the attitude towards research in the profession as a whole.

Chapter 8

CONCLUSION

Today, colleges of education are faced with a dual challenge, to provide teachers of quality for the various and ever-expanding sectors of education and at the same time to look afresh at their own rôle. Present-day society demands that teachers do more than transmit the heritage of the past. It looks to them not to teach the certainties, but to nourish the wonder and curiosity of childhood, to develop resilience and discrimination and to encourage personal fulfilment. It requires not (to use a phrase of Sir Percy Nunn) "the barbarous simplicity of class instruction", but flexible teaching groups, mutual exploration and personal encounter. It expects teachers not merely to teach, but to be in part social workers, able to help their pupils by a knowledge of their environment and their individual problems. As teachers, therefore, it needs highly educated people possessing professional and personal skills.

Today Scotland has a teaching force of some 45,000, and even cautious estimates for the early 'seventies put the need at 52,000.[1] There is now acceptance of the career pattern of married women, and realistic steps are being taken to encourage women to return to teaching after child rearing.[2] All the colleges are expanding (currently 13,000 are in training including 1,600 graduates, almost a quarter of those who graduated from Scottish universities in the previous session), new sources of male recruits are being tapped (750 non-graduate men are in training for primary work) and a major break-through has come with the incursion of the newest university into teacher training.

---

[1] *Education in Scotland in 1967*, p 68.
[2] By the provision of the Teachers' Salaries (Scotland) Regulations, 1966, married women teachers were able to secure incremental placing for half the period of their absence from teaching. Part-time teaching also became pensionable.

Nevertheless, the present situation gives no cause for complacency: women in training still outnumber men by more than 4 to 1, prospective teachers of practical and aesthetic subjects are inadequate for current needs, and well-qualified graduates in mathematics and science scarce. Failure to recruit good honours graduates is a cause for concern. In 1967, for example, Aberdeen College of Education reported that, in the preceding three years, only 4·6 per cent of its graduate students had first class degrees compared with 25 per cent in pre-war years.[1] Latterly, teaching has come to have fewer attractions for men with ordinary degrees, who see little chance of promotion in the new comprehensive system. A recent Jordanhill survey covering over 300 honours and ordinary graduates noted a disturbing proportion of "second choice, uncertain or reluctant entrants to the profession".[2] In the future it may well be that the needs of secondary schools will stimulate other universities to follow Stirling's lead and launch concurrent degree courses, or will lead to novel experiments with the schools themselves taking more responsibility for training graduate teachers.

The deeper challenge is one of purpose and ends. It is perhaps not surprising that students have been critical of aspects of their course work.[3] The times demand consideration of objectives. What do teachers need to know? What sort of persons should they be? How can they be prepared to bridge the gap between the generations, even to face the cultural shock which may await them when they meet their pupils? How can they be helped to understand the emotional and social problems of those who are groping their way to maturity? How can they be encouraged to take children into active partnership in their own education? The questions are inescapable.

For too long, professional training has suffered from the

[1] *Aberdeen College of Education Triennial Report*, 1964-7, pp 6-7. (Aberdeen gives its "wastage" rates as 10 per cent.)
[2] J Elliot, Three articles on graduate entry based on a sample of 317 graduates. (Men students in particular were predominantly working class. Only 7 per cent had fathers holding a university degree.) *Times Educational Supplement* (*Scotland*), 26 April 1968, 3 May 1968, 10 May 1968.
[3] eg, *Higher Education*, Cmnd 2154-VIII, p 896; Paul Kline, An Investigation into the Attitudes to their Teacher Training of Teachers with Two Years' Experience, Unpublished EdB thesis, University of Aberdeen, 1963, p 35. (Two-thirds of those who replied to a questionnaire were hostile to their teacher-training course.)

image of the past. The older forms of apprenticeship, the pupil-teacher system and junior studentships, have long since disappeared. The former prison terminology has been discarded: students are no longer "inmates", nor members of staff "officers". Nor do students today struggle in penury, for the great majority (apart from those whose parents can afford to pay) receive from the central Department, awards which cover their expenses. There still remain survivals from a previous age: terms (such as the "crit" and "parchment"), drab buildings (bleak reminders of the board school era for which they were designed), and conservative attitudes which hinder the adoption of new study patterns and bring problems of discipline.

For too long the influence of the past dominated and depressed teacher education. The changes of recent years have dispelled many of those influences. Today, perhaps the most striking feature is the autonomy of the colleges. It is the new independence combined with the extension in the scope of work, the improvement in facilities and structures of the older colleges (Aberdeen College has now been rehoused and new buildings are planned for Dundee) and the injection of ideas which has brought a liberality unknown before.

Yet many problems remain. The building programme, which began so belatedly, lags far behind current needs. More importantly, if the colleges are to prepare students to work in the spirit of the recent Reports, they must consider not merely the content of their courses and methods of instruction but also the whole problem of personal relationships. Students cannot be encouraged to experiment and to become "critically empirical" in their attitudes unless they can have a sense of confidence in their own competence and judgment. Their continued growth and their capacity for self-renewal will depend very largely on their freedom as students to make mistakes, on their opportunities for genuine inquiry and discussion and on their belief that they are respected as individuals.

In Scottish education the austere traditions have lingered long. In the past many children have left school at the earliest opportunity, conscious of being "rejects" in a system geared to academic achievement. Of those who have gone forward to higher education, too few have had the experience of working independently or have had opportunity of "human exchange", of the sort of conversation and discussion which would have helped them to mature as people. They "have been made to respect authority too soon and too much".[1]

Today the diversity of the teacher's rôle requires that professional preparation should be more than an extension of general culture and an initiation into technical skills. It must include the development of attitudes and insights, the fostering of qualities of character on which personal relationships depend. As Sir James J Robertson, a headmaster for 33 years, has said, the teacher's success in dealing with his pupils "will be a function of a deep and abiding respect for them as persons possessed of human dignity and worth, but denied assurance and understanding which the years somehow bring to us all".[2]

In the context of our own age we have come back to the ideals, intellectual, moral, social and emotional, of the early pioneers of teacher training. John Wood's emphasis on grasp of language, on the comprehension of words, has a significance today when the power of communication is recognised as the key to the quality of life. Similarly, David Stow's emphasis on joyousness and spontaneity in school and playground, and his stress on family relationships between teacher and children are in tune with our own ideas.

A century and a half ago Wood and Stow had the courage and the vision to meet the needs of the new industrial era. The explosive change of a technological age presents a challenge no less profound. On the teacher as the pivot of education, the future depends.

---

[1] "Ill-taught Languages", Derek Bowman, *Times Educational Supplement* (*Scotland*), 17 May 1968.
[2] From "Reflections of a Headmaster". A talk given to a group of secondary school headteachers of the West Riding. Published in *Children in Distress*, Alec Clegg and Barbara Megson, Penguin Education Special, 1968, p 94.

APPENDIX A

I. Extract from the *First Book of Discipline*, which was sanctioned by the General Assembly, 29 May 1560, and subscribed by a great portion of the members of the Privy Council.

"Of necessitie, therefore, we judge it, that every several kirke have one schoolmaister appointed, such a one at least as is able to teach grammar and the Latine tongue, if the town be of any reputation: If it be upaland, where the people convene to the doctrine but once in the week, then must either the reader or the minister there appointed, take care of the children and youth of the parish, to instruct them in the first rudiments especially in the Catechisme . . . And, furder, we think it expedient, that in every notable town, and specially in the town of the superintendent, there be erected a colledge, in which the arts, at least logic and rhetoricke, together with the tongues, be read by sufficient masters, for whom honest stipends must be appointed: As also provision for those that be poore, and not able by themselves nor by their friends to be sustained at letters, and, in speciall, those that come from landward. . . ." In consequence it was envisaged that "first, the youth-head and tender children shall be nourished and brought up in vertue, in presence of their friends. . . . Secondly, the exercise of children in every kirke shall be great instruction to the aged. Last, the great schooles called the universities, shall be replenished with those that shall be apt to learning, for this must be carefully provided that no father, of what estate or condition that ever he may be, use his children at his own fantasie, especially in their youth-head; but all must be compelled to bring up their children in learning and vertue."

II. *Major Legislation*

1696 *Act for Settling of Schools*, William III, cap 26

"That there shall be a School settled and established, and a Schoolmaster appointed in every Parish not already provided, by Advice of the Heritors and Minister of the Parish; and for that Effect, that the Heritors in every parish meet, and provide a commodious House for a School and settle and modify a

218

Sallary to a Schoolmaster, which shall not be under one hundred Merks, nor above two hundred Merks, to be paid Yearly at two Terms, Whitsunday and Martinmas by equal Portions."

1803 *Act for making better provision for the Parochial Schoolmasters, and for making further regulations for the better government of the Parish Schools in Scotland*, 43 Geo 3, cap 54

Future salaries of parochial school masters shall not be "under the sum of 300 merks Scots per annum nor above the sum of 400 merks Scots per annum". They were to be revised every 25 years or fixed accordingly to "the value or average price of a chalder of oatmeal for all Scotland".

The schoolmaster was to be provided with a house "not consisting of more than 2 Apartments including the Kitchen".

1838 *Act to facilitate the foundation and endowment of additional schools in Scotland*, 1 and 2 Vict, cap 87

Additional parish schools to be established, "parliamentary schools", built with aid of a government grant in *quoad sacra* parishes.

The parish schoolmaster's house was now to consist of "no less than two Rooms besides the Kitchen".

1861 *Parochial and Burgh Schoolmasters (Scotland) Act*, 24 and 25 Vict, cap 107

Salaries of schoolmaster were to be not less than £35 nor more than £70.

Heritors were permitted to employ a female teacher to give instruction in "branches of Female Industrial and Household training as well as of Elementary Education". The female teacher's salary was not to exceed £30 a year.

Schoolmasters were no longer required to sign the Confession of Faith. The examination of schoolmasters was withdrawn from the Presbyteries and made the responsibility of the universities.

1872 *Education (Scotland) Act*, 35 and 36 Vict, cap 62

Made provision for the establishment of school boards and the transfer of parochial and burgh schools to the new authorities.

1892 *Education and Local Taxation Account (Scotland) Act*, 55 and 56 Vict, cap 51

Allocated public money to aid the cost of secondary education.

1901 *Education (Scotland) Act*, 1 and 2 Edw 7, cap 9

Abolished exemptions from compulsory attendance at 13. (School leaving age therefore effectively raised to 14.)

1908 *Education (Scotland) Act*, 7 and 8 Edw 7, cap 9

Establishment of medical inspection of school children. Provision of school meals, transport etc became permissive.

1918 *Education (Scotland) Act*, 8 and 9 Geo 5, cap 48

Swept away the parish school boards and established *ad hoc* authorities for each county and for five scheduled burghs. Church Schools were brought into the national system.

1945 *Education (Scotland) Act*, 8 and 9 Geo 6, cap 37

Education to be organised in three progressive stages: primary, secondary and further.   School leaving age to be raised to 15. (In fact it was raised in 1947.)

1965 *Teaching Council (Scotland) Act*, chap 19

Made provision for the control of the teaching profession in such matters as recognition, probation and discipline to pass from the Secretary of State to the General Teaching Council for Scotland.

APPENDIX B

HEADS OF INSTITUTIONS AND LEADING OFFICIALS CONNECTED WITH TEACHER TRAINING, 1835 TO THE PRESENT DAY

I Rectors of the Presbyterian Colleges, 1835 to 1907

GLASGOW

1836-37   Rev John M'Crie

1839-45   Rev Robert Cunningham   Teacher at Edinburgh Hill Street "Academy," and in USA. Later became Rector of Blair Lodge Academy, Polmont (a private foundation)

Church of Scotland

1845-49   Interregnum in Rectorship

1849-67   Joseph Douglas (from Lochmaben Sessional School)

1868-77   James Leitch   formerly Lecturer in History. Wrote Practical Educationalists and their Systems of Teaching. Resigned after student mutiny.

1877-99   *David Ross (Rector of Gartsherrie Academy, had been a pupil teacher, trained in the Normal School '62-3, before becoming classical master in Banff). Author of Fifty Years of the Training System, 1886 Education as a University Subject, 1883

1899   Alex M Williams   formerly Lecturer in English and Science, 1890-9, and at Aberdeen 1887-90

Free Church

1845-49   Robert Hislop   formerly Headmaster of the Senior Practising School. Left to become Rector of Blair Lodge Academy (after Robt Cunningham). (Maurice Paterson, later Rector of Moray House, married his daughter.)

1852-98   Thomas Morrison   formerly Rector of the Free Church School, Inverness. Author of Manual of School Management. (Morrison's brother, Donald, was Rector of Glasgow Academy)

1898- 1902   *John Adams   formerly Rector of Free Church College, Aberdeen. Author of Herbartian Psychology applied to Education, 1897; became first Professor of Education, London University

* University Lecturers

GLASGOW—continued

Church of Scotland	Free Church
	1902-05 *John Alison* (Mathematical master in George Watson's College, Edinburgh)
	1905- *T M Morrison* (died 1908) (Lecturer in Classics and Science) Son of Thomas Morrison – see above

EDINBURGH

Church of Scotland	Free Church
1835-40 *John Wood* (Sheriff of Peebles). (Wood emigrated to USA in 1840)	*Thomas Oliphant*
1841-45 *Thomas Oliphant*	1845-46 *James Fulton* (died in office)
1845-53 *Rev G S Davidson* formerly Assistant to the Professor of Greek, Aberdeen	1846-55
	1855-63 *James Sime* formerly Assistant to the Professor of Natural Philosophy, Edinburgh. Works included *Manual of Religious Knowledge*
1854-86 *James Currie* formerly Master of Heriot's Hospital and Mathematical lecturer for 6 years in the college. Author of many works including *Principles and Practice of Early and Infant School Education.* Died in office	1864- *Maurice Paterson* formerly Assistant at Blair Lodge Academy under Robert Hislop. Resigned on transfer of college to Provincial Committee 1906-7. Author of various articles and editor of a standard series of reading books for schools

1886–
1903   Peter McKinlay
       formerly Chief Assistant to the Rector.
       Trained in the college

1903– Alexander Morgan
       formerly Lecturer in the college

ABERDEEN

Church of Scotland

1874– **Joseph Ogilvie*
       formerly Headmaster of Keith Public School.
       Resigned on transfer of college to Provincial
       Committee 1906-7

Free Church

1875-90 Alexander Ramage
         formerly Headmaster of Charlotte Street
         School, Aberdeen

1890-98 *John Adams* (appointed to become Rector of
         Glasgow Free Church College, 1898)

1898–   *George Smith*
         formerly Rector of Elgin Academy. Appointed
         Director of Studies in the Provincial Centre,
         1906

* University Lecturer

II *Directors of Studies under the Provincial Committees, 1906-59*

GLASGOW

1906-18	Donald Macleod	*formerly* Rector of Hamilton Academy
1919-24	Hugh McCallum	*formerly* Principal Lecturer of the Methods Department. Had earlier been on the staff of the Glasgow Pupil Teacher Institute
1924-40	George A Burnett	*formerly* Director of Studies, Aberdeen
1940-49	William Kerr	*formerly* Assistant Director of Studies
1949-	Henry P Wood	*formerly* Depute Director of Studies

EDINBURGH

1907-20	John King	*formerly* Headmaster of Boroughmuir Higher Grade Public School, Edinburgh
1920-25	Alexander Morgan	*formerly* Rector of the Church of Scotland College
1925-51	Godfrey H Thomson	*also* Professor of Education, Edinburgh University and *formerly* Professor of Education at Newcastle
1951-	William B Inglis	*formerly* Depute Director of Studies and *prior to that* Lecturer in Education, under Dr W Boyd, at Glasgow University

ABERDEEN

P   1906-22   George Smith   *formerly* Rector of the Free Church College

1922-24   George Burnett   *formerly* Master of Method

1924-39   William A Edward   since 1919, first Executive Officer of the newly constituted authority of Roxburgh

1939-   John L Hardie   since 1934, Depute Education Officer of Edinburgh and *previously* Master of Method at Jordanhill, Glasgow

ST ANDREWS

(centres at St Andrews and Dundee under the same Director from 1907)

1906-20   James Malloch   *formerly* Headmaster of Blackness Public School and Lecturer in Education at University College, Dundee. Became Executive Officer of the National Committee, 1920

1920-25   John Davidson   *formerly* Master of Method

1925-41   William W McClelland   *also* Bell Professor of Education at the University of St Andrews. Became Executive Officer of the National Committee in 1941

1941-54   Andrew F Skinner   *also* Bell Professor of Education at the University of St Andrews. Became Professor of Education at the University of Toronto, 1954

1954-59   David Howat   *formerly* Director of Education for Perth and Kinross. He died in 1959

III *Principals of the Colleges of Education under the Scottish Council for the Training of Teachers and the General Teaching Council for Scotland 1959—*

1 *Principals of the old-established colleges (formerly Provincial Centres)*

Jordanhill (Glasgow)	*Moray House (Edinburgh)*	*Aberdeen*	*Dundee*
1959- Sir Henry P Wood, CBE t*see under* Direcors of Studies	1959-66 William B Inglis, OBE *see under* Directors of Studies 1966- Douglas M McIntosh, CBE *formerly* Director of Education, Fife	1959-61 John L Hardie *see under* Directors of Studies 1961- James Scotland *formerly* Principal Lecturer in Education, Jordanhill	1959- David E Stimpson *formerly* Assistant to the Director of Studies

2 *Principals of the Roman Catholic Colleges*

Notre Dame	*Craiglockhart*
1959-65 Sister Mary Rooney Principal since 1946 and *formerly* on the staff of the College. Became Superior 1965 1965- Sister Francis Xavier *formerly* on the staff of the College	1959- Mother Veronica Blount Principal since 1946 and *formerly* on the staff of the College

3 *Principal of Dunfermline College of Physical Education*

1959-70   Nellie Blunden (appointed 1956) *formerly* on the staff of Dartford College of Physical Education, where she had received her training

1970-   Mollie P Abbott *formerly* HMI

4 *Principals of the new Colleges*

Callendar Park (founded 1964)

1964-69   Elizabeth C F Leggatt *formerly* on the staff of Jordanhill

1969-   Charles Brown *formerly* Vice-Principal of Hamilton College of Education

Craigie (founded 1964)

1964-   Ethel M Rennie *formerly* on the staff of Jordanhill

Hamilton (founded 1966)

1966-69   William S Walker *formerly* Principal Lecturer in the Methods Dept, Jordanhill; died 1969

1969-   George Paton *formerly* Assistant Principal, Dundee College of Education

National Committee for the Training of Teachers

Chairmen

1920-23	Professor Alex Darroch
1923-27	The Very Rev John Smith, DD
1927-43	Sir Henry S Keith
1943-49	C W Sleigh, CBE
1949-51	William Fife
1951-55	F R Blair
1955-59	A S Lawson

Executive Officers

1920-26	James Malloch
1926-41	J R Peddie, CBE
1941-59	W W McClelland, CBE

Scottish Council for the Training of Teachers

Chairmen

1959-61	Sir James J Robertson, OBE
1961-67	David Lees, CBE

Secretary

1959-67	George D Gray

General Teaching Council for Scotland

Chairman

1966-	David Lees, CBE

Registrar

1966-	George D Gray

APPENDIX C

I *George Combe, 1788-1858*, Phrenologist

In 1819 Combe wrote *Essays on Phrenology*, and in 1823 he formed Phrenological Society. His chief interest was in education and he advocated a system of national secular education. He taught in and helped to support a school established on his principles, in Edinburgh, in 1848. His voluminous correspondence (in the National Library of Scotland) reveals his extensive contacts. S S Laurie, for example, enburdens himself on his trials as a private tutor and his disappointment at not securing appointment to HM Inspectorate.

An account of Combe's work is given in *Education, its Principles and Practice as developed by George Combe*. Ed William Jolly, London 1879.

Combe visited USA 1838-40 and had some contact with Horace Mann to whom he described Stow's training system.

He described with the aid of a sketch Stow's original normal school in his *Notes on the United States of North America during a Phrenological Visit in 1838-39-40*, vol III, Edinburgh 1841, Appendix 445 *et seq*.

"The buildings consist of a central compartment, and two wings running back in the form of parallelograms, and enclosing on three sides a space used as exercise ground for the normal students. The buildings front the City Road, and a street runs parallel to the boundary wall on the north side. On either side, and behind the buildings, there are vacant spaces occupied as playgrounds, each school having one attached."

He went on to describe the lay-out of the normal school. Standing in front of the seminary there was, he said, on the ground floor, a house for the janitor and rooms for the secretary and rector. On the second floor, there was a hall and classrooms for the normal students, and in the attic storey, a room lighted from the roof, to be used as a classroom for drawing.

On the *right* wing of the building there was, on the ground floor, the infant school and on the second storey, a school of industry in which there were girls of 10 years of age and upwards. In addition to the reading of the Scriptures, to writing and arithmetic they were

229

taught sewing and knitting. Behind the school of industry, were apartments for the master of the infant school.

On the *left* wing of the building there was on the ground floor a juvenile school for children 6-14, under two masters each having an assistant, and on the second storey there was a private seminary.

II *John Kerr, 1824-1907*

Career

Kerr was born at Ardrossan, Ayrshire. His father removed to Skye when the boy was very young and he received part of his education at a parish school in Skye. He attended classes at Glasgow University, 1841-9.

In the latter part of his university career he came under the influence of the new Professor of Natural Philosophy, William Thomson. Thomson converted the old wine-cellar of his house into a physical laboratory and Kerr was one of the students who worked in what was known as the "coal-hole". He was a divinity student at the Free Church College in Glasgow, but did not apparently go on to take up clerical duties. Instead, he taught for a time, before his appointment as Lecturer in Mathematics at the Glasgow Free Church Training College.

Publications

1867   *Elementary Treatise on Rational Mechanics*
1875-88   Papers published in the *Philosophical Magazine* on his two great discoveries, concerned with the electromagnetic character of light: the birefringence produced in glass and other insulators when placed in intense electric field, and the change produced in polarised light by its reflection from the polished pole of a magnet.

Honours

1868   Awarded Honorary LLD, University of Glasgow
1890   Elected a Fellow of the Royal Society
1898   Awarded Royal Medal of the Society
1902   Awarded a Civil List pension of £100 a year

The writer of his obituary notice for the Royal Society noted that Kerr was 51, when he published his first scientific paper. He concluded, "the name of this quiet and unostentatious teacher and experimentalist will be linked for all time with that of Faraday".

Information from *The Times*, 19th August 1907; *Nature* (1907), vol 76, 576-6; *Royal Society, Obituary notices of Fellows deceased,* 1909, i-v.

Extracts on Kerr from the Glasgow Free Church Training College Literary Society Magazine, 1891

OUR LECTURERS

II *Dr Kerr*

There is an idea abroad that Dr Kerr is extremely old. He is familiarly known as "Old John", and whenever any former students pay a visit to the scene of their former struggles and triumphs they are sure to ask, "And how is old Dr Kerr?" As a matter of fact, however, he is not by any means the oldest man in the place, and he is certainly showing no signs of failing strength. So far as appearances go, we may safely conclude that for years to come the classes in the Normal will have the pleasure of receiving Dr Kerr's ministrations.

As a teacher Dr Kerr is unfortunate. He is a thorough master of every subject he teaches, and no one knows better how to make a difficult point perfectly clear, but his classes do not attend to him, so his pearls are cast, so to speak, before – well, perhaps it is better to leave the metaphor incomplete. It is, however, a matter for regret that it is so clearly impossible to attend to Dr Kerr's lessons. He knows pure mathematics as well as any man in Scotland, and his text-book of mechanics was what earned him his degree of LLD, but his methods are not those which are most attractive to young students of science. He loves to state everything as a general proposition, and he is so extremely theoretical in his methods that we find some difficulty in following him. The result is that we condemn his book as useless when as a matter of fact it is too good for us to appreciate it.

Considering the very shabby way in which we treat Dr Kerr, it is pleasant to notice that he always seems perfectly happy. Whenever the noise is so moderate that he can get on somehow, he goes faithfully through his proofs in blissful ignorance of the fact that nobody is following them, and points out their salient features with all the enthusiasm of a lover.

In fact, it is a pity that Dr Kerr did not long ago give his whole time up to study. His heart is in the pursuit of science, and his spare hours have already been fruitful in results of the very highest value. It is to him that science owes the experiments which have shown conclusively the intimate connection that exists between magnetism and light, and thus made a great advance towards the full understanding of the relations between the great physical forces. Every holiday is seized by Dr Kerr as an opportunity for conducting some of the experiments in which he is engaged, and we cannot avoid the conclusion that science would benefit very much more from Dr Kerr's genius if he were to free himself from the distraction of teaching a lot of students who persistently refuse to learn.

Dr Kerr is an intimate friend of Sir William Thomson, another splendid man of science whose teaching does not increase his reputation. It was doubtless at his suggestion that Dr Kerr was elected a Fellow of the Royal Society about a year ago, and a conspicuous token of his friendship is an instrument which Dr Kerr cherishes with quite a fatherly affection, being no less than the second quadrant electrometer that Sir William made, he himself being in possession of the first.

The fact that Dr Kerr is a widower and possesses a daughter has naturally suggested that at some period he must have been in "the state bordering on" matrimony. Many are the stories told of this interesting stage in Dr Kerr's career, and though I cannot guarantee authenticity some of them are quite worth repeating, apart altogether from the question of their genuineness.

Dr Kerr was originally intended to be a minister, and was actually licensed, but even in his student days he gave signs of being absorbed in mathematics. It is said that his aunt would announce that tea was ready, and that in about a quarter of an hour he would look up from the problem in which he had been engaged and ask, "Were you speaking, aunt?"

However, we have wandered a little from our intended narration of Dr Kerr's love experiences.

We are told that it was Mrs Kerr who became enamoured of him, and it is generally assumed that the idea of a proposal of marriage on Dr Kerr's part may be at once dismissed as absurd. However that may be, the story runs that the young lady got her father to engage young Mr Kerr to coach her in various subjects, and that he used to go to her house on certain evenings at six o'clock. One afternoon he was engaged on a problem of unusual intricacy, and after a long study of it he suddenly thought of his engagement for six o'clock. He found that it was half past five, and he had hurried away to the house of the young lady and rung several times before he noticed that the blinds were down and there was a strange absence of traffic in the streets. After a period of silent meditation it gradually dawned upon him that it must be six am.

The paper on Dr Kerr in our last number gave rise to an interesting discussion, and one of the anecdotes we got, relating to Dr Kerr's absence of mind, has been almost paralleled since our last meeting.

*   *   *

It was to the effect that one day on leaving his class he forgot to visit the lecturers' room, and was found shortly afterwards walking leisurely along Sauchiehall Street with his box of chalk in one hand and his pointer in the other.

*   *   *

Only the other week, however, the second year gentlemen saw Dr Kerr walk bravely up the playground, holding up an umbrella in the teeth of the wind and rain. It was only when he collided with the brick wall at the back of Russell Street that he appreciated the situation and walked philosophically back again.

*   *   *

In the class Dr Kerr has been as full of unconscious and of intentional jokes as ever. He no doubt meant to be funny when he told us that some of us were very obliging at assisting him, especially about the end of the hour; but his best joke was evidently unintentional.

*   *   *

A student said that the kinetic energy of a point moving uniformly in a circular path was

$$\tfrac{1}{2}\frac{v}{r};$$

whereupon Dr Kerr asked in an excited tone, "Where did you get that 'half'?"

APPENDIX D

I *Salaries of Scottish School Teachers*

Salaries of dominies* determined by law 1696-1861
(stated in merks until 1861)

	Minimum			Maximum		
1696	£5	11	$1\frac{1}{3}$	£11	2	$0\frac{2}{3}$
1803	16	13	2	22	4	$1\frac{1}{3}$
1828	25	13	3	34	4	$4\frac{1}{2}$
1861	35	0	0	70	0	0

* Applicable only to those dominies who were in charge of parochial schools. (They also drew school fees and sometimes boarding fees.)

Average salaries of certificated teachers 1872-1918[1]

	Men	Women
1873	£110	£58
1883	135	67
1893	135	64
1903	148	74
1913	166	87

[1] From *Reports of Committee of Council on Education*

Minimum salary scales 1919-39 (Certain authorities, notably Glasgow and Edinburgh, paid more)

	Certificated non-graduates		Graduates (General Certificate)		Graduates (Chapter V)	
	Men	*Women*	*Men*	*Women*	*Men*	*Women*
1919	£150–£250	£130–£200	£200–£360	£180–£300	£250–£400	£200–£350
1928	£150–£250	£130–£200	£200–£360	£180–£300	£250–£400	£200–£350

1931-2 cut in salaries was restored in 1935.

National Salary scales 1945—

Examples of revisions which have been triennial or biennial

	Certificated non-graduates	Ordinary Graduates		Honours Graduates	
	Women only	*Men*	*Women*	*Men*	*Women*
1945	£260–£460	£345–£590	£320–£460	£400–£650	£350–£550
1956	£470–£780	*Men and Women** £575–£985 (primary)	£600–£1,040 (secondary)	*Men and Women** 1st and 2nd class degrees £675–£1,200	
1968	£730–£1,465	£860–£1,640	£965–£1,745	£1,075–£2,075	

* Equal pay became fully operative in 1961.

Note: A full-scale study of teachers' salaries relative to changing money values would provide a valuable research topic.

II Statistics for Schools, Scholars and Teachers

Key dates in the history of teacher training	Inspected Schools Public and Grant aided	Children	Certificated teachers
1872 Education Act	2,192	225,300	2,663 (3,759 pupil teachers)
1885 Independence of Scotch Education Department	3,081	455,655	6,365 (3,693 pupil teachers)
1905 Teacher Training under Provincial Committees	3,244	696,381	13,604 (4,191 pupil teachers)
1920 Teacher Training under a National Committee	3,456	870,372	24,792
1959 Teacher Training associated with Scottish Council for Training of Teachers	3,316	892,100	36,984
1967 Institutions autonomous – General Teaching Council	3,164	933,465	42,986

III *Numbers of Teachers in Training 1872 to present day*

	Students		Colleges
1872	729		5
1878	1,039	(thereafter fixed at 860 until 1894)	7
1895	996		9
1905	1,412	(+333 King's Students under Local Committees)	9
1915	2,570	(including 208 graduates)	8
1935	1,770	(including 854 graduates)	8
1955	3,496	(including 475 graduates)	7
1969	12,905	(including 1,649 graduates – in addition 804 are BEd students)	10

APPENDIX E

EARLY EXAMPLES OF TIMETABLES, DUTIES, ETC

I Church of Scotland Normal School, Edinburgh

Timetable (male) 1847

(Extract from Report of Committee of Council on Education, 1847-8, p 521)

Hours am	Monday	Tuesday	Wednesday	Thursday	Friday	Saturday	Sunday
6	Dress and put rooms in order						
7 – 8	Private study and preparation in Library						
8 – 8½	[1]Prayers-Psalmody; Scripture reading and exposition; Prayer						
8½ – 9	Breakfast						
9 –10	[2] English Reading and advanced Geography	[1] McCulloch's Course; special attention to the subject of reading; Bible Lesson of the day given by Rector, or one of the Students	[2] English Reading and Etymology	[1] McCulloch's Course; special attention to the analysis of sentences; Lesson of the day given by Rector, or one of the Students	[1] Lecture on Pedagogics; Themes prescribed, and Exercises returned with comments; Physical Geography, with use of Globes	[5] Sacred Music	[1] Bible History and Doctrine, 9–10½

Hours am pm	Monday	Tuesday	Wednesday	Thursday	Friday	Saturday	Sunday
10— 3	See Elementary School Timetable						
3 – 4	[1] Latin Rudiments, Delectus and Caesar	[1] Senior Students: Virgil, and Adams' Antiquities; [2] Junior Students: Elementary Grammar and Geography	[1] Latin Rudiments, Delectus, and Caesar	Same as on Tuesday	Same as Tuesday	Private study Private study	

4 – 6   Dinner and Recreation
6 – 7   [4] Gaelic Students with Master; the others at private study
7 – 8½ [3] Euclid { Senior Section, Book IV-Algebra, Trigonometry
                  { Junior Section, Book I-Arithmetic, Algebra
8½– 9   Supper
9 – 9½ [1] Prayers
9½–10½ Private Reading; [1] occasional revisal of Latin Rudiments by Junior Students
10½   Retire for the night.   Gas extinguished at 11.

[1] Abstract of Discourses given in and revised

[1] Denotes that the Lesson or Exercise is conducted by the Rector. [2] Head Master. [3] Mathematical Tutor. [4] Gaelic Tutor.
[5] Singing Master.

II Church of Scotland Training College, Edinburgh

Food in boarding house for female students 1858

(Extract from Report of Committee of Council on Education, 1858-9, p 384)

Day	Breakfast	Lunch	Dinner	Tea	Allowance for each Person for a Week
Sunday	Tea, bread and butter	Bread and milk	Broth, beef, potatoes and vegetables	Tea, bread and butter	Tea, 2 ozs; Sugar, $\frac{3}{4}$ and 1 lb; Butter, $\frac{3}{4}$ lb; Beef, $\frac{1}{2}$ lb each time; Bread, 2 loaves; Rolls, 6
Monday	Tea, hot rolls bread and butter	Bread and butter	Broth, apple or Yorkshire dumpling	do	
Tuesday	do	do	Pea-soup, fish, bread and potatoes	do	
Wednesday	do	do	Pea-soup, roast mutton and potatoes	do	
Thursday	do	do	Rice-soup, Scotch collops and potatoes	do	
Friday	do	do	Broth, beef, potatoes and vegetables	do	
Saturday	do	do	Mince collops, cheese, bread and butter	do	

III Episcopal Church College, Edinburgh
Timetable 1869
(Extract from *Report of Committee of Council on Education, 1869-70, p 538*)

Day	7.0	8.0	9.30	10.15	11.0	11.45	12.30	1.15	2.15	4.0	5.0	5.30	6.30	7.15	8.15	9.15 / 10.0
Monday —		Arithmetic*	S Drawing* / J Scripture†	Geography* / Liturgy†	Scripture† / Drawing*	Liturgy† / Geography*	Dinner	Principal's Lecture	Recreation of one hour at least for a general walk	Recreation within the College	Private Study	Private Study	Tea and recreation	School Management‡	Music‡	Prayers and retire
Tuesday —		Arithmetic*	S Drawing* / J —	Geography* / Grammar†	Grammar† / Drawing*	— / Geography*	Dinner	Principal's Lecture	Recreation of one hour at least for a general walk	Recreation within the College	Private Study	Sewing*	Tea and recreation	Private Study	Private Study	Prayers and retire
Wednesday —		Mental Arithmetic*	S Drawing* / J —	Geography* / History†	Scripture† / Drawing*	Liturgy† / Geography*	Dinner	Principal's Lecture	Recreation of one hour at least for a general walk	Recreation within the College	Private Study	Private Study	Tea and recreation	School Management‡	Music‡	Prayers and retire
Thursday —		Arithmetic*	S Drawing* / J —	Geography* / History†	History / Drawing	Geography / Geography	Dinner	Principal's Lecture	Recreation of one hour at least for a general walk	Recreation within the College	Private Study	Sewing*	Tea and recreation	Private Study	Private Study	Prayers and retire
Friday —		Arithmetic*	S Drawing* / J Scripture†	Geography* / Liturgy†	Scripture / Drawing	Liturgy / Geography	Dinner	Principal's Lecture	Recreation of one hour at least for a general walk	Recreation within the College	Private Study	Domestic Economy*	Tea and recreation	School Management‡	Music‡	Prayers and retire
Saturday —		Private Study for Examination	Examination													
Sunday —		Private Study	Morning Service													

Saturday / Sunday (alternate time scale)

Day	9.30	10.0	1.0	2.0	4.0 / 5.0 / 5.30	6.30	8.0	9.0
Saturday	Private Study for Examination	Examination	Recreation			Private Study		
Sunday	Private Study	Morning Service	Recrea-tion	Private Study	Tea / Study		Evensong	Private Study

S Seniors J Juniors * Governess † Principal ‡ Normal Mistress

Q

IV *Free Church Training College, Edinburgh*

Timetables and duties of staff, 1878

(Extract from *Report of Committee of Council*, 1878-9, pp 288-9)

The instruction and the training of the students are conducted by the following staff:—

MALES

No	Names	Degrees	Duties	Annual Salaries £ s d
1	M Paterson	BA Edin	Principal, constantly; scripture, 5 hours; school management, 2 hours; practice of teaching, 3 hours; classics, 6½ hours.	600 0 0
2	W Lees	MA Edin	Lecturer, occasionally; mathematics, 10 hours; science, 2 hours.	160 0 0
3	Jas A Melville	Edin Univ	Lecturer, constantly; English, 5 hours; history, 2 hours; geography, 2 hours; political economy, 1 hour; science, 2 hours.	300 0 0
4	Walter Strang	—	Lecturer, occasionally; music, 4 hours.	150 0 0
5	Victor Richon	BA, LLB Paris	Lecturer, occasionally; French, 4 hours.	112 0 0
6	J H Crawford	MA Edin	Lecturer, occasionally; classics, 6 hours; mathematics, 2 hours; exercises, &c, 7 hours.	100 0 0
7	Jas B Napier	—	Teacher of drawing, 4 hours.	88 0 0
8	Thos Early and Assistant	—	Drill instructors.	10 10 0 each

MALE STUDENTS' TIMETABLE

Hours, and Class of Students		Monday	Tuesday	Wednesday	Thursday	Friday
9–10	II	Drill / English	Latin	English	Drawing	—
	I	English / Drill	Latin	Greek	Latin	—
10–11	II	Scripture	Drawing	Economy	Drill / Geography	English
	I	Drawing	Scripture	Scripture	Drawing / Drill	School Management
11–12	II	Practice of Teaching	Geometry	Practice of Teaching	Algebra	Mensuration
	I	Practice of Teaching	Music	Practice of Teaching	French	Catechism
12–1	II	Algebra	French	Algebra	Music	Teaching
	I	Geography	Geometry	History	Geometry	Algebra
1–2	II	Greek	Music	History	French	Greek
	I	Arithmetic	French	Arithmetic	Music	English
2–3	II	School Management	Physiology	Latin	Latin	Scripture
	I	Greek	Physiology	Latin	English	Latin

NB—II = Students of second year. I = Students of first year.
Science lectures: magnetism and electricity, Wednesday, 3–4; physiology, Friday, 3–4.

244 TEACHER TRAINING IN SCOTLAND

FEMALES

No	Names	Degrees	Duties	Annual Salaries £ s d
1	M Paterson	BA Edin	Principal, constantly; scripture, 4 hours; school management, 2 hours; practice of teaching, 3 hours	Vide male staff
2	M Smith	—	Lady superintendent and head of boarding-house	160 0 0
3	Jas A Melville	Edin Univ	Lecturer, constantly; English, 3 hours; history, 1 hour; geography, 1 hour; arithmetic, 6 hours	Vide male staff
4	W Strang	—	Lecturer, occasionally; music, 2 hours	Vide male staff
5	V Richon	BA, LLB Paris	Lecturer, occasionally; French, 4 hours	Vide male staff
6	Jas B Napier	—	Teacher of drawing, 4 hours	Vide male staff
7	M Shanks	—	Lecturer, occasionally; English, 3 hours; history, 2 hours; geography, 3 hours; arithmetic, 3 hours; practice of teaching, 1 hour; exercises, 2 hours	70 0 0
8	M Miller	—	Lecturer, occasionally; domestic economy, 2 hours; music, 1 hour	30 0 0
9	M Beattie	—	Teacher of sewing, 6 hours	35 0 0
10	Mrs Macpherson	—	Teacher of cooking, 12 lessons	12 12 0
11	Drill instructors	—	—	Vide male staff

FEMALE STUDENTS' TIMETABLE

Hours, and Class of Students		Monday	Tuesday	Wednesday	Thursday	Friday
9–10	II	Scripture	Drawing	Scripture	Drill / Arithmetic	—
	I	Scripture	Arithmetic	Scripture	Sewing / Drill	—
10–11	II	Mental Arithmetic	English	Domestic Economy	Practice of Teaching	Penmanship
	I	Mental Arithmetic	Sewing	Sewing	Practice of Teaching	Drawing
11–12	II	English	Scripture	Geography	Music	Drawing
	I	Drawing	French	Geography	Music	Scripture / History
12–1	II	Sewing	Music	Practice of Teaching	French	Sewing
	I	Catechism	Music	Practice of Teaching	Arithmetic	History
1–2	II	Arithmetic	School Management	Teaching	History	Sewing
	I	English	English	History	School Management	Domestic Economy
2–3	II	English	French	Sewing	Geography	Arithmetic
	I	Arithmetic	Geography	Arithmetic	French	English

NB—II = Students of second year. I = Students of first year.
Science lectures: physiology, Wednesday, 8–9 am; Friday, 8.30–9.30 am.

APPENDIX F

I EXAMPLES OF EARLY UNIVERSITY COURSES IN EDUCATION
(Extracted from David Ross, *Education as a University Subject*
Appendix 1883)

University of Edinburgh—Bell Chair of Education
Course of Lectures by PROFESSOR LAURIE, MA

1.—THE THEORY OR SCIENCE OF EDUCATION

THE END OF EDUCATION.

PHYSICAL CONDITIONS.

PSYCHOLOGY IN RELATION TO THE SCIENCE OF EDUCATION—

I. The Intelligence.
Conclusions from the Intellectual Nature of Man with reference to his Education.

II. Unfolding of Intelligence; or, Periods of Growth.
Conclusions from the Periods of Growth with reference to Education.

III. The Ethical Nature of Man.
Conclusions from the Ethical Nature of Man, with reference to Education

IV. Auxiliaries of the Processes and Growth of Mind.
Conclusions from Mental Growth with reference to Education.
The Science of Education as founded in the preceding Analysis.

2.—THE ART OF EDUCATION

THE EDUCATIVE PROCESS IN GENERAL FROM THE ETHICAL POINT OF VIEW.

I. The Real in the Educative Process—
(A) With a View to Right Judgment.
(1) The Real-Naturalistic with a view to the Elements of Right Judgment.
(2) The Real-Humanistic with a view to the Elements of Right Judgment.
(B) The Real in Education with a view to evoking the Ethical Sentiments.

246

II. The Formal in the Educative Process.
(A) Intellectual, Naturalistic, Humanistic.
(B) Ethical; with a view to Habituation to Right and Good Action.

3.—METHODICK

1. Methodick with a view to Instruction and Assimilation.
2. Methodick with a view to Power of Judgment or Discrimination.
3. Methodick with a view to Habituation to Right and Good Action.

4.—METHODOLOGY

COLLECTION OF THE PRINCIPLES AND RULES OF METHOD IN INSTRUCTION.

I. The Application of these Rules to Real Studies, viz.—
Intellectual, Naturalistic, Humanistic, and Ethical.
II. The Application to Formal Studies—
(A) Intellectual Habit.
(B) Ethical Habit.
Motives and Punishments—
(a) Inner and Attractive.
(b) Outer and Coercive.
End of the Art of Education.

5.—SCHOOLS AND THE TEACHER

School Rooms, Furniture, Apparatus, Text Books, System of State Schools, Technical Schools, Girls' Schools. The Teacher and his Education.

6.—THE HISTORY OF EDUCATION

Early Education, China, India, Persia; Greek and Roman Education; The Renaissance; Erasmus, Colet, Luther, Melanchthon; Montaigne; Ascham, Sturm; Bacon and Realism; Ratke and; Comenius; the Jesuits; Milton, Locke, Rousseau, Bassedow, Campe; Pestalozzi, Jacotot; Bell, Lancaster; Fröbel, Richter, Diesterweg; Arnold, Spencer, Bain. History of Education in Scotland; Primary Schools, Gymnasiums, and Real Schools in Germany.

(Arrangements were also made whereby selected schools were visited with a view to the observation of school-organization and methods.)

University of St Andrews—Bell Chair of Education

Course of Lectures by PROFESSOR MEIKLEJOHN, MA

This Chair contemplates the instruction and training of teachers in the Science and Art of Teaching; and the subject is divided into Three Parts:

I. THE THEORY.—The *Psychology* of the growing mind—an attempt to estimate the mode, rate, and kind of growth by experiment; and an inquiry into the relation of various kinds of knowledge to the mind, and the influence of certain thoughts, emotions, and sets of circumstances upon the character. The growth of the senses, the memory, the understanding, the reason, the will, the imagination, the social emotions. The relation of the religious, moral, and intellectual sides of human nature to each other. The building up of a sound understanding, the formation of a just habit of action. The theories and writings of the best thinkers upon education.

II. THE HISTORY.—History of the notions regarding education, the chief educational ideas of the East, of Greece and Rome, of the Jews, of Early, Medieval, and Reformed Christianity, of the Jesuits, and of the great men who have practised, or thought and written on, education. Bacon, Selden, Milton, Locke, Jean Paul, Gœthe, Herbert Spencer; the educational ideas and processes of Comenius, Pestalozzi, Ratich, Jacotot, Diesterweg, Fröbel, &c.; the educational aims, beliefs, habits, and processes of the national systems which exist in Germany, France, England, and other countries.

III. THE PRACTICE.—The processes employed in the schools of this country—the relation of these processes to the growth of the mind, and their value considered as means to ends—the teaching of languages—the difficulties, either inherent in the language or adherent to the circumstances under which it is taught. The difference of aim in teaching classical and modern languages, and the consequent difference in means. Science, especially the sciences of observation, and the necessary conditions under which these must be taught. The more usual school subjects—such as History, Geography, Grammar, English, Composition, &c. Text-books—the mental outfit of a Teacher, his aims, his practical ends, and the means to these; his difficulties, his rewards; the nature and limitations of his profession, its advantages.

II ADAMS'S COURSE IN EDUCATION AT UNIVERSITY OF GLASGOW
Extracts from *University of Glasgow Calendar, 1901-2*, pp 77, 495-6

EDUCATION
THEORY, ART, AND HISTORY OF EDUCATION
This Lectureship was instituted by the University in 1894

Lecturers   1894. DAVID ROSS, MA, BSc, LLD
              1899. JOHN ADAMS, MA, BSc

The Education Class meets daily at 3.30 pm. The course consists of one hundred lectures qualifying for graduation in Arts.

A. THEORY.—Application of Logic, Psychology and Ethics to Education; child mind; temperament; suggestion; habit; will; character.

B. ART.—Communication between minds; language; illustration; graphic methods; sequence of studies; form and matter.

C. HISTORY.—Conspectus of educational systems; development of educational ideals; comparative education.

Books for class work.—Davidson's *Aristotle and the Ancient Educational Ideals; Herbartian Psychology applied to Education* (Isbister); Locke's *Thoughts on Education*; Herbert Spencer's *Education*; Ascham's *Scholemaster*, Book I.

Examination paper in Education (1901) for ordinary Degree of MA

FIRST PAPER—THREE HOURS

1. Explain and discuss the place of Music in Hellenic Systems of Education.

2. Relate Aristotle's Educational System to his theory of the State.

3. Give the substance of Locke's teaching as to (*a*) Sauntering, (*b*) Reasoning with Children, (*c*) Breeding, (*d*) Learning to read, (*e*) Learning by heart.

4. Contrast the views of Locke and Mr Herbert Spencer with regard to Physical Education.

5. Estimate the Natural Reactions Theory of punishment as presented by Rousseau and Spencer.

6. Expound the Herbartian theory of the formation of Apperception Masses, and note educational applications.

7. Give, with a running commentary, Rousseau's views on the teaching of Drawing and of Geography.

8. Explain the following, giving the Context in each case:—
   (*a*) From Rousseau's *Emile*.
      (1) The happiest treatise on Natural Education.
      (2) Present interest is the grand motive power.
      (3) I am preaching to you a difficult art.
   (*b*) From Spencer's *Education*.
      (1) The natural history of Society.
      (2) The leisure part of Education.
      (3) Do not expect from a child any great amount of moral goodness.

SECOND PAPER—THREE HOURS

1. Explain exactly the nature of Habit; and let your answer bring out the meaning of (a) instinct, (b) plasticity, (c) impulse, (d) accommodation.

2. Explain *briefly* the following terms (a) the *free* arts, (b) the strongest motive, (c) the socius, (d) the quadrivium, (e) continuum, (f) Chantry Schools.

3. Describe the general nature of fatigue, and indicate the relation between the practice effect and the fatigue effect in mental work. From our knowledge of fatigue, what conclusions may we draw for our guidance in the work of teaching?

4. Give an account of the three stages in the systematic development of the content of the mind.

5. Show the importance of the distinction between retaining and recalling as functions of Memory. Mark off the sphere of memory from that of imagination in the ordinary work of reproducing past experiences.

6. Distinguish between (a) correlation and co-ordination in the development of the child's powers, (b) convergent and divergent association, (c) spontaneous and voluntary attention.

7. What are the essentials of the Socratic Method? To which subjects may it be best applied in school? What limitations are necessary in order that it may be successfully used with children?

8. The place of Imitation as a motor influence in Education; *or* the Influence of the idea of Development on Educational Theory.

APPENDIX G

I *Aberdeen Provincial Centre*
Outline of Courses in Ethics, Logic and Psychology in
(1) 1923-4, (2) 1931-2

Extracts from Aberdeen Training Centre Handbooks

1 Courses 1923-4

Ethics

1. The nature and scope of Ethics; relation to Education.

2. The psychological bases of moral action. The moralisation of instincts and desires. Phenomenon of Will. Sketch of what self-realisation for human being involves.

3. Stages in moral growth. The authority of Conscience. Worth of Sanctions of Morality.

4. Character. Relative importance of heredity and environment in formation of character. Defects of character and their remedies. Function of Punishment.

5. Motive, Intention. Consequences as subject of moral judgment.

6. Different theories of moral end. Pleasure for pleasure's sake. Duty for duty's sake. Happiness as defined by Plato and T. H. Green.

7. The individual and society.

Books recommended—

G. A. Johnston, "An Introduction to Ethics"; J. S. Mackenzie, "Manual of Ethics"; J. H. Muirhead, "Elements of Ethics"; J. Dewey and J. H. Tufts, "Ethics"; MacGunn, "The Making of Character"; Plato, "Republic"; J. Seth, "A Study of Ethical Principles".

Logic

1. The nature of Logic and its divisions.

2. Knowledge and language; terms, their kinds; connotation and denotation.

3. Definition and its fallacies.

4. Division and classification.

5. Propositions, their kinds and interpretations.

6. Opposition and immediate inference.

7. Deductive inference; function, rules and fallacies of the syllogism.

8. Inductive inference—The method of establishing general laws.

9. The estimation of evidence; observation, experiment and testimony.

10. Perfect Induction—Induction by Simple Enumeration; Induction by discovery of cause.

11. Principle of Uniformity of Nature—Scientific definition of Cause.

12. Mill's Methods of Induction.

13. Induction of Verification of Hypothesis.

14. Reasoning from Analogy.

15. Logic and Education.

Books recommended—
Prof. Jevons, "A Primer of Logic"; L. J. Russell, "Logic from Standpoint of Education"; Welton, "The Logical Basis of Education"; Welton and Monahan, "Intermediate Logic".

Psychology

I. Analysis—First Year

1. Introduction. The study of psychology. Value of experiment in psychological method.

2. The stream of consciousness; its general conditions; the subconscious and the unconscious in mind.

3. Mind and body, the facts as to their relation. Sensation, Feeling, Will.

4. Characteristics of Consciousness—(1) Apperception, Activity, Work, and Fatigue.

5. Characteristics of Consciousness—(2) Habit, Adaptation, Association.

6. Perception, Imagery, Idea.

7. The perception of space—Illusions of perception

8. Sensation. Introductory—Visual Sensations, facts and theories.

9. Sensation—Tactual, Auditory and Sensations.

10. Mental elements and combinations—Self-consciousness—Resumé.

II. Development—Second Year

1. Mind and Life; the function of mind in evolution; animal psychology.
2. Reflex and instructive action: their relation to consciousness.
3. Imitation, Play; development of intelligence in animals.
4. Assimilation and association of ideas.
5. Memory, its forms and conditions.
6. Factors in the mental development of the child, individual, social, etc.
7. Suggestion, Judgment, Belief.
8. Feeling, Emotion, Temperament.
9. Development of Imagination—Types of Mental Imagery.
10. Mental Activity—General conditions of mental growth and decay. Conclusion.

Books recommended for study—
First Course—Mellone and Drummond, "Elements of Psychology"; Wm McDougall, "Physiological Psychology"; C Myers, "Experimental Psychology"; L Witmer, "Analytical Psychology"; Wm James, Text-book of Psychology"; E B Titchener, "Text-book of Psychology."

Second Course—W B Drummond, "An Introduction to Child-study"; Francis Galton, "Inquiry into Human Faculty"; Ed Claparède, "Experimental Pedagogy" (trans. Lough and Holman); H J Watt, "Economy and Training of Memory"; Dr Drever, "Instinct in Man"; Dr Rusk, "Experimental Education"; Wm McDougall, "Social Psychology."

2 Courses 1931-2

Ethics

1. The nature and scope of Ethics: its relation to Education.
2. The psychological basis of morality.
3. The meaning of morality; its relation to the intrinsic values.
4. Stages in moral growth.
5. Methods of developing character.
6. Different theories of the moral end.

Books recommended—
Muirhead, "Elements of Ethics"; Hobhouse, "The Rational Good"; Everitt, "Moral Values"; Ross, "Social Psychology"; Burt, "The Young Delinquent"; Adler, "The Education of Children."

Logic

1. The nature of Logic and its divisions.
2. The Logic of terms and its application to teaching.
3. Propositions and their meanings.
4. The evaluation of evidence.
5. Induction: the scientific methods.
6. Analogy.
7. Immediate Inference and Deduction.
8. Inference in children.

Books recommended for reference—

Welton and Monahan, "Intermediate Logic"; Wolf, "Text-book of Logic"; Joseph, "Introduction to Logic"; Westaway, "Scientific Method"; Stebbing, "A Modern Introduction to Logic."

Psychology

There are three courses on Psychology: (i) Graduates attend sixty of the seventy-five lectures which constitute the Ordinary Course at the University; (ii) those who are not Graduates attend a Special Course of sixty lectures; (iii) those who wish to study Infant Psychology attend a Special Course of thirty lectures which includes practice in the application of mental tests to children.

The Course for two-year students covers the following subjects:—

1. The aims and data of Psychology.
2. The introspective and objective methods of studying mental facts.
3. The body in relation to the mind.
4. Sensation.
5. Perception.
6. Imagination.
7. Memory.
8. Reasoning.
9. Learning.
10. Feeling and desire.
11. Instinct and emotion.
12. The development of character.
13. The applications of Psychology.
14. Mental tests.

II *National Committee for the Training of Teachers*
EDUCATION—FINAL JOINT EXAMINATION
Friday, 30th May, 1924.   10 AM to 12.30 PM

Answer FIVE questions, viz., the whole of Section A, TWO questions from Section B, and ONE question from Section C. Twenty marks are assigned to each question.

Section A
(The whole of this Section should be answered)

1. What principles should guide the teacher in drawing up the curriculum for any stage of advancement, eg, the Infant School, *or* the Senior Division, *or* the Secondary School?

Show how any *one* of the subjects of instruction—eg, Nature Study, *or* Arithmetic, *or* History—would be affected by the application of these principles.

2. Enumerate the chief educative agencies, other than the school itself, under which the pupil is brought during school life, and estimate the influence which each exerts on the growth of his mind and character.

Section B
(Two questions to be answered)

3. What is meant by the "Corporate Life" of the school? Estimate its effect upon the individual pupil, and suggest any ways in which it may be promoted and utilised.

4. What light does the study of Fatigue in school throw upon the problems of school organisation and class management?

5. What do you understand by "Interest"? Can it be regarded as an aim in Education? How is Interest related *either* to effort *or* to attention?

6. Write short notes, not exceeding ten lines each, on any *four* of the following:—Auto-education, the Recapitulation Theory, the Discipline of Natural Consequences, the Dalton Plan, the Play-way, the Project Method.

7. Explain and comment on the following statement:—

"Education is the instrument used by society for conserving its culture and providing efficient men and women for carrying forward the work to be done."

8. Discuss the advantages and disadvantages of class teaching and individual work respectively.

Section C

(One question to be answered)

9. Describe the general features of Greek education, as exemplified *either* at Athens, *or* at Sparta, *or* in the ideal system of Plato. Compare in some detail the part played by physical training in Greek education and in Scottish education of to-day.

10. Why was the Renascence an epoch in the history of education? Remark on some of its merits and defects, as exemplified in the schools of the Jesuits.

11. What does Rousseau mean by "negative education," and how long does he propose that it should last? Give illustrations.

12. Describe the educational ideals of the Scottish Reformers. To what extent have they been realised in modern legislation and in the practice of our schools to-day?

National Committee for the Training of Teachers
Central Executive Committee

Education- Final Joint Examination

27th May 1932   10 am to 12.30 pm

Answer five questions, viz., Section A; three questions from Section B; and one question from Section C. Twenty marks are assigned to each question.

Section A

(This question must be answered)

1. Comment on the following quotation from Pestalozzi: "We must bear in mind that the ultimate end of education is not perfection in the accomplishments of the school but fitness for life, not the acquirement of habits of blind obedience and of prescribed diligence, but a preparation for independent action.

Section B

(Three questions to be answered)

2. "Not only is the practice of a craft a corrective of day-dreaming and a preparation for the right use of leisure, but it provides a social training peculiarly valuable in the case of adolescents."
Discuss this statement fully.

3. "Regulations make for more, not less, liberty."
What bearing has this view on freedom in the schools?

4. What are the theoretical bases of the project method and other methods which make use of "purposeful activity"?

5. "The 'Primary School Child' as such is only a lay figure, convenient for us to hang our educational generalisations upon. But Tommy Smith and Mary James and Dick Harrison, all ten years of age last month, have almost as many differences as likenesses."

Describe the more important of these differences, and discuss the educational adjustments which should be made in respect of them.

6. Write brief notes on any *two* of the following:—

(*a*) Home work.

(*b*) Standardised attainments tests.

(*c*) The provision made in Scotland for gifted children.

(*d*) Frequency of use as an index of educational values.

(*e*) Juvenile delinquency.

Section C

(One question to be answered)

7. How far does Aristotle's distinction between liberal and illiberal studies hold to-day?

8. Examine critically Rousseau's views about rewards and punishments.

9. Can Locke be regarded as an upholder of the theory of formal discipline?

10. Compare the educational principles and practice of Dr Montessori with those of any one other educator.

R

SELECTED BIBLIOGRAPHY

1 MANUSCRIPT SOURCES

Address by Mr David Caughie on the presentation to him of a Silver Salver and Purse of Sovereigns on the Occasion of his Jubilee as a teacher, 6 January 1868 (transcribed from the original MS by R R Rusk, May 1926)

Committee Book, Drygate School, 1829-31

Donaldson Papers, Papers of Sir James Donaldson (Principal of St Andrews, 1886-1910) St Andrews Library

Letters including letters of David Stow (National Library of Scotland)

letters of S S Laurie (National Library of Scotland)

letters of Henry Craik and John Struthers on teacher training (HM Record Office)

Literary Magazine of Free Church Training College, Glasgow, 1891

Logbooks of Glasgow Schools including the former St John's Sessional School (Annfield School)

Minutes of the Committee of Education of the Free Church of Scotland Assembly's Committee on the Normal Seminary, Glasgow, 1845-85

Minutes of the Committee of the Church of Scotland Normal College, Glasgow, 1872-7

Minutes of the Currie Club (former students of the Edinburgh Church of Scotland College), 1860-99

Students Diary, Marion MacCorquodale, Chapter III, Glasgow Provincial Committee, 1927-8

Visitors' Book, Glasgow Church of Scotland Normal Committee, 1849

Visitors' Book, Edinburgh Church of Scotland Normal Committee, 1845-50

Visitors' Book, Edinburgh Church of Scotland Ladies' Committee, 1845-52

2 TYPESCRIPT SOURCES

John Adams 1857-1934, *Biographical Notes*, R R Rusk, 1961

Carnegie Dunfermline Trust, Ian Thomson (Scottish School of Physical Education)

Life of Sister Mary of St Wilfrid by a Sister of Notre Dame

Memoranda on Conferences of Teachers of Logic, Psychology and Ethics in Scottish Training Colleges, 1924-34
Papers of the Director of Studies, Glasgow Training Centre, 1926
Reflections on the Fulton Report. (Report of the National Advisory Council (England) on the Training and Supply of Teachers, 1962), R R Rusk
To be a Pupil Teacher, Isobel Law, 1965

3 MATERIAL ISSUED BY TRAINING AUTHORITIES, ETC

Chronicle of Aberdeen Demonstration School, J C Milne, 1930 (cyclostyled)
Dundee Training College 1906-56 (official jubilee history)
Handbooks, Magazines, Prospectuses, Registers and *Timetables* of the colleges and training centres (some available from 1906 onwards; the majority from 1921)
Notre Dame Training College, Dowanhill, Glasgow (Book of the) *Golden Jubilee, 1895-1945*
Minutes
  Minutes of King's Students' Committees, 1896-1906
  Minutes of the National Committee for the Training of Teachers, Central Executive Committee, 1921-59
  Minutes of the Provincial Committees, 1906-59
  Minutes of the Scottish Council for the Training of Teachers, 1959-66
  Minutes of the General Teaching Council for Scotland, 1966-69
Reports
  Reports of Committees of University Senates
  Reports of the Committee of the General Assembly for increasing the means of Education in Scotland particularly in the Highlands and Islands
  Reports of the Education Committee to the General Assembly of the Free Church of Scotland
  Reports of the Glasgow Educational Society's Normal Seminary, Glasgow, Collins, 1836-40
  Triennial Reports of the Colleges, 1959-68
  University Calendars

4 OFFICIAL PUBLICATIONS

Minutes and Reports of the Committee of Council on Education
Circulars, Memoranda, Regulations and Reports of Scottish Education Department (previously the Scotch Education Department)
Report of the Committee appointed to inquire into Certain Questions Relating to Education in Scotland, 1887-8

*Reports of Select Committees of the House of Commons on the State
of Education in Scotland*, 1834 and 1838
*Report of Select Committee of the House of Commons on Teachers'
Training and Registration Bills*, 1891 (evidence of S S Laurie)
Reports of Royal Commissions
  Argyll Commission (on Schools in Scotland), 1865-8
  Colebrooke Commission (on Endowed Schools and Hospitals), 1873-5
  Kinnear Commission (under the Universities Act of 1889), 1900
  Taunton Commission vol VI (*Report on Certain Burgh Schools in
    Scotland*), 1868
Reports of the Advisory Council on Education in Scotland
  Training of Teachers (Cmd 6723), 1946
  Primary Education (Cmd 6973), 1946
  Secondary Education (Cmd 7005), 1947
Reports of Committees and Working Parties
  The Teaching Profession in Scotland (Wheatley Report) (Cmnd
    2066), 1963
  From School to Further Education (Brunton Report), 1963
  Higher Education (Robbins Report) (Cmnd 2154), 1963
  Primary Education in Scotland, 1965

5 JOURNALS (all present-day journals unless otherwise stated)

Education for Teaching
Educational News (published in 1876-1918 – superseded by *Scottish
  Educational Journal*)
Infant School Magazine (editions 1834-69)
Education in the North
Scottish Educational Journal (published 1852-7 and 1918 to present
  day)
Scottish Educational Studies
Times Educational Supplement
Times Educational Supplement (Scotland)

6 BOOKS, ARTICLES, UNPUBLISHED THESES

ADAMS, JOHN *Errors in School: their causes and treatment*, London,
  University of London Press, 1927
— *Herbartian Psychology applied to Education*, London, Isbister,
  1897
— *Primer on Teaching with special reference to Sunday School work*,
  Edinburgh, Clark, 1903
— *Education and the New Teaching*, London, Hodder and Stoughton,
  1918

ADAMS, JOHN *The Teacher's Many Parts*, London, University of London Press, 1930

BAIN, ANDREW *Education in Stirlingshire from the Reformation to the Act of 1872*, Scottish Council for Research in Education, Publication No LI, London, University of London Press, 1965

BARCLAY, WILLIAM *The Schools and Schoolmasters of Banffshire*, printed in Banff, 1925

BARNARD, HENRY *Normal Schools and other Agencies and Means designed for the Professional Education of Teachers*, 11th edition, Hartford, USA, Case and Co, 1851

BARRON, JAMES *The Northern Highlands in the Nineteenth Century*, 3 vols, printed in Inverness, 1907

BELFORD, A J *Centenary Handbook of the Educational Institute of Scotland*, Edinburgh, Educational Institute of Scotland, 1946

BONE, T R (ed) *Studies in the History of Scottish Education*, Scottish Council for Research in Education, Publication No 54, London, University of London Press, 1967

BONE, T R *School Inspection in Scotland 1840-1966*, Scottish Council for Research in Education, Publication No 57, London, University of London Press, 1968

BOYD, WILLIAM *Education in Ayrshire through Seven Centuries*, Scottish Council for Research in Education, Publication No XLV, London, University of London Press, 1961

— "Growing Points in Scottish Education", *New Era in Home and School*, July-August 1935, vol 16, no 7

BOYD, WILLIAM AND RAWSON, WYATT *The Story of the New Education*, London, Heinemann, 1965

BUCHANAN, ROBERT *The Schoolmaster in the Wynds or How to educate the Masses*, Glasgow, Blackie, 1850

CAMPBELL, WILLIAM "Scotland – Teachers-in-Service", *Year Book of Education*, London, Evans, 1953

CHALMERS, THOMAS *Churches and Schools for the Working Classes*, Edinburgh, Lowe, 1845

CHRISTISON, ALEX *The General Diffusion of Knowledge, one great cause of prosperity in North Britain*, Edinburgh, P Hill, 1802

CLELAND, ELIZABETH *The Church of Scotland Training College in Aberdeen: Record of the Classes from 1874-5 to 1894-5*, Aberdeen, Adelphi Press, 1896

— *The Church of Scotland Training College in Aberdeen: Record of the Classes, 1895-6 to 1906-7*, Aberdeen, Adelphi Press, 1907

CLARKE, J *Short Studies in Education in Scotland*, London, Longman, 1904

R*

CLARKE, J (ed)   *Problems of National Education*, London, Macmillan, 1919

COMBE, GEORGE   *Notes on the United States of North America during a Phrenological Visit in 1838-39-40*, Edinburgh, Maclachlan and Stewart, 1841

CORMACK, A A   *William Cramond 1844-1907. Schoolmaster at Cullen*, printed in Banff, 1967

CRAIK, HENRY   *The State in its Relation to Education*, London, Macmillan, 1884

CURRIE, JAMES   *Principles and Practice of Early and Infant School Education*, London, Hamilton, Adams & Co, 1857

DAVIE, GEORGE   *The Democratic Intellect*, Edinburgh, University of Edinburgh Press, 1961

DEAN, IRENE F M   *Scottish Spinning Schools*, Scottish Council for Research in Education, Publication, No I, London, University of London Press, 1930

DEWAR, DUNCAN   *A Student of St Andrews a Hundred Years Ago. His Accounts*, (ed P R S Lang) Glasgow, Jackson, 1926

DONALDSON, GORDON   *The Scots Overseas*, London, Hale, 1966

DOUGLAS, G C M   *The Scotch Training College*, Glasgow, Erskine (undated pamphlet but probably written 1883-4)

FERGUSON, T   *The Dawn of Scottish Welfare*, Edinburgh, Nelson, 1948

FITCH, J   "The Universities and the Training of Teachers", *Contemporary Review*, December 1876, vol 29

FRASER, WILLIAM   *Memoir of the Life of David Stow*, London, Nisbet, 1868

— *The State of our Educational Enterprises*, Glasgow, Blackie, 1858

Gaelic-Speaking Children in Highland Schools, Scottish Council for Research in Education, Publication No XLVII, London, University of London Press, 1961

GUNN, JOHN   *Maurice Paterson, Rector of Moray House*, Edinburgh, Nelson, 1921

HITCHMAN, P J   "Reading and Recitation in Teacher Training in the Nineteenth Century", *Researches and Studies*, November 1963, no 26, University of Leeds

HOUSEMAN, ROBERT E   David Stow. His Life and Work 1793-1864, MEd thesis, University of Manchester, 1938

INGLIS, W B   "Scottish Tradition of Public Education", *Year Book of Education*, London, Evans, 1957

INSH, G PRATT   *Life and Work of David Stow*, Edinburgh, Lindsay, 1938

JESSOP, J C   *Education in Angus*, Scottish Council for Research in

Education, Publication No II, London, University of London Press, 1931

JOLLY, WILLIAM *Education – its Principles and Practice as developed by George Combe*, London, Macmillan, 1879

— "The Professional Training of Teachers", *Fortnightly Review*, (New Series), September 1874, vol xvi

KAY-SHUTTLEWORTH, JAMES *Public Education as affected by the Minutes of the Committee of Privy Council from 1846 to 1852*, London, Longman, 1853

— *Four Periods of Public Education*, London, Longman, 1862

KENNEDY, ALEX *The Teacher in the Making*, Edinburgh, Oliver and Boyd, 1944

KENNEDY, W *Moray House and its Surroundings*, Edinburgh, Nelson, 1883

KERR, JOHN *Memories Grave and Gay*, Edinburgh, Nelson, 1902

— *Leaves from an Inspector's Log Book*, Edinburgh, Nelson, 1913

KLINE, P An Investigation into the Attitudes to their Teacher Training of Teachers with Two Years' Experience, EdB thesis, University of Aberdeen, 1963

KNOX, H M Educational Writings of Simon Somerville Laurie, PhD thesis, University of Edinburgh, 1949

— "Simon Somerville Laurie: 1829-1909", *British Journal of Educational Studies*, vol x, no 2, May 1962

— *Two Hundred and Fifty Years of Scottish Education*, Edinburgh, Oliver and Boyd, 1953

LAURIE, SIMON S *Reports to the Trustees of the Dick Bequest*, Edinburgh, Constable, 1865, 1890, 1904

— "Training Schools in Scotland", *The Museum*, July 1862, vol 3, no 6

— *The Training of Teachers and other Educational Papers*, London, Kegan Paul, 1882

LAW, ALEXANDER *Education in Edinburgh in the Eighteenth Century*, Scottish Council for Research in Education, Publication No LII, London, University of London Press, 1965

LEITCH, JAMES *Practical Educationalists and their System of Teaching*, Glasgow, Maclehose, 1876

LEWIS, G *Scotland a Half Educated Nation*, Glasgow, Collins, 1834

Lists of Schoolmasters teaching Latin 1790, ed D J Withrington, Miscellany X, Scottish History Society, 4th Series, vol 2, Edinburgh, 1965

MCCLELLAND, WILLIAM "Social Aspects of the Teacher's Preparation", *New Era in Home and School*, April 1936, vol 17, no 4

MACCOLL, D *Among the masses or Work in the Wynds*, London, Nelson, 1867

MALCOLM, C A AND HUNTER, J N *Moray House*, Edinburgh, Moray House, 1948

MANN, HORACE *Report of an Educational Tour of Germany, France, Holland and of Great Britain and Ireland*, ed W B Hodgson, London, Simpkin, 4th edition, 1857

MENZIES, G ALLAN *Reports to the Trustees of the Dick Bequest*, Edinburgh, Constable, 1836, 1844, 1854

MEIKLEJOHN, J M D *Inaugural Address, Chair of Education, University of St Andrews*, Edinburgh, R M Cameron, 1876

MONCREIFF, RT HON LORD *An Educational Retrospect. Address delivered on the occasion of the opening of a new Board School*, Glasgow, Morrison, 1886

MORGAN, ALEXANDER *Makers of Scottish Education*, London, Longmans, 1929

— *Rise and Progress of Scottish Education*, Edinburgh, Oliver and Boyd, 1927

— *Two Famous Old Edinburgh Colleges. A Century of Teacher Training*, Edinburgh, Church of Scotland Committee on Education, 1935

— "The Training of Secondary Teachers", *The Secondary School Journal*, May 1909, vol 2, pt 2

MUIR, G W "Some Thoughts on the Administration of Teacher Education", *Journal of Educational Administration*, October 1964, vol 11, no 2

Necessity of a Reform in the Parochial System of Scotland, by one who has long witnessed its existing defects in a letter to the Rt Hon Andrew Rutherford MP, Edinburgh, Black, 1848

NISBET, JOHN D (ed) *Scottish Education Looks Ahead*, Edinburgh, Chambers, 1969

NEILL, A S *Is Scotland Educated?*, London, Routledge, 1936

OGILVIE, JOSEPH *Aberdeen Church of Scotland Training College*, Aberdeen, Albany Press, 1907

OSBORNE, G S *Scottish and English Schools. A Comparative Study of the Past Fifty Years*, London, Longmans, 1966

PILLANS, JAMES *Principles of Elementary Teaching chiefly in reference to the Parochial Schools of Scotland*, Edinburgh, Black, 1825

— "Rationale of Discipline" (in *Contributions to the Cause of Education*), London, Longman, 1856

— "Seminaries for Teachers", *Edinburgh Review*, July 1834, vol 59, no 120

REA, F G *A Schoolmaster in South Uist, Reminiscences of a Hebridean Schoolmaster 1890-1913*, London, Routledge, 1964

RICH, R W *The Training of Teachers in England and Wales during the Nineteenth Century*, Cambridge, Cambridge University Press, 1933

ROBERTSON, JAMES J *Godfrey Thomson*, Edinburgh, Moray House, 1964

— *The Scottish Solution. Religious and Moral Education in the Schools of Scotland*, Edinburgh, Church of Scotland Committee on Education, 1954

ROSS, DAVID *A Minister of Education. His Position and Functions*, Glasgow, Maclehose, 1885

— *Education as a University Subject: its History, Present Position and Prospects*, Glasgow, Maclehose, 1883

— *Fifty Years of the Training System*, Glasgow, Maclehose, 1886

— *The Art of Questioning*, Glasgow, Maclehose, 1891

— *The Residue and Equivalent Grant*, Edinburgh, J Lindsay, 1892

RUSK, R R *A History of Infant Education*, London, University of London Press, 1933

— *Introduction to Experimental Education*, London, Longmans, 1912

— "Sir John Adams: 1857-1934", *British Journal of Educational Studies*, November 1961, vol x, no 1

— *The Training of Teachers in Scotland*, Edinburgh, Educational Institute of Scotland, 1928

SADLER, MICHAEL *Sir John Adams. A Lecture in his Memory*, London, Oxford University Press, 1935

SAUNDERS, L J *Scottish Democracy 1815-40*, Edinburgh, Oliver and Boyd, 1950

Scottish Montessori School by a Sister of Notre Dame. London, Sands, 1932

SELLAR, A C *Scotch Educational Progress 1864-87. An address at the opening of one of the Govan Board Schools 1887*, Glasgow, Malcolm, 1887

SIMPSON, I J *Education in Aberdeenshire before 1872*, Scottish Council for Research in Education, Publication No XXV, London, University of London Press, 1947

SKINNER, ANDREW F "Professional Education", *Year Book of Education*, London, Evans, 1953

SMITH, JOHN *Broken Links in Scottish Education*, London, Nisbet, 1913

SOCIETY IN SCOTLAND FOR PROPAGATING CHRISTIAN KNOWLEDGE *An Account of the Society in Scotland for Propagating Christian Knowledge*, Edinburgh, 1774

SOCIETY IN SCOTLAND FOR PROPAGATING CHRISTIAN KNOWLEDGE *The State of the Society in Scotland for Propagating Christian Knowledge*, Edinburgh, 1729

STODDARD, A M *John Stuart Blackie*, Edinburgh, Blackwood, 1896

STOW, DAVID *Granny and Leezy. A Scottish Dialogue. Grandmother's visit to the First Infant Training School*, London, Longman (6th edition), 1860

— *Infant Training. A Dialogue Explanatory of the System adopted in the Model Infant School, Glasgow*, Glasgow, Collins, 1833 (published anonymously by "a Director")

— *National Education. The Duty of England in regard to the Moral and Intellectual Elevation of the Poor and Working Classes*, London, Hatchard, 1847

— *The Training System adopted in the Model Schools of the Glasgow Educational Society. A Manual for Infant and Juvenile Schools which includes a system of Moral training suited to the Condition of Large Towns*, Glasgow, Blackie, 1845 (earliest extant edition was published under the title of *Moral Training, Infant and Juvenile*, 1834)

STRONG, JOHN *A History of Secondary Education in Scotland*, Oxford, Clarendon Press, 1909

THOMSON, S P *Life of Lord Kelvin*, London, Macmillan, 1910

UNIVERSITY OF LONDON INSTITUTE OF EDUCATION *Studies and Impressions*, 1902-52, London, Evans, 1952

VERNON, P E "The Contributions to Education of Sir Godfrey Thomson", *British Journal of Educational Studies*, May 1962, vol X, no 2

WADE, N A *Post Primary Education in the Primary Schools of Scotland 1872-1936*, London, University of London Press, 1939

WEBB, IDA M Women's Physical Education in Great Britain 1800-1966, MEd thesis, University of Leicester, 1967

WILSON, JOHN *Tales and Travels of a School Inspector*, Glasgow, Jackson, Wylie, 1928

WOOD, H P "Teacher Training in Scotland", *Advancement of Science*, March 1964, vol 20, no 88

WOOD, JOHN *Account of the Edinburgh Sessional School*, Edinburgh, Oliver and Boyd, 5th edition, 1840

INDEX

Aberdeen Church of Scotland College, 86, 113, 114
  Rectors, 223
Aberdeen College of Education, 198, 200n, 206-7, 210, 215, 216
Aberdeen Free Church College, 86, 113, 114, 130
  Rectors, 223
Aberdeen Provincial Centre, 149, 151, 164, 164n, 166, 166n, 178-9, 192, 251-4
Aberdeen Provincial Committee, 144, 147
  Directors of Studies, 225
Aberdeen School Board, 108
Aberdeen University, 25, 87, 96, 105
  desire to participate in teacher training, 98, 114, 114n, 117, 144-5
  lectureship in education, 119, 223
  local committee established, 119-120
  link with training centre, 144, 145, 145n
  education degrees, 157, 199, 201
Abolition of school fees, 107, 121
Academies, 21, 24, 65, 71, 73, 104, 104n
Acts, see Legislation
Adams, John, 108n, 158, 183
  Rector in Aberdeen and Glasgow, 128-31, 221, 223
  University courses, 131, 132, 248-250
  views of, 140
Advanced Divisions, 168-9, 184
Advisory Council on Education, 172, 173, 187, 188-9, 193, 194, 207
Argyll Commission, 82, 83, 84, 112
Arnold, Matthew, 59, 98, 108n, 112, 132
Assembly Schools, 40
  training of teachers for, 40-1

Bachelor of Education Degree, 157, 166, 181, 183, 184
  new degree, 199-200, 200n, 201, 206, 209, 237
Bain, Alexander, 105, 247
Ballard, P B, 132
Bearsden, see Notre Dame
Bell, Andrew, 28
  monitorial system of, 29, 30
  University endowment, 96
Bell Chairs of Education, 246, 247
Blackie, John Stuart, 25
Blind
  courses for teachers of, 163
Boarding and Teacher Training, 55, 62, 69, 102, 238, 241
  provision for women, 68, 69, 80, 103, 150, 166, 166n, 184, 197, 240
Board Schools, 88, 89-90, 134
  used for teaching practice, 115, 148-9
Book of Discipline, see Knox, John
Boyd, William, 145, 165-6, 182-3, 184, 186-7, 224
Brunton Report, 202, 202n
Burgh Schoolmaster, 22, 71
Burgh Schools, 14, 21-2, 23, 104, 134
  pupil teachers in, 60
  certificated teachers in, 65, 71, 73
Burnett, George, 174, 224, 225
Bursaries, see Church Bursaries
Bursary Competition, 145, 151
Burt, Cyril, 158, 253

Calisthenics, 63n, 91
Callendar Park College, 197, 198, 205, 209, 227
Calvinism, Influence of, 13, 23, 24
Cambridge Local Examination, 134
Carlyle, Thomas, 129

267

Catholic Poor School Committee, 123

Caughie, David, 34, 36

Central Classes for Pupil Teachers, see Pupil Teachers

Central Institutions, 136, 139, 139n, 162

Certificate (Teacher's)
early certificates, 42, 42n
grading of, 70, 70n
under 1906 Regulations and Amendments, 139, 169, 170, 171, 175
post-war changes in, 195, 201, 202

Certificate Examination
taken by ex-pupil teachers, 61
taken by practising teachers, 70, 109, 118-19, 135
taken by parish schoolmasters, 70, 72, 72n
examination papers, 175-6, 255-7

Certificated Teachers
new mobility of, 71
estimate of by Argyll Commissioners, 83
numbers required after 1872, 86
salaries, 234-5

Chalmers, Thomas, 15, 32, 51

"Chapter III" Students
under 1906 Regulations, 139, 145, 147-8, 149
under later Regulations, 169, 170, 171
Article 39, 149, 171, 180
end of system, 201

"Chapter V" Students
under 1906 Regulations, 139, 149, 150, 156, 163
under later Regulations, 169, 170, 171, 191
end of system, 201

"Chapter VI" Students
under 1906 Regulations, 139, 149, 155, 158
under later Regulations, 169, 171, 184
end of system, 201, 202

Cheltenham College, 75n

Child Guidance Clinics, 165-6, 166n, 182

Church Bursaries
for entrance to Normal School, 61, 75, 77, 78
for Normal School students to attend University, 82, 94, 137

Church Ministers
aspirations of dominies to become, 18
aspirations of trained teachers, 65, 75-6
"stickit ministers", 19

Church of Scotland and Teacher Training
early association, 40, 49, 68
effect of Disruption, 53, 58
reaction to Minutes of 1846, 58
religious instruction for students, 86
end of Church control, 125, 135
compensation for Church buildings, 138
1906 arrangements for religious instruction, 138, 189

Church of Scotland Colleges, see under Aberdeen, Edinburgh and Glasgow

Church of Scotland Education Committee, 75

Churches and Teacher Training, 135, 136, 137, 138
See Church of Scotland and Teacher Training, Episcopal College, Free Church, Roman Catholic Colleges

Clydebank Mutual Service Association, 183

Cockburn, Lord, 23, 24

Codes, see also Revised Code
Code of 1873, 93
Code of 1895, 119
Code of 1899, 126n

Coleridge, Derwent, 66

Colleges of Education
new designation, 194
Boards of Studies in, 194
developments in 1950s, 195-6, 206-7
developments in 1960s, 211-12, 214
Principals, 226-7

Combe, George, 44n, 46n, 229

Committees of Management, 162, 163, 194
Concurrent System
early years of, 93, 94, 99-100, 113
under Provincial Committees, 120, 146, 147-8, 150-1, 172
opinions of, 179-180, 189
at Stirling University, 211
Cousin, Victor, 43, 43n, 45
Craigie College, 197, 205, 209, 227
Craiglockhart College, 162-3, 171, 174, 198, 205-6, 226
Craik, Sir Henry, 107, 107n, 110, 118n, 122n, 126
views on teacher training, 116-17, 133
Criticism Lessons, 45, 46, 48-9, 92-3, 131, 177, 205, 216
Cross Commission, 112
Cruden, Major, 113, 154
Cuisenaire, 196
Currie Club, 124
Currie, James, 68, 76, 82n, 222

Dalton Plan, 176
Darroch, Professor, 145, 152, 156, 157, 163, 228
Day School Certificate, 169, 171
Deaf
courses for teachers of, 163, 208
Decroly, 165
Department of Science and Art at South Kensington, 79
Dey, Dr, 133
Dick Bequest, 18n, 19n, 22n, 66, 66n, 71, 96, 98
Dickens, Charles, 64, 64n
Discipline in colleges, 103, 191, 216
Disruption, 51, 52
Dominie, see Parish Schoolmaster tradition of, 192
Donaldson, Principal, 114, 146
Dowanhill, see Notre Dame
Drever, James, 153, 166, 181, 183
Drygate School, 33-7, 39, 45
Dundas Vale Normal School, 46, 48, 229
later use of, 46n
see also Glasgow Church of Scotland College
Dundee, 116-17

Dundee College of Education, 198, 200n, 206-7, 210, 216, 226
Dundee Infant School, 40
Dundee School Board, 87n, 108
Dundee Sessional School, 60
Dundee Training Centre, 146, 147, 149, 150, 151
new building, 164, 164n
inter-war years, 166, 167, 174, 179, 182, 212
Directors of Studies, 225
Dundee University, BEd Degree, 200
Dundee University College, 116, 164
local committee, 119-120, 133, 147
links with training centre, 150, 167, 195
Dunfermline, 154
Dunfermline College
foundation, 154-5
inter-war period, 163, 167, 178, 184
wartime and post-war, 187, 197, 198, 227

Eaglesham, E J R, 207n
Edgar, John, 147n
Edinburgh Church of Scotland Normal School, 52-3
boarding house, 53, 54, 240
buildings and equipment, 86-7, 91-2
link with University, 115, 133
old students, 124, 124n
Rectors, 76, 222
timetable, 238
Edinburgh Free Church Normal School, see Moray House
Edinburgh High School, 22, 23, 24, 28
Edinburgh Infant School, 40
Edinburgh Infant School Society, 41
Edinburgh Provincial Committee, 146-7, 152-3
Directors of Studies, 224
Edinburgh School Board, 108
Edinburgh Sessional School, 29-32, 38, 40
incorporates a Normal School, 40-1, 49, 50

Edinburgh Training Centre, 145, 149, 151, 152
    popularity of concurrent course, 157
    new buildings, 157
    See also Moray House
Edinburgh University
    Chair of Education, 95, 96, 246
    concern for teacher training, 115, 117
    Degree of BEd, 157
    Diploma of Literate in Arts, 97
    Diploma in Education, 115, 119, 133, 209
    links with Moray House, 167, 183, 187, 195
    new BEd, 199, 209
Educational Institute of Scotland, 71, 71n, 95, 105, 142, 170, 199, 204n
Emergency Training Scheme, 188, 193
English Teacher Training, *see* Scottish and English Teacher Training
Episcopal Church, 62
Episcopal College, 62, 69, 77, 80, 87, 88, 122, 138, 152, 162, 171
    Principals, 241
Episcopal Schools, 85, 121-2
Established Church, *see* Church of Scotland
Explanatory System, *see* Intellectual System

Fearon, D R, 83-4, 83n
Fitch, Sir Joshua, 105n
Fleming, Charlotte, 207n
Forsyth, David, 104, 104n
Free Church
    efforts for education, 51-2
    response to Privy Council policy, 57, 58, 62, 94
    bursaries for University study, 82, 94
    religious instruction for students, 86
    transference of colleges, 135, 138
    See also under Aberdeen, Glasgow and Moray House
Free Church Schools, 52, 70, 88

Froebel Training, 163
Freud, 163, 164n
Further Education
    preparation of teachers of, 209
    Colleges of, 212, 212n

Gaelic-speaking students, 21 40, 41
    boarding accommodation, 53-4, 70, 239
    effect of Revised Code on, 77-8
    problems of training, 78, 110
    special courses, 178, 192
Gallery System, 33, 34, 34n, 48, 59n, 60
    See also "Simultaneous" Method
Geddes Axe, 168
General Teaching Council, 203n, 203-4, 211, 226, 228
Gibson, John, 57
Gill, John, 75n
Glasgow Church of Scotland College
    site and facilities, 52, 92
    student mutiny, 103
    Rectors, 104, 221-2
    See also Dundas Vale
Glasgow Educational Society, 42, 43-4, 45
    establishes Normal School, 46-7, 48, 49, 50
Glasgow Education Committee, 164, 170
Glasgow Endowment Fund, 94
Glasgow Free Church College, 52, 53, 62, 63, 67
    organisation of work, 74, 79, 100, 113
    social life, 103, 124
    Rectors, 67-8, 128, 129-130, 221-2
Glasgow Provincial Committee, 146-7, 164, 173
    Directors of Studies, 224
Glasgow St John's Parochial School (Annfield School), 45
Glasgow School Board, 94
    classes for pupil teachers, 108
    views on teacher training, 115, 142
Glasgow Training Centre, 145, 149, 151
    See also Jordanhill

Glasgow University
  proposed Chair of Education, 96,
    105
  Lectureship in Education and
    Education Course, 119, 221,
    248-50
  local committee, 120
  education degrees, 157, 199, 200
  social life of students, 174-5
Govan School Board
  central classes for pupil teachers,
    108
  higher grade schools, 112n
  junior student system, 142
Gray, George D, 228
Gymnastics in colleges, 63, 63n, 113,
  128, 154-5

Hadow Report, 186
Hamilton Academy, 141
Hamilton College of Education, 197,
  205, 209, 227
Handicapped Children, Reports on,
  193
Herbart, 129
  See also Psychology
Heriot-Watt College, 201
Heriot-Watt University, 211
Hetherington, Hector, 146n
Higher Grade Schools, 112, 112n,
  120, 134, 140, 161, 168
Holmes, Edmund, 132
Homerton College, 75n
Horne, R, 41
Hullah, John, 91, 92
Hunnybun, W H, 123

Infant School Magazine, 40
Infant School Society
  in Edinburgh, 41
  in Glasgow, 33, 40
Inglis, W B, 143, 181, 184n, 187,
  193, 224, 226
In-service Courses, 196, 202n, 205,
  209, 212
Inspectorate and Teacher Training
  duties prior to 1906, 80, 81, 117,
    119, 127
  duties under Provincial Com-
    mittees, 146
  views on training, 115, 172
  end of inspection, 194

Institutes of Education (England),
  189, 195
Intellectual System, 31-2, 41, 54-5
Intermediate Certificate, 127, 134,
  138, 140
Inverness, 21, 40, 78, 221

Johnson, Dr, 16, 20
Joint Committee of the Provincial
  Committees, 147, 151
Jordanhill College
  building, 164, 164n, 198
  developments in inter-war years,
    166, 174, 178, 184
  developments in post-war years,
    188, 192, 197, 198, 200n, 206-7,
    208, 209, 210, 215
  Directors of Studies and Principal,
    224, 226
Junior Students, 140, 141n, 143, 151
Junior Student Centre, 140-1, 141n,
  143
Junior Student Certificate, 139, 141,
  143
Junior Student System, 138, 142,
  150, 151, 169, 216

Kay, James (later Kay-Shuttle-
  worth), 30, 47-8, 56, 56n, 58, 67
Kelvin, Lord, See Thomson, Pro-
  fessor W
Kennedy-Fraser, D, 164n
Kerr, Rev John, 63, 63n, 74, 79,
  124-5, 230-3
Kerr, John, HMI, 81, 82, 93, 106,
  113, 114
King's Students, 133, 134, 136, 237
Knight, Rex, 183n
Knox, John, 14, 218

Laban, Rudolf, 198
Ladies' Committee, 68
Lady Literate in the Arts, 114-15,
  119n
Lancaster, Joseph, 28, 37
  Monitorial System of, 29, 31
Latin (or Classics)
  in Normal Schools, 54, 57, 63, 64,
    76, 91, 112, 239, 243
  in Parish Schools, 22, 24, 59, 60,
    66n, 73, 111, 112

Laurie, Professor S S,
    interest in teacher training, 65-7,
        68, 69, 75, 78, 82, 86, 98-9, 115
    inspector for Dick Bequest, 81
    education as a University subject,
        95-6, 97, 98, 115, 119, 133-4,
        145, 246
Leaving Certificate, 112, 119, 121,
    127, 134, 139, 140, 141, 142,
    151, 152, 168, 169, 170, 173
Legislation
    Act of 1696, 15, 218-9
    Act of 1803, 27, 219
    Act of 1838, 219
    Act of 1861, 71, 78, 219
    Act of 1872, 85, 219
    Act of 1882, 112n
    Act of 1892, 219
    Act of 1901, 220
    Act of 1908, 220
    Act of 1918, 160, 220
    Act of 1945, 188, 220
    Act of 1963, Industrial Training
        Act, 212n
Leitch, James, 103, 221
Leith School Board, 108
Lewis, George, 43, 45
Local Committees, 119, 133, 134-5,
    137
Locke, John, 105, 247, 248, 249
Lowe, Robert, 72, 73-4, 95

McAllister, Anne H, 193
McClelland, W W,
    work at Dundee, 165n, 167-8, 174,
        179, 180, 181, 182, 183, 208n,
        225
    Executive Officer of the National
        Committee for the Training of
        Teachers, 182, 189, 193, 228
McIntosh, D M, 208, 208n, 226
McNair Report, 189
Madras College, 99, 99n
Malloch, James
    work at Dundee, 133, 147, 150,
        225
    Executive Officer of the National
        Committee, 163, 228
Manchester University, 163
Mann, Horace, 23
Master of Education degree, 199, 201

Meiklejohn, Professor, 97, 247
Mentally   Defective   Children,
    courses for teachers of, 163-4
Merit Certificate, 120, 126, 127, 140
Minutes of Committee of Council
    on Education
    of 1846, 55-6, 58, 72
    of 1853, 62
Monitorial System, 28, 29, 30-2
    teacher training in, 40-1
Montessori Methods, 165, 176
Moray House
    buildings and equipment, 52, 86,
        92, 147, 148, 164, 164n,
    Rectors, Directors of Studies,
        Principals, 68, 142, 168, 187,
        208, 222-3, 224, 226
    nineteenth century developments,
        70, 101, 123, 150
    training centre under provincial
        committee, 156, 163, 168, 171,
        176, 178, 179, 181
    College of Education, 183, 187,
        192, 200n, 206-7, 208-9, 210
Morgan, Alexander, 9, 147, 157,
    223, 224
Morris, Ben, 207n
Morris, Sir Philip, 191n
Morrison, Thomas, 67, 80, 101,
    102-3, 104, 124, 221
Morrison, T W, 147, 222
Mount Pleasant College, 88, 122

Nasmyth, James, 24
National Committee for the Train-
    ing of Teachers, 160-4, 167,
    168, 171, 172, 173, 193
    Central Executive Committee of,
        161, 163
    Chairmen and Officers, 228
    Committee   of   Directors   and
        Assessors, 193
    Common   Examination   Papers,
        255-7
Navigation
    in Parish Schools, 22
    in General Assembly Schools, 40
    in Training Colleges, 112
Neill, A S, 109, 116n
New Education Fellowship, 165
Newsom Report, 202

Normal School, 46, 65-6, 67, 92
North East
  education in, 20, 66-7, 71
  See also Dick Bequest
Notre Dame College
  foundation and early years, 122,
    123, 138, 158
  College School, 141
  comes under National Committee
    for Training of Teachers, 162,
    163
  developments in inter-war years,
    166, 171, 176
  developments in post-war years,
    197, 198, 205-6
  Principals, 226
  Sister of, *see* Sister
Nunn, Percy, 158, 214

Oban High School, 110
Ogilvie, Joseph, 86, 119, 147, 223
Owen, Robert, 33
Oxford Local Examination, 134

Paisley Grammar School, 143
Parchment, *see* Certificate (Teach-
  er's)
Parish Schoolmasters, 9, 16-20, 21,
    24, 27, 66-7, 70-1, 72, 72n
  comparison with certificated
    teachers, 65, 77, 83
  salaries of, 71, 234
Parish Schools, 14, 15, 16-18, 20, 21,
    23, 24
  pupil teachers in, 59, 60, 112
  become Board Schools, 85, 134
Paterson, Maurice, 68, 100, 124,
    147, 221, 222-3, 242, 244
Pestalozzi Methods, 33, 247, 248
Pillans, Professor, 15, 28-9, 42, 43-4,
    95
Playfair, Lyon, 137
Poor Law Schools, *see* Workhouse
  Schools (England)
Preliminary Training, 152, 169, 170,
    173
  See also Junior Student System
Presbyterial licensing of school-
  masters, 17
  visitation of schools, 19, 45
Primary School, Report on, 204

Probationary period of teaching, 70,
    75, 139, 203
Provincial Centres, *see* Training
  Centres
Provincial Committees
  establishment of, 136, 137, 138
  early years of, 143, 144, 145, 149,
    155, 157
  under National Committee for the
    Training of Teachers, 161, 163
  end of system, 194
  Directors of Studies, 224-5
Prussian Education, Influence of,
    43-4
Psychology
  Faculty psychology, 97, 105, 113,
    128, 131
  Herbartian psychology, 128, 129,
    131, 249
  experimental psychology, 152, 159,
    164, 166
  developments   in   provincial
    centres, 146, 152, 153, 164, 165,
    175, 176, 177, 180, 186, 207,
    252-3, 254
  included in syllabuses, 246, 248,
    249, 252, 254
Pupil Teachers
  selection and studies, 59, 60, 60n,
    61, 71
  effect of Revised Code on, 77, 77n,
    89-90
  improvements in training, 93, 100,
    108-9
  qualities of, 90, 108, 121
  numbers of, 236
Pupil Teacher System, 55-8, 59, 68,
    108-9, 111, 112, 138
  assessment of, 140, 142, 144

Qualifying Examination, 140, 168,
    184
Queen's Scholars, 91, 97, 99
Queen's Scholarships, 55, 56, 57, 61,
    62, 72, 75, 115, 119, 121
Queen's Students, 119, 120, 133
Queen's Studentships, 119, 120
Quick, R H, 113

Ramage, George, 86, 223
Ramsay, Professor, 74n, 93, **117-18**

Register of Teachers
  proposals for, 107, 131
  establishment of, 203, 203n
Regulations of 1906,138,139,140,148
  See also separate Chapters
Regulations of 1922, 163
Regulations of 1924, 169, 177n
Regulations of 1931, 173, 175, 177n
Regulations of 1948, 191
Regulations of 1965, 201, 202
Revised Code, 72-3, 77, 90, 107
  applied to Normal Schools, 73, 73n, 74, 75, 76
  applied to pupil teachers, 77, 77n
Rich, R W, 66n
Robertson, Sir James J, 196, 217, 228
Roman Catholic Colleges, 10, 122
  See also Craiglockhart and Notre Dame
Roman Catholic Schools, 85, 88, 111, 121-2, 205
Ross, David, 104-5, 111, 119, 124, 131, 135, 221, 246
Royal College of Science and Technology, 201
Rural Schools, teacher preparation for, 11, 78, 112, 178-9, 192, 206
Rusk, R R
  student recollections, 113, 129-130
  studies in Germany, 183
  work in provincial centres, 164, 166, 180, 253
  Director of the Scottish Council for Research in Education, 181
  views of, 195n

Sabbath School, *see* Sunday Schools
Sadler, Sir Michael, 129, 132
St Andrews Provincial Committee, 146, 147, 155, 157
  Directors of Studies, 225
St Andrews Training Centre, 147n
St George's Training College, 134, 134n, 156, 163, 205
St Margaret's College, *see* Craiglockhart
St Mark's College, 62, 66
Salaries
  parish schoolmasters, 10n, 15, 22, 71, 234

certificated teachers, 71, 87, 234
Salary Scales, 160, 168, 172, 188, 234-5
School Boards, 85, 88n, 88-9, 112, 160
  connected with teacher training, 91, 108, 115, 135, 136, 146
Scotch (later Scottish) Education Department and Teacher Training, 100, 103-4, 113, 114, 117, 118, 127, 138, 142-3, 146, 152, 157, 161-2, 170, 175, 194, 216
Scottish Certificate of Education, 206, 206n
Scottish compared with English education, 10, 66, 106, 139-140, 166
Scottish compared with English teacher training, 10, 55, 66, 67, 69, 102, 105-7, 116, 133, 185, 191, 203, 211
Scottish Council for Research in Education, 181, 208n
Scottish Council for Training of Teachers, 194, 194n, 196, 197-8 203-4, 205, 226, 228
  Committee of Principals, 199
Scottish Education Inquiry Committee, 114, 116
Scottish School of Physical Education, 178, 184, 209
Scottish Universities Commission, 116, 117
"Scottish Solution", 10, 205
Scottish Youth Leadership Association, 187
Secondary School Committees, 138-9
Senior Students, 139
Senior Studentship, 138
Sessional Schools, 64, 70
Sewing Mistresses, 78
Side School, 27, 110
Sime, James, 68, 222
Simpson, James, 44n
"Simultaneous" Method, 34, 38, 45, 50, 54-5, 60, 76
Sister Monica, 156, 156n
Sister Marie Hilda, 166
Sister Mary of St Wilfred, 122-3, 138

Smith, George, 147, 223, 225
Snodgrass, Neill, 165n
Social Workers, Training of, 187, 208, 212, 214
Society in Scotland for Propagating Christian Knowledge, 20-1
Society of the Sacred Heart, 162-3
See also Craiglockhart College
Sociology, 187, 206, 208
South Uist, 111
Special Recruitment Scheme, 188, 190, 191
Spencer, Herbert, 105, 247, 248, 249
Stirling University, 211, 215
Stornoway, 110
Stow, David
pioneer work with children, 32-4, 36, 39
comparison of methods with those of John Wood, 37-8
trains teachers, 40, 41, 42n, 46-7, 68, 52
official positions, 45, 46
views on teacher training, 9, 12, 39, 45, 49, 54, 57n, 131
invited to become HMI, 47-8
death and influence of, 74-5, 75n
home used for students, 80
assessment, 217
Strathclyde University, 211
Struthers, John, 95n, 108n
influence on teacher training, 126, 136, 144-5, 147, 154-5
Student Mutiny, 103, 221
Student Representative Councils, 166
Sunday Schools, 9, 28, 33, 49
Supplementary Courses, 127, 149, 157, 168
Sutherland, John, 193

Taunton Commission, 83n
Teachers
numbers, 236
numbers in training, 237
Teacher's Certificate, *see* Certificate
Temple, Frederick, 59
Thomson, Professor Sir Godfrey H, 168, 182, 187, 207-8, 224
research activities, 180, 181, 183-4
Thomson, Professor W, 63, 230, 232

Thouless, R H, 183
Training Centre
establishment of, 136, 139, 143
organisation and assessment, 148, 163, 170, 173, 176, 177, 184
postwar developments, 190, 194-5
See under Aberdeen, Dundee, Edinburgh and Glasgow
Training Colleges, 92, 112
Training System, *see* "Simultaneous" Method

United Free Church, 135n, 164
Universities and Teacher Training
effect of combined University and College course, 121
suggestions for strengthening connection, 130, 135, 137
effect of new Arts Ordinances, 150
links with Provincial Committees and National Committee for Training of Teachers, 162
University Diploma Courses, 157, 180, 207
proportions of graduates entering teacher training, 168, 214
new BEd degrees, 199-201

Valentine, C W, 146
Vernon, P E, 180, 181, 183, 187

Welsh, Dr, 43
Wesleyans
send students to Glasgow, 47, 53
establishment of own College, 75n
Wheatley Committee, 203
Wilderspin, Samuel, 33, 37, 40, 43
Williams, A M, 147, 221
Women Students
as pupil teachers, 60
in Normal Schools, 61, 68, 79, 80, 87, 101-2
comparison with men students, 77, 100-1
enter Universities, 119, 120
inter-war and post-war years, 167, 192, 195, 195n

Women Teachers
  Stow's views on, 39
  career opportunities, 61-2, 78
  compared with men teachers, 78-9
  assessment, 87
  celibacy in interwar years, 168
  wastage in postwar years, 196
  salary scales, 234-5
  numbers, 236
Wood, Sir Henry P, 186, 197, 209,
  224, 226

Wood, John
  work in Edinburgh Sessional
    School, 26, 29, 30-2
  methods compared with those of
    Stow, 37-8
  trains teachers, 40, 41
  emigrates, 51-2
  assessment, 217
Workhouse Schools (England), 41, 47

Youth Leaders, training of, 187, 218

Publications of the Scottish Council for Research in Education

I   SCOTTISH SPINNING SCHOOLS   (With illustrations)
     By IRENE F M DEAN, FRHistSoc   25p (5/-) net

II   EDUCATION IN ANGUS
     By J C JESSOP, MA, PhD, FRHistSoc   (out of print)

III CURRICULUM FOR PUPILS OF TWELVE TO FIFTEEN
     YEARS   (Advanced Division)   (out of print)

IV   GROUP TEST FOR COLOUR BLINDNESS
     By M COLLINS, MA, BEd, PhD, and J DREVER, MA,
     BSc, DPhil   (out of print)

V   THE INTELLIGENCE OF SCOTTISH CHILDREN
                                          (out of print)

VI   ACHIEVEMENT TESTS IN THE PRIMARY SCHOOL
     By GREGOR MACGREGOR, MA, BSc, FEIS
                                          (out of print)

VII A HISTORY OF SCOTTISH EXPERIMENTS IN RURAL
     EDUCATION
     By JOHN MASON, MA, PhD   (out of print)

VIII THE HISTORY OF MATHEMATICAL TEACHING IN
     SCOTLAND
     By DUNCAN K WILSON, MA, BSc, PhD
                                          (out of print)

IX   THE PROGNOSTIC VALUE OF UNIVERSITY ENTRANCE
     EXAMINATIONS IN SCOTLAND   (out of print)

X   TESTS OF ABILITY FOR SECONDARY SCHOOL
     COURSES
     By FRANK M EARLE, MEd, DSc   (out of print)

XI   CITY AND RURAL SCHOOLS
     By ALEX S MOWAT, MA, BEd   (out of print)

XII THE STANDARDISATION OF A GRADED WORD
     READING TEST
     By P E VERNON, MA, PhD   20p (4/-) net
     Test cards reprinted from the above:
     1 THE GRADED WORD READING TEST
                                          2½p (6d) per copy
     2 THE BURT (Rearranged) WORD READING TEST
                                          2½p (6d) per copy

XIII STUDIES IN ARITHMETIC, Volume I   75p (15/-) net

XIV SCOTTISH PRIMARY SCHOOL ORGANISATION
                                          (out of print)

XV   THE INTELLIGENCE OF A REPRESENTATIVE GROUP
     OF SCOTTISH CHILDREN
     By A M MACMEEKEN, MA, BEd, PhD   (out of print)

XVI AN ANALYSIS OF PERFORMANCE TEST SCORES OF A
     REPRESENTATIVE GROUP OF SCOTTISH CHILDREN
     By Sir GODFREY THOMSON, PhD, DSc, DCL,
     FEIS(Hon)   (out of print)

XVII   THE ASSESSMENT OF EDUCATIONAL FILMS
(out of print)

XVIII STUDIES IN ARITHMETIC, Volume II   £1 net

XIX   SELECTION FOR SECONDARY EDUCATION
By WILLIAM McCLELLAND, CBE, MA, BSc, BED,
FRSE, FEIS   25p (5/-) net

XX   THE EARLY DEVELOPMENT OF NUMBER CONCEPTS
(out of print)

XXI   THE TEACHING OF ARITHMETIC
By JOHN MORRISON, MBE, MA, BSc   5p (1/-) net

XXII   EVACUATION IN SCOTLAND
Edited by WILLIAM BOYD, MA, BSc, DPHIL, DLITT,
LLD   25p (5/-) net

XXIII THE TERMAN-MERRILL INTELLIGENCE SCALE IN
SCOTLAND
By D KENNEDY-FRASER, MA, BSc, FRSE, FEIS
5p (1/-) net

XXIV   THE SCOTTISH COUNCIL FOR RESEARCH IN EDUCA-
TION: ITS AIMS AND ACTIVITIES *(Revised Edition)*
(out of print)

XXV   EDUCATION IN ABERDEENSHIRE BEFORE 1872
By IAN J SIMPSON, MA, PHD   25p (5/-) net

XXVI   STUDIES IN READING, Volume I   75p (15/-) net

XXVII MENTAL TESTING OF HEBRIDEAN CHILDREN
By CHRISTINA A SMITH, MA, BED   5p (1/-) net

XXVIII ADDITION AND SUBTRACTION FACTS AND PRO-
CESSES   *(out of print)*

XXIX   PROMOTION FROM PRIMARY TO SECONDARY
EDUCATION
By DOUGLAS M McINTOSH, CBE, LLD, MA, BSc,
BED, PHD, FRSE, FEIS   5p (1/-) net

XXX   THE TREND OF SCOTTISH INTELLIGENCE
37½p (7/6) net

XXXI   AIDS TO EDUCATIONAL RESEARCH COMPRISING
BIBLIOGRAPHIES AND TOPICS FOR RESEARCH
(Revised Edition) 12½p (2/6) net

XXXII TRADITIONAL NUMBER RHYMES AND GAMES
By F DOREEN GULLEN, MA, BLITT   *(out of print)*

XXXIII THE WRITING OF ARABIC NUMERALS
By G G NEILL WRIGHT, MA, BED, DLITT
52½p (10/6) net

XXXIV STUDIES IN READING, Volume II   37½p (7/6) net

XXXV   SOCIAL IMPLICATIONS OF THE 1947 SCOTTISH
MENTAL SURVEY   52½p (10/6) net

XXXVI THE TEACHING OF ARABIC NUMERALS
By G G NEILL WRIGHT, MA, BED, DLITT
12½p (2/6) net

XXXVII PATTERNS OF ERROR IN THE ADDITION NUMBER FACTS
By J M THYNE, MA, EdB   52½p (10/6) net

XXXVIII HEARING DEFECTS OF SCHOOL CHILDREN
52½p (10/6) net

XXXIX LEFT-HANDEDNESS: LATERALITY CHARACTERISTICS AND THEIR EDUCATIONAL IMPLICATIONS
By MARGARET M CLARK, MA, EdB, PhD   £1 net

XL STUDIES IN SPELLING   75p (15/-) net

XLI EDUCATIONAL AND OTHER ASPECTS OF THE 1947 SCOTTISH MENTAL SURVEY   75p (15/-) net

XLII ELEVEN-YEAR-OLDS GROW UP
By J S MACPHERSON, MA, BSc, EdB   75p (15/-) net

XLIII HOME ENVIRONMENT AND THE SCHOOL
By ELIZABETH FRASER, MA, EdB, PhD
52½p (10/6) net

XLIV TEACHING LEFT-HANDED CHILDREN
By MARGARET M CLARK, MA, EdB, PhD
12½p (2/6) net

XLV EDUCATION IN AYRSHIRE THROUGH SEVEN CENTURIES
By WILLIAM BOYD, MA, BSc, DPhil, DLitt, LLD
£1 net

XLVI THE LEVEL AND TREND OF NATIONAL INTELLIGENCE
By JAMES MAXWELL, MA, BEd   25p (5/-) net

XLVII GAELIC-SPEAKING CHILDREN IN HIGHLAND SCHOOLS   52½p (10/6) net

XLVIII THE SCOTTISH SCHOLASTIC SURVEY 1953
£1·25p (25/-) net

XLIX AITHRIS IS OIDEAS   37½p (7/6) net

L THE ATTAINMENTS OF SCOTTISH TEN-YEAR-OLDS IN ENGLISH AND ARITHMETIC   25p (5/-) net

LI EDUCATION IN STIRLINGSHIRE FROM THE REFORMATION TO THE ACT OF 1872
By ANDREW BAIN, MA, EdB, PhD   £1·50p (30/-) net

LII EDUCATION IN EDINBURGH IN THE EIGHTEENTH CENTURY
By ALEXANDER LAW, OBE, MA, PhD
£1·50p (30/-) net

53 AGE OF TRANSFER TO SECONDARY EDUCATION
By J D NISBET, MA, BEd, PhD, and
N J ENTWISTLE, BSc, PhD   62½p (12/6) net

54 STUDIES IN THE HISTORY OF SCOTTISH EDUCATION 1872-1939   £1·87½p (37/6) net

55 THE SCOTTISH STANDARDISATION OF THE WECHSLER INTELLIGENCE SCALE FOR CHILDREN
57½p (11/6) net

56 **RISING STANDARDS IN SCOTTISH PRIMARY SCHOOLS: 1953-63**   Boards £1·12½p (22/6) net
    Paper 80p (16/-) net

57 **SCHOOL INSPECTION IN SCOTLAND 1840-1966**
    By T R BONE, MA, MEᴅ, Pʜᴅ   £1·50p (30/-) net

58 **SIXTEEN YEARS ON**
    By JAMES MAXWELL, MA, BEᴅ
    Boards £2·10p (42/-) net
    Paper £1·50p (30/-) net

59 **THE TRANSITION TO SECONDARY EDUCATION**
    By J D NISBET, MA, BEᴅ, Pʜᴅ and N J ENTWISTLE,
    BSc, Pʜᴅ   £1·25p (25/-) net

60 **A BIBLIOGRAPHY OF SCOTTISH EDUCATION BE-FORE 1872**
    By JAMES CRAIGIE, OBE, MA, Pʜᴅ, FEIS
    £4·50p (90/-) net

61 **A HISTORY OF THE TRAINING OF TEACHERS IN SCOTLAND**
    By MARJORIE CRUICKSHANK, MA, Pʜᴅ
    £2·50p (50/-) net

62 **A STUDY OF FIFTEEN-YEAR-OLDS**   £2·10p (42/-) net

THE SCOTTISH PUPIL'S SPELLING BOOK
Parts I-V 10p (2/-) each   Teacher's Book 75p (15/-) each

MANUAL FOR THE SCOTTISH STANDARDISATION OF THE WECHSLER INTELLIGENCE SCALE FOR CHILD-REN   25p (5/-) net
(Available only to users of the Wechsler Scale and on application to the Council)

SCHOLASTIC SURVEY TESTS IN ENGLISH AND ARITHMETIC (as used in Publications No XLVIII, L and 56)
20 tests £1